THE IDEALS GUIDE TO
AMERICAN CIVIL WAR
PLACES

★ 150 YEARS SESQUICENTENNIAL ★

THE IDEALS GUIDE TO
AMERICAN CIVIL WAR
1861 ## PLACES 1865

SECOND EDITION

BY JULIE SHIVELY

ideals®

NASHVILLE, TENNESSEE

The Ideals Guide to American Civil War Places, Second Edition
ISBN-13: 978-0-8249-5913-5

Published by Ideals Publications
A Guideposts Company
Nashville, Tennessee
www.idealsbooks.com

A special thanks to Lt Col. Keith Gibson, Director,
VMI Hall of Valor Civil War Museum, for his
invaluable contribution in reading and offering
suggestions to this manuscript.

Cover design by Katie Jennings
Designer, Eve DeGrie
Production, Marisa Jackson
Editors, Nancy Skarmeas, Joan Biddle
Editorial Research, Elizabeth Kea

Cover and title page photograph: Union artillery battery, East Cemetery Hill, Gettysburg National Military Park.
Back Cover: Spring Grove Cemetery and Arboretum, Cincinnati, OH.

The Library of Congress has cataloged the first edition as follows:

Shively, Julie, 1964–
    The Ideals guide to American Civil War places / Julie Shively.
        p.   cm.
    Includes index.
    (alk. paper)
    1. United States—History—Civil War, 1861–1865—Battlefields Guidebooks. 2. Historic
sites—United States Guidebooks. 3. United States—History—Civil War , 1861–1865—Campaigns. I. Title. II. Title: Guide to American Civil War places.
E641.S55 1999
973.7'3—dc21   99-33645
                                                                                                          CIP

Printed and bound in the U.S.A.

10 9 8 7 6 5 4 3 2 1

*This book is dedicated to my husband, Al, whose service in the U.S. Marine Corps—from
Vietnam through Desert Storm—gave him perspective, insight, and knowledge of wartime
decisions which, during our discussions of the various battles and campaigns of the Civil War,
were of infinite value to me. For this, and for his enduring love, he remains my personal hero.
—JS*

TABLE OF CONTENTS

INTRODUCTION

A century and a half have passed since the time of our nation's greatest internal crisis. The United States Civil War spanned five years and was fought on battlefields that stretched from Pennsylvania to Florida, from North Carolina to New Mexico, and included most of the states and territories in between. Three million men saw combat, and more than 600,000 Americans were killed in battle. Thousands more died after the war from wounds or illnesses contracted during the conflict.

The election of Abraham Lincoln in 1860 made the inevitable war a reality. As president, Lincoln was committed to keeping the nation whole and set forth his aim in his first inaugural address in 1861. "One section of our country believes slavery is right, and ought to be extended, while the other believes it is wrong, and ought not to be extended. This is the only substantial dispute. . . . Such will be a great lesson of peace; teaching men that what they cannot take by an election, neither can they take it by a war—teaching all, the folly of being the beginners of a war."

Today, some of the Civil War battlefields are now housing developments, parking lots, and shopping malls. Many, however, remain intact and commemorate our country's tumultuous past. In museums and parks, those who fought are remembered, and in cemeteries, row upon row of markers provide silent testimonies of war. This book guides readers, state by state, through the vital and intriguing places of this conflict. For the second edition, new color photographs and up-to-date site information have been added—just in time for the 150th anniversary years and the commemorative events that will take place to mark them.

Though much time has passed, these historic places still have stories to tell. Walk the battlefields of Shiloh, Vicksburg, Gettysburg, and others, and the ghosts of the past seem to rise from these hallowed grounds. Visit the Civil War museums of Virginia, Florida, Tennessee, and elsewhere, and marvel at the crude weapons of war and primitive medical devices that managed to keep some of the wounded alive. Kneel at the graves of those soldiers who fought, not for selfish or vain reasons, but the Southerners out of fear of a vanishing society and the unknown future, and the Northerners for the continuance of the Union. And silently thank both sides who—at last—began the process of real freedom for all Americans.

ABOUT THE AUTHOR

A graduate of the United States Air Force Academy in political science, Julie Shively is a United States Air Force Reserve historian at the Air Force Historical Research Agency, where she writes and edits Air Force unit histories. She holds a master's degree in education and an education specialist degree in math and science. Shively teaches high school algebra in Gwinnett County, Georgia, where she lives with her husband and four cats.

Chronological List of
Major Battles and Engagements

The following list of battles is by no means comprehensive but merely provides a glimpse of the enormity of the American Civil War.

 ## 1861

Apr. 12–15 ....Ft. Sumter, SC
July 21 ....First Manassas, VA (Bull Run)
Aug. 10..................Springfield, MO (Wilson's Creek)
Sept. 12–20 ....Lexington, MO
Oct. 21 ....Ball's Bluff, Leesburg, VA (Edward's Ferry, Harrison's Landing)
Nov. 7 ....Galveston Harbor, TX
Dec. 20..................Dranesville, VA

 ## 1862

Jan. 19–20 ....Mill Springs, KY (Logan's Cross Roads)
Feb. 8 ....Roanoke Island, NC
Feb. 12–16 ....Ft. Donelson, TN
Mar. 6–8 ....Pea Ridge, AR
Mar. 8–9 ....Hampton Roads, VA
Mar. 23 ....Winchester, VA (First Kernstown)
Mar. 26, 28............Glorieta Pass, NM (Apache Canon)
Apr. 6–7 ....Shiloh, TN (Pittsburg Landing)
Apr. 18–28 ....Forts Jackson and St. Philip, LA
Apr. 29–30 ....First Corinth, MS
May 31–June 1......Fair Oaks, VA
June 8 ....Cross Keys, VA (Union Church)
June 9 ....Port Republic, VA
June 27 ....Gaines' Mill, VA
June 27 ....First Cold Harbor, VA
June 27 ....Chickahominy, VA
July 1 ....Malvern Hill, VA
Aug. 9....................Cedar Mountain, VA (Slaughter Mountain, Cedar Run, and Mitchell Station)
Aug. 28–30............Second Manassas, VA (Bull Run)
Aug. 30..................Richmond, KY
Sept. 1 ....Chantilly, VA
Sep. 13–15 ....Harpers Ferry, WV
Sept. 17 ....Antietam, MD (Sharpsburg)
Sept. 19–20 ....Iuka, MS

Oct. 3–4 ....Second Corinth, MS
Oct. 8 ....Perryville, KY
Dec. 7....................Prairie Grove, Fayetteville, AR
Dec. 11–13.............Fredericksburg, VA
Dec. 28–29.............Chickasaw Bayou, Vicksburg, MS
Dec. 31–Jan. 2.......Stones River, TN (Murfreesboro)

1863

Jan. 1 ....Galveston, TX
Feb. 3 ....Fort Donelson, TN (Cumberland Ironworks)
Mar. 4–5 ....Unionville, TN (Spring Hill, Thompson's Station)
May 1 ....Port Gibson, MS
May 1–3 ....Chancellorsville, VA
May 18–July 4.......Siege of Vicksburg, MS
June 9 ....Brandy Station, VA
June 17–20 ....Aldie, Middleburg, and Upperville, VA
June 23–30 ....Rosecrans's Campaign: Murfreesboro to Tullahoma, TN
July 1–3 ....Gettysburg, PA
July 10–Sep 6........Siege of Fort Wagner, Morris Island, SC
Sept. 18–20 ....Chickamauga, GA
Nov. 17–Dec. 4......Siege of Knoxville, TN
Nov. 24–25 ....Chattanooga, TN

1864

Apr. 8–9 ....Mansfield and Pleasant Hills, LA/TX
May 5–6 ....Wilderness, VA
May 7–Sept. 2........Atlanta Campaign
May 8–18 ....Spotsylvania Court House, VA
May 9–13 ....Sheridan's Cavalry Raid, VA
May 13–16 ....Resaca, GA
May 15 ....New Market, VA
May 23–26 ....North Anna River, VA
May 25–29 ....Dallas GA, Pickett's Mill, New Hope Church, and Allantoona Hills
June 1–12 ....Second Cold Harbor, VA
June 10 ....Brice's Crossroads, near Guntown, MS
June 15–Apr. 1......Siege of Petersburg, VA
June 27 ....Kennesaw Mountain, Marietta, GA (Big Shanty)
July 22 ....Atlanta, GA
July 23–24 ....Kernstown and Winchester, VA
July 28–Sep 3........Siege of Atlanta, GA
Aug. 5–23...............Mobile Bay, Forts Gaines and Morgan, AL
Aug. 31–Sept. 1 .....Jonesboro, GA
Sept. 19–22 ....Winchester and Fisher's Hill, VA
Sept. 26–27 ....Ironton, MO (Pilot Knob)
Sept. 28–30 ....New Market Heights, VA (Laurel Hill)
Oct. 19 ....Cedar Creek, VA

Nov. 29–30 ....Spring Hill and Franklin, TN
Dec. 24–Jan. 13.....Fort Fisher, NC

1865

Feb. 5–7 ....Dabney's Mills, Hatcher's Run, VA
Feb. 27–Mar. 25 ....Sheridan's raid into VA
Mar. 26–Apr. 9 ......Siege of Mobile, AL
Apr. 1 ....Five Forks, VA
Apr. 2 ....Fall of Petersburg, VA
Apr. 3 ....Fall of Richmond, VA, Confederate Capital
Apr. 6 ....Sailor's Creek, VA
Apr. 9 ....Appomattox Court House, VA, Lee surrenders to Grant
Apr. 14 ....Assassination of President Abraham Lincoln
May 10 ....Irwinsville, GA, Capture of Jefferson Davis
May 12–13 ....Palmito Ranch, TX
May 26 ....Final surrender, Lt. Gen. Kirby Smith to Maj. Gen. Canby

EXPLANATORY NOTES

A compass denotes those sites directly related to the battle described in the previous pages.

▪ The green marks on the maps represent the general location of the places. Although interstates, federal highways, and some state highways are included for orientation, space limitations prevent precise directions. In some states, the state map is not complete and shows only that area of the state that contains a Civil War place. In other states, some of the Civil War places are not included on the map because of space restrictions. Please refer to the information on the site provided in each state chapter for more specific directions.

Map abbreviations:

Am. .... American	Headqtrs... Headquarters	Nat'l. .... National
Btlfd. .... Battlefield	Hist. .... Historic	Pk. .... Park
Ch. .... Church	Is. .... Island	Plant.......... Plantation
Conf. .... Confederate	Mem.......... Memorial	Pt. .... Point
Ctr. .... Center	Mon.......... Monument	Soc. .... Society
CW........... Civil War	Mt. .... Mount	St. .... State
Dept. .... Department	Mtn. .... Mountain	Vis. Ctr. ..... Visitor's Center
Ft. .... Fort	Mus. .... Museum	

ALABAMA

The Alabama state legislature voted to leave the Union on January 11, 1861, making the state the fourth to secede. Alabama then played host to the first Confederate capital, at Montgomery, where representatives from the Confederate states elected Jefferson Davis their president and drafted a Confederate constitution. One hundred thousand Alabamans fought for the Confederate cause, and sixteen generals named the state as their birthplace. Still, Alabama's greatest contributions to the war effort were probably its industrial and agricultural resources. The state's ironworks armed the Confederate troops, while Alabama's farms fed soldiers throughout the South.

Alabama was among the least fought over Southern states during the war. No large-scale Federal campaigns penetrated into the state; instead troops, both Northern and Southern, passed though the state on their way to battle elsewhere. Alabama's most significant battle was fought over Mobile Bay and the city it protected.

Alabama today features Civil War sites as varied as the state's many contributions to the Confederacy, sites which remember the soldiers, the citizens, the laborers, and the leaders who were part of Civil War Alabama.

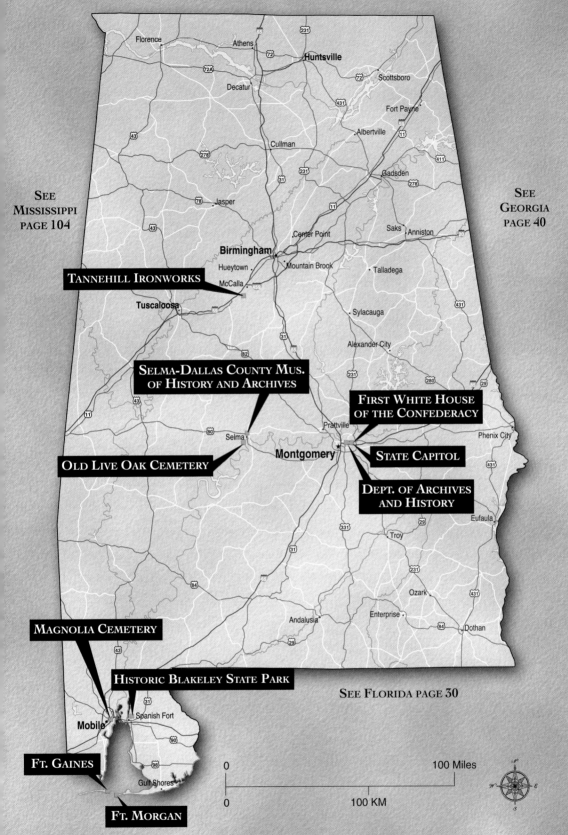

SEE TENNESSEE PAGE 168

SEE
MISSISSIPPI
PAGE 104

SEE
GEORGIA
PAGE 40

Florence
Athens
Huntsville
Scottsboro
Decatur
Fort Payne
Albertville
Cullman
Gadsden
Jasper
Saks Anniston
Center Point
Birmingham
Hueytown
Mountain Brook
Talladega
McCalla
Tuscaloosa
Sylacauga
Alexander City
Prattville
Selma
Phenix City
Montgomery
Eufaula
Troy
Ozark
Andalusia
Enterprise
Dothan

TANNEHILL IRONWORKS

**SELMA-DALLAS COUNTY MUS.
OF HISTORY AND ARCHIVES**

**FIRST WHITE HOUSE
OF THE CONFEDERACY**

OLD LIVE OAK CEMETERY

STATE CAPITOL

**DEPT. OF ARCHIVES
AND HISTORY**

MAGNOLIA CEMETERY

HISTORIC BLAKELEY STATE PARK

SEE FLORIDA PAGE 30

Spanish Fort

Mobile

FT. GAINES

Gulf Shores

FT. MORGAN

0   100 Miles

0   100 KM

THE BATTLE OF MOBILE BAY

August 5, 1864

The Union victory at Mobile Bay effectively blocked the last port available for Confederate blockade running.

In 1862, the ports of New Orleans and Pensacola fell to the Union, leaving Mobile, Alabama, as the major Confederate port in the Gulf of Mexico. Forts Morgan and Gaines protected the entrance to Mobile Bay, and the Confederates had mined the channel with torpedoes.

In the summer of 1864, the Union navy set up a blockade to prevent Confederate ships from leaving the port. When the North learned that Rear Admiral Franklin Buchanan intended to run the blockade with the ironclad *Tennessee*, the situation came to a head. Rear Admiral David Farragut ordered fourteen Union wooden ships be lashed in pairs with the larger of each pair facing Fort Morgan. Farragut planned to run the ships in a line past the Confederate forts and engage the *Tennessee*.

The Union's run began at 5:30AM on August 5. The day started inauspiciously, as the USS *Tecumseh* encountered the minefield, was hit, and quickly sank. The next ship in line, the *Brooklyn*, spied buoys dead ahead, suspected them to be the minefield boundary, and reversed engines. This stalled all the ships behind and exposed them to heavy fire from Fort Morgan. Farragut, lashed to the rigging of the USS *Hartford* to keep from falling from his perch, demanded a reason for the delay. When told about the underwater torpedoes and the sailors' reluctance to move through the minefield, he called out, "Damn the torpedoes, full speed ahead!" The Federal ships passed the minefield untouched. (Fourteen of the *Hartford*'s crew received Congressional Medals of Honor.)

When Farragut finally encountered Buchanan on the *Tennessee*, Farragut began what he later called "one of the fiercest naval combats on record." Throughout the day, three Union ironclads clashed with the *Tennessee* and its accompanying three gunboats, but the ship withstood the barrage. The only damage inflicted upon the *Tennessee* came from the *Manhattan*'s fifteen-inch, solid shot. Overpowered and overwhelmed, the *Tennessee* finally surrendered. Fort Gaines fol-

Fort Gaines and Mobile Bay

lowed within days, but Fort Morgan held out for more than two weeks before it also surrendered to the Union. The city of Mobile, however, remained in Southern hands until the end of the war, although its naval significance was erased by the Union victory at Mobile Bay.

Cannon, Fort Gaines

"You shall not have it to say when you leave this vessel that you were not near enough to the enemy, for I will meet them, and then you can fight them alongside of their own ships; and if I fall, lay me on one side and go on with the fight."

Rear Adm. F. Buchanan

SOUTHERN COMMANDERS:
Rear Adm. F. Buchanan
Capt. J. D. Johnston

STRENGTH: 2200

CASUALTIES: 312

Tannehill Ironworks Historical State Park

12632 Confederate Parkway, McCalla, AL
PHONE: 205-477-5711
WEB: www.tannehill.org
HOURS: Open daily sunrise to sunset.
ADMISSION: Free.

Tannehill Ironworks was the largest producer of ordnance, skillets, pots, and ovens for the Confederate army. At its height, Tannehill produced up to twenty tons of iron a day. However, as part of Union General James Wilson's raid on Alabama war industry sites, Tannehill Ironworks was burned to the ground on March 31, 1865. Today, more than 1,500 acres are preserved for hiking, camping, and recreation. From spring through autumn, blacksmiths, millers, and craftsmen are available to demonstrate their time-honored trade. Artifacts of the nineteenth century iron industry are displayed in the Iron and Steel Museum.

Selma-Dallas County Museum of History and Archives

4 Martin Luther King Street, Selma, AL
PHONE: 334-874-2197
HOURS: Monday – Saturday 10AM – 4PM.
ADMISSION: A fee is charged.

The museum is housed in a Victorian-era railway passenger station built on the site of the Confederate Naval Gun Foundry and Ordnance Works and adjacent to the C.S. Navy Yard where the ironclad warships C.S.S. *Tennessee*, *Huntsville* and *Tuscaloosa* were built. The Museum has under its care a VII inch Brooke Rifled Cannon which was the first of many produced onsite and which served on the *Tennessee*. The Foundry and

Photograph on display, Selma-Dallas County Museum of History and Archives

Works were burned by Federal troops after the Battle of Selma. It is estimated that two-thirds of all munitions used by the Confederacy late in the war were produced in Selma. On hand are examples of shot and shell produced here as well as a copy of foundry Commandant Catesby ap R Jones's log book covering in detail the production of the Selma-made cannon as well as other items relating to Selma's war period. Also on display are hundreds of interesting items and one-of-a-kind collections relating to all periods of Selma and Dallas County's history.

Old Live Oak Cemetery

Dallas Avenue, Selma, AL
PHONE: 334-874-2161
WEB: www.SelmaAlabama.com
HOURS: Open daily except Sundays.
ADMISSION: Free.

Listed on the National Historic Register, Old Live Oak Cemetery contains the remains of many Confederate soldiers as well as some notable civilians. These include Elodie Todd Dawson, staunch Confederate supporter and sister-in-law of Abraham Lincoln; N. H. R. Dawson, Confederate colonel who later was appointed U.S. Commissioner of Education; John Tyler Morgan and Edmund Winston Pettus, both Confederate generals who later became U.S. senators; Catesby ap Roger Jones, commander of the Confederate ironclad *Merrimac* and of the Greater Confederate Naval Gun Foundry and Ordnance Works at Selma; Lt. General William J. Hardee CS, author of "Rifle and Light Infantry Tactics" and Commandant of Students at West Point; and the Reverend Arthur Small, a Presbyterian minister who died in the Battle of Selma.

FIRST WHITE HOUSE OF THE CONFEDERACY

644 Washington Avenue, Montgomery, AL
PHONE: 334-242-1861
WEB: www.firstwhitehouse.org
HOURS: Open weekdays; closed state holidays.
ADMISSION: Free.

The First White House of the Confederacy was the executive residence of President Jefferson Davis and his family while the capital of the Confederate States of America was in Montgomery, Alabama. Completely furnished with original period pieces

Photo above: Jefferson Davis's bedroom

First White House of the Confederacy

from the 1850s and 1860s, the 1835 Italianate style House is open to the public. It has been listed on the National Register of Historic Places since 1974.

ALABAMA STATE CAPITOL

600 Dexter Avenue, Montgomery, AL
PHONE: 334-242-3935
E-MAIL: capitoltours@preserveala.org
WEB: www.preserveala.org
HOURS: Open daily except Sunday; closed state holidays.
ADMISSION: Free.

In February 1861, Confederate President Jefferson Davis delivered his inaugural address from the Alabama State Capitol. Built in 1851, the Greek Revival building contains twin, two-story, spiral staircases and a ninety-foot-high rotunda. The first Confederate Constitution was written in its senate.

ALABAMA DEPARTMENT OF ARCHIVES AND HISTORY

624 Washington Avenue, Montgomery, AL
PHONE: 334-833-4437
HOURS: Open Tuesday – Saturday; closed state holidays.
ADMISSION: Free.

Located across the street from the capitol, the Alabama Department of Archives and History contains exhibits on the Confederacy, the Civil War, and the presidency of Jefferson Davis. The department's collection of Confederate flags is the largest in the state and among the largest in the nation.

FORT GAINES HISTORIC SITE

109 Bienville Boulevard, Dauphin Island, AL
PHONE: 251-861-6992
WEB: www.dauphinisland.org
HOURS: Open daily;
closed Thanksgiving, Christmas Eve, and Christmas Day.
ADMISSION: A fee is charged for adults; children are discounted.

Battlements and soldiers' living quarters at the fort may still be seen. A self-guided tour takes approximately one hour. Past annual events have included a Battle of Mobile Bay Commemorative, Christmas at the Fort, and Colonial Events.

Latrines, Fort Gaines

Cannon, Fort Gaines Historic Site

MAGNOLIA CEMETERY

1202 Virginia Street, Mobile, AL
PHONE: 251-208-7307
E-MAIL: friendsmagnolia@bellsouth.net
HOURS: Cemetery grounds:
7AM – 5:30PM; Office: Monday – Friday
(excluding City Holidays) 7:30AM – 4PM.
ADMISSION: Free.

Confederate Rest, Magnolia Cemetery, Mobile, AL

Opened by the City of Mobile in 1836, this is the second oldest and only active municipal cemetery in Mobile. Confederate Generals Braxton Bragg, James Hagan, Adley Gladden, Danville Leadbetter and Jones Withers are interred here as is the youngest Confederate General, John H. Kelly. Kelly was promoted to general at nineteen for his actions at Chickamauga. He died on September 4, 1864 as a result of wounds received during the Battle of Franklin, TN. Over eleven hundred Confederate casualties are buried in the Confederate Rest Section of Magnolia, and hundreds more are buried in private, family lots in the cemetery. Hundreds of Union casualties are interred in the Mobile National Cemetery adjacent to Magnolia. Many of these soldiers, both Confederate and Union, were killed during the battles of Fort Blakeley, Spanish Fort, and Mobile Bay. Lieutenant J. L. Moses fired the last cannon at the Battle of Blakeley.

HISTORIC BLAKELEY STATE PARK

34745 Alabama Highway 225, Spanish Fort, AL near Mobile, Alabama
P.O. Box 7279, Spanish Fort, AL 36577
PHONE & FAX: 251-626-0798
E-MAIL: blakeleypark@aol.com
WEB: www.blakeleypark.com
HOURS: Open daily 9AM to dusk for day visitors, longer for campers.
ADMISSION: A fee is charged.

Historic Blakeley State Park was created in 1981 when the State of Alabama established the Historic Blakeley Authority to protect the 3,800 acres on the Blakeley National Register of Historic Places because of its unique history and diverse natural attractions.

Some 2,000 acres of land under the auspices of Blakeley Park are preserved and available to the public. Historic sites preserved include early Native American sites, historic Indian sites, the site of the now "ghost town" of the 1814 Town of Blakeley, and both Confederate and Union breastworks of the April 9, 1865 Civil War battle of Fort Blakeley.

Participating in the 1865 battle, fought hours after Gen. Robert E. Lee had surrendered to Gen. Ulysses S. Grant, effectively ending the Civil War, were some 6,000 U.S. Colored Troops, as African-American regiments were called then, which was the third largest incident of African-American troops to fight in the Civil War.

Blakeley Park periodically holds reenactments demonstrating the living history of the Union artillery attack and the brief but furious battle that ended the siege April 9, 1865. Miles of Civil War breastworks and the earthen fortifications known as redoubts are located inside the park. Equally outstanding are the many miles of nature trails among the woodlands.

Camping facilities feature a full-service wooded RV campground and a primitive campground for tents and pop-ups. Twenty-four hour staffing provides information and security to visitors in the family-oriented campground. Charter and periodic public walk-on eco-tours into the Mobile-Tensaw River Delta aboard the park's 50-passenger pontoon boat from the park's dock on the Tensaw River are offered as well as other programs.

Photo top left: Battle of Blakeley monument

Photo bottom left: Artillery firing

FORT MORGAN HISTORIC SITE

51 Alabama Highway 180 West, Gulf Shores, AL
PHONE: 251-540-7127

HOURS: Open daily.

ADMISSION: A fee is charged; children, seniors, and groups are discounted.

Much of Fort Morgan remains in excellent condition and is still standing. A self-guided tour is available of the site, and candlelight tours focusing on the Civil War are held Tuesday evenings at 7PM in June and July, weather permitting. Fort Morgan features a museum, an information center, and an annual living history encampment that commemorates the Battle of Mobile Bay and the Siege of Fort Morgan.

Photo left: Interior wall, Fort Morgan

Photo below: Aerial view of Fort Morgan

ARKANSAS

Arkansas offered the Confederacy little in the way of agricultural, industrial, or transportation resources; but it did produce 60,000 volunteers to fight for the Southern rebellion. In May of 1861, the state legislature voted near unanimously to secede. The one vote for remaining loyal to the Union came from the northwestern Ozarks region, where the Confederacy was trusted as little as any other form of government. Ironically, it was in that northwestern corner of the state—not in the slaveholding counties of the south and east—that the Civil War first came to Arkansas, in battles at Pea Ridge and Prairie Grove, both of which helped the Union secure control of the state.

A frontier state at the time of the Civil War, Arkansas is still largely rural, and its battlefields have not been hemmed in or swallowed up by development. Much in Arkansas remains unchanged; especially at the Civil War battlefields, where it is not too difficult to imagine the sights and sounds of the long-ago conflict.

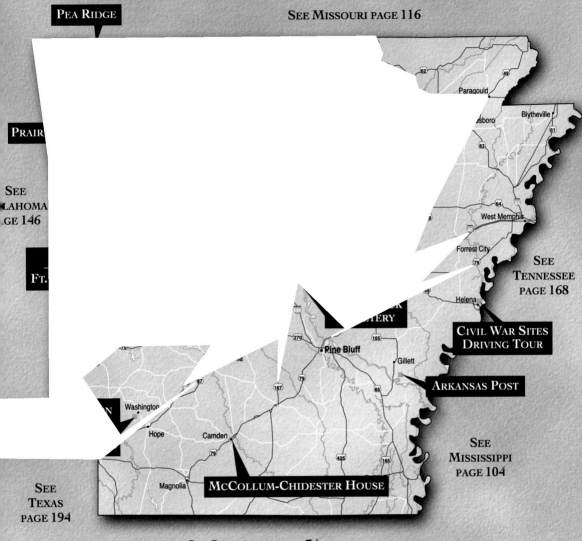

PEA RIDGE

SEE MISSOURI PAGE 116

Paragould

Blytheville

PRAIR

SEE
LAHOMA
GE 146

West Memphis

FT.

Forrest City

SEE
TENNESSEE
PAGE 168

Helena

CIVIL WAR SITES
DRIVING TOUR

Pine Bluff

Gillett

ARKANSAS POST

SEE
MISSISSIPPI
PAGE 104

Washington

Hope

Camden

SEE
TEXAS
PAGE 194

Magnolia

McCOLLUM-CHIDESTER HOUSE

SEE LOUISIANA PAGE 74

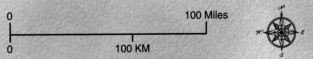

0   100 Miles

0   100 KM

THE BATTLE OF PEA RIDGE (ELKHORN TAVERN)

March 6–8, 1862

Although it took place in Arkansas, this battle secured Missouri for the Union and led to Union victory in Arkansas.

"I have never thought that General Curtis has received the credit he was entitled to. . . . This campaign demonstrated early in the war what could be accomplished by a small Army 300 miles away from any rail or water communication"

G. M. Dodge about Maj. Gen. S. R. Curtis (pictured above)

General Sterling Price, former governor of Missouri and Confederate sympathizer who led a Pro-Confederate State Guard, menaced the Union army after the battle of Wilson's Creek and threatened to disrupt the Union advance down the Mississippi River. The North had to suppress Price who had joined the Confederate troops in February 1862. On the other side, the Confederates were determined to invade and retake Missouri through the new Confederate Army of the West under Major General Earl Van Dorn. In December of 1861, Brigadier General Samuel R. Curtis took command of the Union army in Missouri, and his first objective was to drive Rebel factions from the state. With this in mind, Curtis marched to Springfield and forced Confederate sympathizers, led by Price, into Arkansas. Once there, Price's men joined with Confederates under General Ben McCulloch; their combined forces came under the command of General Van Dorn.

On March 6, Curtis and his troops marched near Pea

Pea Ridge National Military Park

Cannon at Elkhorn Tavern, Pea Ridge National Military Park

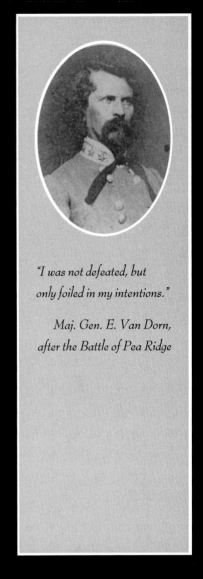

Ridge to Elkhorn Tavern, along Little Sugar Creek. That evening, Van Dorn also reached Little Sugar Creek but chose to come around the rear of the Union from the north. Curtis learned of the flanking movement and turned his twenty-one guns about. Price and McCulloch split up due to their difference in speed, so McCulloch turned toward Leetown. Curtis attacked both Confederate divisions the morning of March 7. Darkness finally halted the fighting. During the night, Curtis and Van Dorn repositioned their men to continue fighting around Elkhorn Tavern in the morning. The Confederates held their own until their artillery ammunition ran out due to ordnance trains being separated from the main body of the army. Then the Southern rout began into the heart of Arkansas. This ended any serious threat to Missouri.

SOUTHERN COMMANDERS:
Maj. Gen. E. Van Dorn
Maj. Gen. S. Price

STRENGTH: 16,500

CASUALTIES: 1,500

PEA RIDGE NATIONAL MILITARY PARK

15930 Highway 62E, Garfield, AR
PHONE: 479-451-8122
WEB: www.nps.gov/peri
HOURS: Open daily; closed Thanksgiving, Christmas, and New Year's Day.
ADMISSION: A fee is charged for adults or per car; children and seniors are discounted.

With more than 4,300 acres of the Pea Ridge Battlefield contained within its boundaries, this military park might be one of the best-preserved Civil War battle sites in the U.S. The park includes a reconstruction of Elkhorn Tavern on its original site. The tavern is open for tours from Memorial Day until Labor Day weekend. Markers outline key events of the battle on a seven-mile self-guided tour. A ten-mile hiking trail is also available. The Visitor's Center features a thirty-minute movie, "Thunder in the Ozarks," on events before, during, and after the battle; and a new museum houses exhibits pertaining to the battle. Living history programs occur throughout the year.

PRAIRIE GROVE BATTLEFIELD STATE PARK

506 E. Douglas Street, Prairie Grove, AR
PHONE: 479-846-2990
WEB: www.arkansasstateparks.com/
prairiegrovebattlefield
HOURS: Open daily 8AM – one hour after sunset; Hindman Hall: open daily 8AM – 5PM; closed major holidays.
ADMISSION: Admission to park grounds is free. Museum and house tours charge a fee; children are discounted.

The 838-acre Prairie Grove Battlefield State Park includes Hindman Hall Museum and Visitor Center, a picnic area and playground, a monument area, a historic building area, and the Borden House and orchard which sit atop the Prairie Grove ridge which stretches east to west for about two miles. The Confederate Army positioned itself on

Photo above right: Hindman Hall Visitor Center and Battlefield Museum

Photo below right: Morrow House

this high ground, covering the entire length with its battle lines by the end of December 7, 1862. The remaining park acreage includes part of the Prairie Grove valley and slope where the Union Army advanced during the battle. In addition, the park has several resources useful for interpreting the battle, the effects of the Civil War on the region, and the history of the park. These range from an artifact collection to buildings, monuments, and interpretive signs.

The Archibald Borden House is believed to be on the original site of the first Borden House, which was destroyed by Union soldiers who set it on fire the day after the battle. The John Morrow House served as headquarters for Confederate General Hindman prior to the Battle of Prairie Grove. Among the exhibits at the Hindman Hall Museum are Civil War artifacts and displays on the soldier's life. A five-mile driving tour to the western overlook and one-mile walking trail over the most contested part of the battlefield are also available.

FAYETTEVILLE NATIONAL CEMETERY

700 Government Avenue, Fayetteville, AR
PHONE: 479-444-5051
WEB: www.cem.va.gov
HOURS: Open daily sunrise to sunset.
ADMISSION: Free.

Fayetteville National Cemetery was established in 1867, and the bodies of 1,210 soldiers were moved from the battlegrounds of Pea Ridge, Prairie Grove, and Fayetteville to this final resting place; a great portion of the interred are unknown. During World War II, the layout was revised and five sections were added. Each year Memorial Day services commemorate the soldiers buried here.

HEADQUARTERS HOUSE

118 East Dickson Street, Fayetteville, AR
PHONE: 479-521-2970 (Washington County National Historical Society)
E-MAIL: info@headquartershouse.org
WEB: www.headquartershouse.org
HOURS: Open Wednesday afternoons or by appointment.
ADMISSION: A fee is charged; children are discounted.

Headquarters House

Headquarters House was built in 1853 by a Northern sympathizer and judge who was imprisoned for his political views. At various times, the house served as headquarters for both the Union and Confederate commanders. The Battle of Fayetteville was partially fought on the house grounds, and a hole made by a minié ball is still visible in one of the doors. Commemorations of the Battle of Fayetteville occur here each April.

FORT SMITH NATIONAL HISTORIC SITE

47 South 3rd Street, Fort Smith, AR
PHONE: 501-783-3961
HOURS: Open daily 9AM – 5PM; closed
Christmas and New Year's Day.
ADMISSION: $4/person; children under 15
free; America the Beautiful pass admits
4 people free.

Originally a Union fort, Fort Smith fell into
Confederate hands in 1861, then was recaptured by Union forces in 1863. Until the end of
the war, it remained as a base for Federal operations in Arkansas. The Visitor's Center offers
self-guided walking tours, artifacts, exhibits,
and a fifteen-minute film on the history of the
fort. Marked walking trails along the Arkansas
River lead to the site of the first fort.

Photo above right: Fort Smith National Historic Site

*Photo below right: Bastion #3, Fort Smith
National Historic Site*

FORT SMITH NATIONAL CEMETERY

522 Garland Avenue and South 6th Street, Fort Smith, AR
PHONE: 479-783-5345
WEB: www.cem.va.gov
HOURS: Open daily 7:30AM – sunset.
ADMISSION: Free.

More than 1,500 unknown soldiers are buried at Fort Smith National Cemetery. Also interred at the
cemetery are Confederate Generals James B. McIntosh who fought and died at Pea Ridge, Richard
C. Gatlin who was the Adjutant General of North Carolina, and Alexander Early Steen who fought
and died at Prairie Grove. The cemetery's office houses a few pictures on the area's military history.

HISTORIC WASHINGTON STATE PARK
CONFEDERATE STATE CAPITOL

Franklin Street, Washington, AR
PHONE: 870-983-2684
WEB: www.historicwashingtonstatepark.com
HOURS: Open daily; closed Christmas, New Year's Day, and Thanksgiving.

1836 Courthouse, Historic Washington State Park

ADMISSION: A fee is charged for historic demonstrations and guided tours.

Historic Washington State Park served as the state capital between 1864 and 1865. The park features a nineteenth-century museum village, which includes the building that served as the Confederate capitol in Arkansas, a restaurant, print museum, several historic houses, a blacksmith shop, and a weapons museum. There is an annual reenactment of the Civil War experience at the park the first weekend of November.

McCollum-Chidester House Museum

926 Washington Street, Camden, AR
PHONE: 870-836-9243
HOURS: Open Wednesday – Saturday; closed major holidays.
ADMISSION: Adults $5; students $2.

The city of Camden was occupied by Northern forces in 1864. During the occupation, Gen. Frederick Steele, commander of the force, used this house as his headquarters.

McCollum-Chidester House Museum

Little Rock National Cemetery

2523 Confederate Boulevard, Little Rock, AR
PHONE: 501-324-6401
WEB: www.cem.va.gov
HOURS: Open daily, dawn until dusk; office open 8AM – 4:30PM.
ADMISSION: Free.

The grounds of Little Rock National Cemetery were originally used as a Union camp. After Union troops evacuated, the Confederates used the area in which to bury their dead. In 1868, the cemetery was established as a national cemetery. The Union and Confederate dead were separated until a law was passed in 1937 to take the separation away. Approximately 10,000 Civil War soldiers are buried here. The Confederate markers are slightly more pointed than the Union gravestones. Legend has it that the Confederates used pointed stones to prevent Union soldiers from sitting on the markers. Services are held on Memorial Day.

Minnesota Monument

MOUNT HOLLY CEMETERY

12th Street and Broadway, Little Rock, AR
HOURS: Open daily.
ADMISSION: Free.

Mount Holly Cemetery, established in 1843, is the final resting place of executed Confederate spy David O. Dodd and five Confederate generals.

Mount Holly Cemetery

OLD STATE HOUSE MUSEUM

300 West Markham Street, Little Rock, AR
PHONE: 501-324-9685
HOURS: Monday – Saturday 9AM – 5PM; Sunday 1PM – 5PM. Closed Thanksgiving, Christmas Eve, Christmas Day, and New Year's Day.
ADMISSION: Free.

The Old State House, now a museum of Arkansas history, served as the state's capitol from 1836 to 1911. In 1861, it was the site of the Arkansas Secession Convention and served as the seat of Confederate government until 1863, when Union troops moved into Little Rock. The building then served as the seat of the Federal government until the end of the war. The Old State House Museum maintains a collection of Civil War battle flags, not currently on view. The museum plans a series of five Civil War related exhibits from 2011 – 2015. Guided and self-guided tours are available.

Old State House Museum

ARKANSAS POST NATIONAL MEMORIAL

1741 Old Post Road, Gillett, AR
PHONE: 870-548-2207
WEB: www.nps.gov/arpo
HOURS: Open daily; closed major holidays.
ADMISSION: Free.

During the Civil War, the Confederates tried to maintain control of the Arkansas River by erecting an earthen fort at this site. In 1863 the Union destroyed the fort and gained control of the river. The museum features a 22-minute film covering Arkansas Post history including details of the battle. The park also offers accessible trails along the bayous and to the location where much of the battle occurred.

Post Bend Lake as seen from Arkansas Post National Memorial

JACKSONPORT STATE PARK

205 Avenue Street off Arkansas Highway 69, Jacksonport, AR
PHONE: 870-523-2143
WEB: www.arkansasstateparks.com
HOURS: Open daily; museum open Tuesday – Saturday
8AM – 5PM, Sunday 1PM – 5PM.
ADMISSION: $3.25 adults; $1.75 children 6 –12; children under 6 free.

Because of its access to both the Mississippi and Arkansas Rivers, Jacksonport was of prime importance during the war and was occupied by both the Confederate and Union armies. Five generals used the town as their headquarters. On June 5, 1865, Confederate Gen. Jeff Thompson, the "Swamp Fox of the Confederacy," surrendered 6,000 troops to

Jacksonport State Park

Lt. Col. C. W. Davis at the Jacksonport Landing. The 162-acre park sits on the White and Black Rivers. On the grounds are a museum and a Civil War monument. Camping is allowed for a fee.

CIVIL WAR SITES DRIVING TOUR

226 Perry Street, Helena, AR
PHONE: 870-817-7400
HOURS: Open weekdays.
ADMISSION: Free.

The Civil War Sites Driving Tour features important sites of the July 4, 1863, Battle of Helena, won by Union forces. The tour also features the Confederate Cemetery, where Confederate casualties from the Battle of Helena are interred. Brochures of the driving tour, which features four Union battery sites located on private property, are available at Helena City Hall.

FLORIDA

Despite having seen little battle, Florida's borders contain a diverse collection of Civil War history. Throughout the state, Florida's Civil War past is evident in its fortresses, museums, and historical sites. Although it was the southernmost state of the Confederacy, many of Florida's strategic forts and cities were controlled by Union forces. Dry Tortugas Fort, the largest all-masonry fort in the Western Hemisphere, was held by the North throughout the war.

With access to both the Atlantic Ocean and the Gulf of Mexico, Florida's peninsular location has made it a key tactical position since the Spanish first arrived in 1513. Castillo de San Marcos, the country's oldest surviving fort, was occupied by both Confederate and Union forces. Similarly, Fort Clinch in Fernandina Beach and Fort Barrancas in Pensacola were also controlled by both armies at different times during the Civil War. St. Marks Lighthouse, now a National Wildlife Refuge, was the site of a Confederate lookout tower, which Union forces attempted to burn twice.

The war's grip stretched as far south as Key West, where Fort Zachary Taylor boasts one of the nation's largest collections of Civil War armament. Each February a reenactment of the Battle of Olustee commemorates the only major battle fought in Florida. After defeat, Union forces returned to Jacksonville, and the state of Florida was secured as part of the Confederacy.

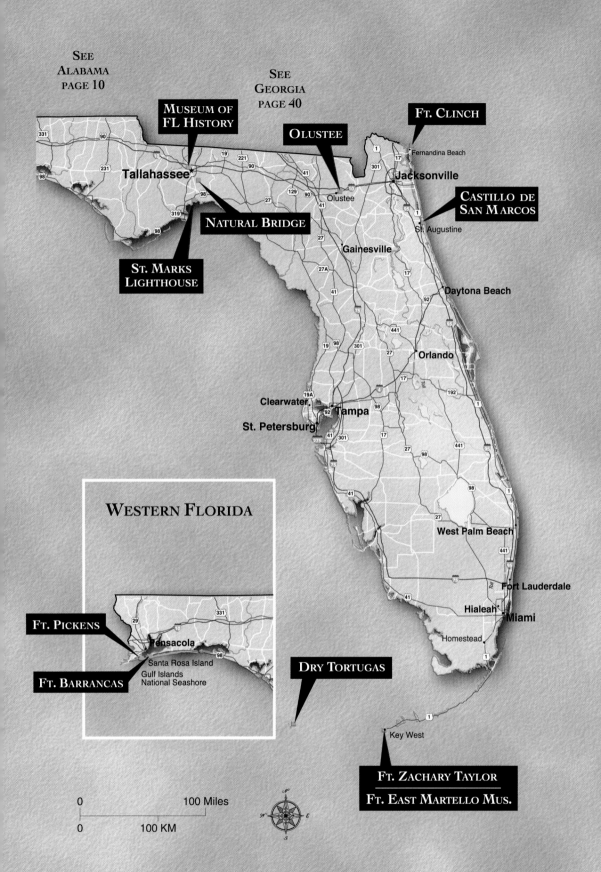

SEE
ALABAMA
PAGE 10

SEE
GEORGIA
PAGE 40

MUSEUM OF
FL HISTORY

OLUSTEE

FT. CLINCH

Fernandina Beach

Tallahassee

Jacksonville

CASTILLO DE
SAN MARCOS

Olustee

St. Augustine

NATURAL BRIDGE

Gainesville

ST. MARKS
LIGHTHOUSE

Daytona Beach

Orlando

Clearwater

Tampa

St. Petersburg

WESTERN FLORIDA

West Palm Beach

FT. PICKENS

Pensacola

Fort Lauderdale

Santa Rosa Island
Gulf Islands
National Seashore

Hialeah

Miami

FT. BARRANCAS

DRY TORTUGAS

Homestead

Key West

FT. ZACHARY TAYLOR

FT. EAST MARTELLO MUS.

0   100 Miles

0   100 KM

"Have met the enemy at Olustee and now falling back. Many wounded. Think I may be compelled to go to Baldwin, but shall go to Barber's immediately. . . . A devilish hard rub."

Brig. Gen. T. A. Seymour

NORTHERN
COMMANDER:
Brig. Gen. T. A. Seymour

STRENGTH: 5,500

CASUALTIES: 1,861

THE BATTLE OF OLUSTEE

February 20, 1864

The only major Civil War battle in Florida.

In December of 1863, President Abraham Lincoln issued the Proclamation of Amnesty and Reconstruction, offering pardon and amnesty to all Confederate supporters, except for government and military leaders, who would pledge their support to the Union. Included in the proclamation was a provision for Union loyal governments to be set up in states where ten percent of voters had pledged such loyalty. Lincoln had high hopes for Florida, where Union support ran high in the northern part of the state.

In February of 1864, Lincoln sent General Truman A. Seymour's Union troops to northern Florida. Included in Seymour's division were the men of the Fifty-fourth Massachusetts

Olustee Battlefield State Historic Site

Infantry, the African-American unit that had fought at Fort Wagner, South Carolina, under Colonel Robert Gould Shaw.

Seymour's force of approximately 5,000 soldiers landed at Jacksonville and moved inland. Seymour hoped to block the Southern supply line which extended into Florida. Despite the Federal blockade, the peninsula provided numerous ports for Confederate privateers and navy ships.

On February 20, Seymour's men met a Confederate force under Brigadier General Joseph Finegan east of Lake City at Olustee. The two sides, evenly matched in strength, fought through the afternoon in a bloody conflict. The Confederate forces, however, proved stronger, and the Union troops retreated to Jacksonville. The Confederates did not pursue; and once safely inside Jacksonville, the Union controlled the city for the remainder of the Civil War.

After Olustee, fighting in Florida increased. Smaller battles were fought in Gainesville, Marianna, Fort Myers, and Natural Bridge. The Confederate District of Florida surrendered to the Union on May 10, 1865.

"I pressed forward my cavalry force last night in the direction of Baldwin. I have received no report from them yet, but think that the enemy has abandoned Baldwin and retired to Jacksonville."

Brig. Gen. J. Finegan

SOUTHERN COMMANDER:
Brig. Gen. J. Finegan

STRENGTH: 5,000

CASUALTIES: 946

Cannon, Olustee Battlefield State Historic Site

FORT BARRANCAS

901 Taylor Road, Pensacola, FL
PHONE: 850-455-5167
WEB: www.nps.gov/guis
HOURS: Open daily.
ADMISSION: Free.

Fort Barrancas has been restored and is a part of the Gulf Island National Seashore. The original fort was occupied by Confederate forces from 1861 until they withdrew in May 1862. Although artillery fire was exchanged with nearby Fort Pickens, Fort Barrancas was never attacked. A Visitor Center and 2PM guided tours are available, and on Saturdays only, a guided tour of nearby Advanced Redoubt is given at 11AM.

Fort Barrancas from across the bay

FORT PICKENS

1400 Fort Pickens Road, Pensacola Beach, FL
PHONE: 850-934-2600 (Gulf Island National Seashore)
WEB: www.nps.gov/guis
HOURS: Open daily.
ADMISSION: A fee is charged by the car; over 62 are free.

Built over five years from 1829 to 1834, this fort was occupied by Union troops throughout the war. Fort Pickens is the site of the first Civil War battle in Florida. The steadfast refusal to surrender in the face of repeated demands by a numerically-superior force was a great rallying point for Unionists during the Secession Winter of 1861. When Federal forces refused to evacuate the fort, Confederate troops attacked unsuccessfully. In 1862 Southern leaders moved their troops to more active areas and abandoned their positions in the Pensacola area. A Visitor Center and guided tours are available.

Photo right:
Casemates, Fort Pickens

Cannon, Fort Pickens

MUSEUM OF FLORIDA HISTORY

500 South Bronough Street, Tallahassee, FL

PHONE: 850-245-6400
WEB: www.museumoffloridahistory.com
HOURS: Open daily; closed Thanksgiving and Christmas.
ADMISSION: Free.

This state history museum includes Civil War military armament, soldiers' personal effects, home-front artifacts, and Confederate battle flags carried by Florida units.

*Photo above: Civil War-era revolver,
Museum of Florida History*

*Photo right: Civil War encampment,
Museum of Florida History*

NATURAL BRIDGE BATTLEFIELD STATE HISTORIC SITE

Natural Bridge Road, Woodville, FL
PHONE: 850-922-6007
HOURS: Open daily.
ADMISSION: $3/car.

On March 6, 1865, Confederate troops, including cadets and home guards, defeated Union troops as they attempted to cross St. Marks River at Natural Bridge. This historic site features a monument outlining the battle and a listing of the names of the Confederate soldiers who took part in the battle. Self-interpretive plaques are also available. Each March the site hosts a reenactment of the Battle of Natural Bridge.

Confederate monument, Natural Bridge Battlefield State Historic Site

ST. MARKS LIGHTHOUSE

St. Marks National Wildlife Refuge, 1255 Lighthouse Road, St. Marks, FL
PHONE: 850-925-6121
WEB: www.fws.gov/saintmarks
HOURS: Open daily.
ADMISSION: A fee is charged.

During the Civil War, Customs Collector Alonzo B. Noyes ordered the oil and lenses to be removed and stored at the town of St. Marks. Confederates used the tower for a lookout, but repeated shelling by the Union stopped the practice. After the war, the tower was repaired and the height was raised to 73 feet. The light was relit in 1867. Although visitors are not currently permitted in the structure, the wildlife refuge around the site is open.

Photo right: St. Marks Lighthouse

OLUSTEE BATTLEFIELD STATE HISTORIC SITE —

U.S. Highway 90, Olustee, FL
PHONE: 386-758-0400
WEB: floridastateparks.org
HOURS: Open daily.
ADMISSION: Free.

The Olustee Battlefield State Historic Site represents the largest Civil War battle in Florida. Trails with interpretive markers offer a self-guided walk through the battle site. Each February the Battle of Olustee is reenacted. A visitor center features several Civil War artifacts.

FORT CLINCH STATE PARK

2601 Atlantic Avenue, Fernandina Beach, FL
PHONE: 904-277-7274
WEB: floridastateparks.org
HOURS: Open daily.
ADMISSION: A fee is charged.

The Union began construction of Fort Clinch in 1847 but never completed it. The partially finished building was occupied by Confederate forces from 1861 until threat of a Union naval expedition forced evacuation in March 1862. For the remainder of the war, Union troops occupied Fort Clinch. Guided tours of the fort are available. A reenactment of sentry duty and drills takes place on the first weekend of each month. Special Union garrison reenactments are scheduled for the first weekend of each month, and Confederate garrison reenactments take place during the month of October.

Fort Clinch State Park

CASTILLO DE SAN MARCOS NATIONAL MONUMENT ━━

1 South Castillo Drive, Augustine, FL
PHONE: 904-829-6506
WEB: www.nps.gov/casa
HOURS: Open daily; closed Christmas.
ADMISSION: A fee is charged for adults; seniors are discounted; children 15 and under are free.

The Castillo de San Marcos (called Fort Marion during the Civil War) was originally built by the Spanish between 1672 and 1695. Confederate forces occupied the fort from 1861 until a threat from Union naval forces caused them to withdraw in 1862. Several times a day, rangers give informative talks and guided tours; information and exhibits are available inside the fort.

DRY TORTUGAS NATIONAL PARK ━━━━━━━━━━

Key West (08 miles offshore in the Gulf of Mexico), FL
PHONE: 305-242-7700 (includes transportation information to island)
WEB: www.nps.gov/drto
HOURS: Open daily.
ADMISSION: A fee is charged; children under 17 are free.

The largest all-masonry fort in the Western Hemisphere, Fort Jefferson was garrisoned by Union troops throughout the Civil War. It also served as a military prison. Exhibits and self-guided tours of the fort are available.

FORT ZACHARY TAYLOR HISTORIC STATE PARK ━━

End of Southard Street through Truman Annex, Key West, FL
PHONE: 305-292-6713
WEB: floridastateparks.org/forttaylor
HOURS: Open daily.
ADMISSION: A fee is charged.

Fort Zachary Taylor Historic State Park

Construction on Fort Zachary Taylor began in 1845 and was completed in 1866. To aid in the coastal blockade, Union troops quickly secured Fort Zachary Taylor at the outset of the war and occupied it for the war's entirety. Cannon inside the fort comprise one of the largest groups of Civil War heavy artillery in existence. Tours of Fort Zachary Taylor are given twice daily. In February the park hosts a heritage festival at the site which provides a living history showcase.

FORT EAST MARTELLO MUSEUM

3501 South Roosevelt Boulevard, Key West, FL
PHONE: 305-296-3913
WEB: www.kwahs.org
HOURS: Open daily 9:30AM – 4:30PM; closed Christmas Day.
ADMISSION: Adults $6, Seniors (62+) and AAA $5, Children $3.

Designed after the nearly impregnable coastal Martello watchtowers in Italy, Fort East Martello was never completed. Built to defend Fort Zachary Taylor from Confederate attack, Fort East Martello with its eight-foot thick walls could have withstood fierce enemy bombardment during the Civil War. However, no battles ever took place and today its casemates, citadel and court-yard are home to a vast collection of Key West art and artifacts from the early Calusa natives to the present day residents.

Fort East Martello Museum

GEORGIA

Georgia, the most populous and prosperous state in the Deep South, was early to secede from the Union and quick to make its first contributions to the Confederacy in the form of materiel and food. Georgia's factories provided powder, arms, shoes, and uniforms; its farms produced corn and hogs. In addition, with 1,400 miles of railroad tracks, Georgia could move food, supplies, and men quickly and efficiently. Whereas there were early Civil War naval battles off the Georgia coast, it was not until the fall of 1863 at Chickamauga that large-scale land warfare came to Georgia, and not until the following spring when Union General William T. Sherman began his long march through the state—first from Chattanooga to Atlanta, and then from Atlanta to Savannah—that interior Georgia felt the full brunt of the Civil War. When Sherman left Savannah in January of 1865, Georgia's active role in the Civil War was over.

In all, more than 550 battles or skirmishes were fought on Georgia soil, and the state sent 100,000 men to fight for the Confederacy. Georgia's support of the Confederate cause was complete, and thus the destruction and devastation of the Civil War touched the state in every corner. Although much of Georgia's Civil War heritage has been lost to development and neglect, Civil War sites are abundant throughout the state, and in recent decades Georgia has made renewed efforts to preserve the evidence and artifacts of its Civil War past.

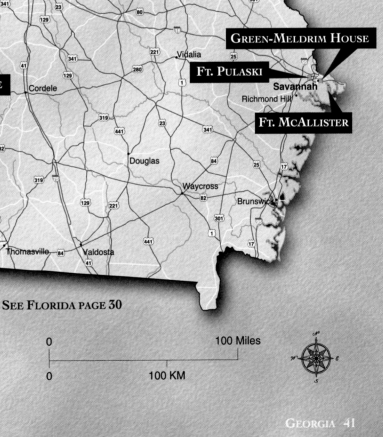

See Tennessee page 168

See North Carolina page 132

CHICKAMAUGA AND CHATTANOOGA

Fort Oglethorpe

See
South Carolina
page 158

KENNESAW MTN.

PICKETT'S MILL

Kennesaw
Marietta

Dallas

MARIETTA
CEMETERY

R. TOOMBS HOUSE

A. H. STEPHENS SITE

Washington

Atlanta

STONE MTN.

Crawfordville

ATLANTA CYCLORAMA

OAKLAND CEMETERY

South Augusta

NAT'L. CIVIL WAR
NAVAL MUS. AT
PORT COLUMBUS

Macon

GREEN-MELDRIM HOUSE

Columbus

Vidalia

FT. PULASKI

Andersonville

Savannah

ANDERSONVILLE

Cordele

Richmond Hill

FT. MCALLISTER

See
Alabama
page 10

Albany

Douglas

Waycross

Brunswick

Thomasville

Valdosta

See Florida page 30

0   100 Miles

0   100 KM

THE BATTLE OF CHICKAMAUGA

September 18–20, 1863

This battle near the Tennessee border was the last great Confederate victory.

The city of Chattanooga, in southeastern Tennessee near the Georgia border, was a link to the Deep South by rail and, therefore, a strategic military objective for the Union. In 1863 the city was protected by Confederate General Braxton Bragg. Through a series of blunders, both sides stumbled into the Battle of Chickamauga.

In early September 1863, Union General Ambrose Burnside took Knoxville, northeast of Chattanooga. Meanwhile, Major General William Rosecrans's army began to advance upon Chattanooga from the Tennessee River. Outnumbered and outflanked, General Bragg withdrew from Chattanooga south to LaFayette, Georgia, to regroup, obtain reinforcements, and prepare for an attack. Rosecrans learned of the Confederate retreat and concentrated his army, moving them north on the LaFayette Road toward Chattanooga. Bragg, lacking accurate information as to the Union army's

Second Minnesota Monument, Chickamauga and Chattanooga National Military Park

Chickamauga and Chattanooga National Military Park

whereabouts, belatedly seized all the crossings over Chickamauga Creek to keep Rosecrans from the LaFayette Road and to force the Union army away from Chattanooga.

On the evening of September 18, a Union brigade came upon Confederate soldiers who had captured Reed's Bridge on the northern end of the Chickamauga Creek. Believing that this was the only Confederate unit across the creek, the Union army rejoined its corps and, in the morning, turned east into the forest between LaFayette Road and Chickamauga Creek. Throughout the day, both sides fed the battle just to maintain stability. Neither side wanted a fight in the thick terrain. Fighting began at dawn and ended in a stalemate; the Union still held LaFayette Road, but in a defensive position.

The next morning, fighting resumed with no advancement on either side until, acting on false information, Rosecrans moved a division of his men to plug a reported hole in his line. The hole did not exist, but one was created by the move, and the Confederates moved through the gap and cut the Union army in half. The Union army broke and retreated. When the Confederate army did not actively pursue them, Union forces reorganized and marched into Chattanooga; they had lost the battle but had gained the city.

Bragg came under sharp criticism for his decision not to pursue and destroy Rosecrans's army. Left unharassed, the Federals fortified Chattanooga. Chickamauga was the bloodiest two-day battle of the war. Combined, the two sides lost almost 35,000 men.

CHICKAMAUGA AND CHATTANOOGA NATIONAL MILITARY PARK

3370 LaFayette Road, Fort Oglethorpe, GA

PHONE: 706-866-9241

WEB: www.nps.gov/chch

HOURS: Open daily, except Christmas.

ADMISSION: Free. ($3 entrance fee for adults 16 and older to Point Park, a unit of the Lookout Mountain Battlefield.)

* Note: See Tennessee for additional information concerning the battles of Chickamauga and Chattanooga.

Chickamauga and Chattanooga National Military Park consists of various units spanning Tennessee and Georgia. The Chickamauga Battlefield consists of 5,300 acres, while Lookout Mountain Battlefield, Orchard Knob, Missionary Ridge, Wauhatchie, and Moccasin Bend National Archeological District consist of over 4,000 acres of preserved land. This park is the first of five National Military Parks authorized by Congress between 1890 and 1899. It was officially dedicated in September 1895.

Each year special programs, such as guided tours of battlefield areas and Civil War living history encampments, are presented at Chickamauga Battlefield and Lookout Mountain Battlefield to commemorate the Battle of Chickamauga and Battles for Chattanooga. These events take place near

First Wisconsin Cavalry Monument (foreground) and Wilder Brigade Monument (background), Chickamauga and Chattanooga National Military Park

Brotherton Cabin, Chickamauga and Chattanooga National Military Park

the anniversaries of the battles (September for Chickamauga and November for Lookout Mountain).

The Chickamauga Battlefield Visitor Center features exhibits on the Battle of Chickamauga, the Claud and Zanada Fuller Collection of American Military Shoulder Arms, a 7-minute fiber optic map presentation and a 23-minute orientation film depicting the Battle of Chickamauga. The Lookout Mountain Battlefield Visitor Center houses various audiovisual programs and exhibits, including the 13 x 30 foot painting by James Walker, titled "The Battle of Lookout Mountain."

Photo above right: Chickamauga and Chattanooga National Military Park Headquarters

Photo below right: Chickamauga and Chattanooga National Military Park

THE BATTLE OF KENNESAW MOUNTAIN

June 27, 1864

Kennesaw Mountain was a decisive battle in General William T. Sherman's campaign to capture Atlanta for the Union.

In his campaign to reach and take Atlanta for the Union during the spring of 1862, Major General William T. Sherman, with a force of 100,000 men, began his advance toward the city on May 4 from the northwest corner of Georgia, 100 miles from Atlanta. His route was laid out along the railroad lines connecting Atlanta with Nashville, which were his connection to his supply base in Tennessee. Blocking his way was rugged terrain and 65,000 Confederate soldiers under the command of General Joseph E. Johnston.

Sherman's advance was marked by strategy more than by battle. The Confederates would set up lines of defense, the Union would outflank them, then the Confederates would move south to reset their defenses. By mid-June, Sherman was only thirty miles from Atlanta. On June 27, the general decided to make an aggressive assault on the Confederates so intent upon blocking his way. He chose Kennesaw Mountain, just outside Atlanta, as the site of this assault.

Kennesaw Mountain National Battlefield Park

Illinois Monument, Kennesaw Mountain National Battlefield Park

At 8:00AM, the Union struck twice at Confederate defenses on Kennesaw. The day was stiflingly hot and humid, and because the Union was unfamiliar with the thick, dense, and swampy terrain, they met with little success. The lines collided and came to a standstill, in many places falling into hand to hand combat, naming the most bloody area "Dead Angle."

By midday, the battle was over; the Confederates had held their ground against the powerful Union forces, and Union losses were triple that of the South. Still, the loss was only a minor setback for the Union. By September Sherman had taken Atlanta.

"More of their best soldiers lay dead and wounded than the number of British veterans that fell in General Jackson's celebrated battle of New Orleans."

Gen. J. E. Johnston

PICKETT'S MILL STATE HISTORIC SITE AND BATTLEFIELD

4432 Mt. Tabor Church Road, Dallas, GA
PHONE: 770-443-7850
WEB: www.GeorgiaStateParks.org
HOURS: Open daily
Thursday – Saturday 9AM – 5PM;
closed major holidays.
ADMISSION: $2.75 – $4.

Pickett's Mill is the site of a May 27, 1864, battle between General Johnston's Confederates and General Sherman's Union troops during Sherman's March to Atlanta. This battlefield, located just

Pickett's Mill State Historic Site and Battlefield

north of Atlanta, is wonderfully preserved. Original earthworks are intact, and brochures are available for a self-guided tour. Visitors may view a film on the battle and tour the site on several walking trails. Each year a commemoration of the battle takes place the first weekend after Memorial Day.

KENNESAW MOUNTAIN NATIONAL BATTLEFIELD PARK

900 Kennesaw Mountain Drive, Kennesaw, GA
PHONE: 770-427-4686
WEB: www.nps.gov/kemo
HOURS: Open daily dawn to dusk; closed major holidays
ADMISSION: Free.

Self-guided auto tours are the best way to tour this park, and each stop has wayside exhibits. The visitor center provides information for touring the park, as well as a twenty-minute movie.

A battlefield tour interprets the site, and many trails provide hiking opportunities. Included within the park are earthworks, cannon emplacements, a monument to Georgia's soldiers, and a monument to the 400 Illinois soldiers who died here. Call the visitor center for information on frequent special events.

Photo left: Kennesaw Mountain National Battlefield Park

MARIETTA NATIONAL CEMETERY

500 Washington Avenue, Marietta, GA
PHONE: 1-866-236-8159
HOURS: Open daily.
ADMISSION: Free.

This is the burial site of more than 10,000 Union casualties from the battles of New Hope Church, Pickett's Mill, and Kennesaw Mountain. Several special services are held during the year and include Four Chaplains' Day in February, Memorial Day in May, POW/MIA Day in September, Veterans Day in November, and Pearl Harbor Day in December.

Marietta National Cemetery

ATLANTA CYCLORAMA AND CIVIL WAR MUSEUM

800 Cherokee Avenue, Atlanta, GA
PHONE: 404-658-7625
WEB: www.atlantacyclorama.org
HOURS: Tuesday – Saturday 9:15AM – 4:30PM; closed major holidays.
ADMISSION: A fee is charged; children and seniors discounted.

This Civil War cyclorama, *The Battle of Atlanta*, is the largest painting in the U.S. It was completed in 1886 by German artists. Also on site are exhibits related to Atlanta's involvement in

Atlanta Cyclorama

the Civil War as well as a Civil War diorama. The cyclorama is located in the center of Atlanta's Grant Park, named for Col. Lemuel Grant, a native of the city.

HISTORIC OAKLAND CEMETERY

248 Oakland Avenue SE, Atlanta, GA
PHONE: 404-688-2107
WEB: www.oaklandcemetery.com
HOURS: Open daily.
ADMISSION: Free; a fee is charged for walking tours.

Established in 1850, this forty-eight-acre cemetery contains the graves of 3,900 known and 3,000 unknown Confederate soldiers who died in battle and hospitals in and around Atlanta. The Confederate Section also includes headstones of sixteen Union soldiers; the Confederate Obelisk, dedicated in honor of the Confederate Army in 1874; and The Lion of Atlanta, unveiled in 1894, dedicated to the unknown Confederate dead. Other notable Atlantans who are interred here include Margaret Mitchell, author of *Gone with the Wind*; Bishop Wesley Gaines, bishop of AME church and founder of Morris Brown College; Carrie Steele Logan, founder of the first orphanage for black children in Atlanta; and Bobby Jones, the golfer. Guided walking tours are available on Saturdays and Sundays and on weekdays if arranged in advance.

STONE MOUNTAIN PARK AND MUSEUM

U.S. Highway 78 East, Exit 8, Stone Mountain, GA
PHONE: 770-498-5690
WEB: www.stonemountainpark.com
HOURS: Open daily.
ADMISSION: A fee is charged.

This 3,200-acre park features a large monument to Confederate leaders. Carved into the face of the mountain are Confederate Generals Lee and Jackson and Confederate President Jefferson Davis. An Antebellum Plantation and a museum showing how the community was affected by the Civil War are also located in the park.

ROBERT TOOMBS HOUSE STATE HISTORIC SITE

216 East Robert Toombs Avenue, Washington, GA
PHONE: 706-678-2226
WEB: www.gastateparks.org
HOURS: Tuesday – Saturday 9AM – 5PM; closed major holidays.
ADMISSION: A fee is charged; children are discounted.

After the Civil War, Confederate General Robert Toombs, an outspoken secessionist who was appointed by Confederate President Jefferson Davis to act as Secretary of State to the Confederacy, refused to take the Oath of Allegiance to the United States. When Federal troops came to

Robert Toombs House State Historic Site

arrest him, Toombs fled to Cuba. He returned in 1867 when his last child died. President Johnson did not arrest Toombs nor require him to swear an oath. Toombs's restored home contains
family furnishings and may be viewed in self-guided tours.

ALEXANDER H. STEPHENS HISTORIC SITE

456 Alexander Street NW, Crawfordville, GA

PHONE: 706-456-2221
WEB: www.gastateparks.org
HOURS: Wednesday – Sunday
9AM – 5PM, closed major holidays.
ADMISSION: A fee is charged.

Liberty Hall, the home of Confederate Vice President Alexander H.
Stephens, contains many period
furnishings, as well as some which
belonged to the Stephens family.
Also of interest are Stephens's grave
and a Confederate museum.

Liberty Hall, Alexander H. Stephens Historic Site

THE BATTLE OF FORT PULASKI

April 10–11, 1862

This battle displayed the deadly accuracy of modern weapons, specifically the rifled cannon.

Fort Pulaski, located on Cockspur Island off Georgia's northern coast, sits at the mouth of the Savannah River and guards the city of Savannah. The British originally realized Cockspur's strategic position and constructed Fort George, which was abandoned in 1776. After the War of 1812, Congress authorized reconstruction of Fort George which was completed in 1847 and renamed Pulaski. In 1861 volunteer militia from Savannah began repairs on the fort in the name of the Confederate States of America.

On November 7, 1861, Union forces captured Hilton Head Island, South Carolina, and prepared to take Cockspur Island through siege. Their first step was to erect batteries on neighboring Big Tybee Island. The walls of Fort Pulaski were seven-feet thick, and the fort was defended by forty-eight guns. Confederate General Robert E. Lee, who in 1830 as a lieuten-

Cannon on Terreplein, Fort Pulaski National Monument

Cannon and casemates, Fort Pulaski National Monument

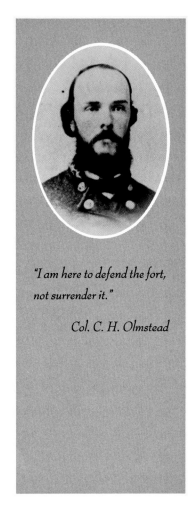

"I am here to defend the fort, not surrender it."

Col. C. H. Olmstead

ant designed the dike system at Fort Pulaski, declared that a Union cannon could make it difficult for Fort Pulaski but could not breach its walls. His opinion was based on his knowledge of the fort's construction and also the one-mile separation between Cockspur and Big Tybee. Lee was correct as far as traditional, smooth-bore cannon were concerned. On Big Tybee, however, the Union had a rifled cannon with spiraled grooves to give the projectiles more distance and accuracy.

Under the cover of darkness, the Union worked to construct eleven batteries—two of which contained the deadly rifled cannon—on Big Tybee Island. After months of preparation, Union guns opened fire on April 10, 1862, concentrating on the southeast side of Fort Pulaski. The cannon picked away at the wall until, by nightfall, the fortress was half its thickness on its besieged side. During the night, the Confederates repositioned their cannon, replacing those destroyed by Union fire. In the morning, however, the Union continued its relentless firing. By noon, the southeast wall of the fort was breached, and Union gunfire was exploding against the powder magazine. Confederate Colonel Charles H. Olmstead knew there was nothing else to do but surrender.

At 2:00AM on April 11, fearing a devastating explosion from the magazine, Olmstead reluctantly raised the white flag. Losses were limited to one killed on each side; nearly four hundred Confederates, however, were taken prisoner, and both sides learned the deadly power of the rifled cannon.

THE NATIONAL CIVIL WAR NAVAL MUSEUM AT PORT COLUMBUS

1002 Victory Drive, Columbus, GA
PHONE: 706-327-9798
WEB: civilwarnavalmuseum.com
HOURS: Open daily 9AM – 5PM; closed Christmas.
ADMISSION: A fee is charged.

This museum features the remains of two Confederate gunboats, the CSS *Chattahoochee* and the CSS *Jackson*, as well as weapons, uniforms, paintings, and other artifacts related to both Confederate and Union forces. The museum also houses an exhibit illustrating the ingenuity of the Confederate navy (of which fifty percent were in the United States Navy prior to the war) to counter the Union naval warfare.

ANDERSONVILLE NATIONAL HISTORIC SITE

Georgia Highway 49, 6 miles from Georgia Highway 26, Andersonville, GA
PHONE: 229-924-0343
WEB: nps.gov/ande
HOURS: Open daily; museum closed Thanksgiving Day, Christmas Day, and New Year's Day.
ADMISSION: Free.

Historic monuments scattered among Civil War burials, Andersonville National Cemetery

The largest and most notorious of Civil War prisons, Andersonville saw more than 45,000 prisoners pass through its gates. Nearly 13,000 died here. The Confederate officer in charge, Capt. Henry Wirz, was the only Civil War soldier to be tried and hanged as a war criminal. While the park's National Prisoner of War Museum honors all American prisoners of war from all the nation's wars, there are extensive Civil War artifacts, as well as a library with an oral history archive of former POWs. Former American prisoners of war volunteer to serve as hosts at the museum.

Portions of the original palisade and gate have been rebuilt, and white stakes show the location of the stockade and the "deadline," a line which a prisoner could not cross without being shot. The 12,920 prisoners who died in Andersonville are buried near the prison site in what is now the Andersonville National Cemetery. Defensive earthworks built by slave labor to protect the prison from a possible Union attack are also present.

The films *Echoes of Captivity* and *Voices from Andersonville* are shown at the museum and introduce visitors to both the Civil War story of Andersonville and the experience of American prisoners of war throughout history. A self-guided driving tour is available on CD at the museum.

FORT PULASKI NATIONAL MONUMENT

U.S. Highway 80 East, 15 miles east of Savannah, GA
PHONE: 912-786-5787

WEB: www.nps.gov/fopu
HOURS: Open daily 9AM – 5PM; closed major holidays.
ADMISSION: A fee is charged; children 15 and under are free.

Fort Pulaski National Monument

The visitor center of the 5,623-acre Fort Pulaski National Monument features a video giving the history of the fort and the battle. The museum features artifacts from Civil War-era cannons. Audio stations provide interesting commentary during the self-guided walking tour of the fort. Walls marked by Union fire testify to the ferocity of the battle.

GREEN-MELDRIM HOUSE

14 West Macon Street, Savannah, GA
PHONE: 912-233-3845
HOURS: Tuesday, Thursday, and Friday 10AM – 4PM; Saturday 10AM – 1PM; closed December 15 – January 15 and 2 weeks prior to Easter.
ADMISSION: Donations are accepted.

Built in the early 1850s, Green-Meldrim House was occupied by Union Gen. William T. Sherman, who made it his headquarters. Tours of the Gothic Revival house, which has been designated a National Historic Landmark, are available.

FORT MCALLISTER HISTORIC PARK

3894 Fort McAllister Road, Richmond Hill, GA
PHONE: 912-727-2339
WEB: www.gastateparks.org
HOURS: Open daily.
ADMISSION: A fee is charged; children are discounted.

After withstanding Federal naval assault for more than two years, Fort McAllister was captured by the Union during Sherman's March to the Sea in December 1864. The park features the preserved fort itself, as well as a museum with exhibits of Civil War artillery, a gun collection, and uniforms. Also on display are artifacts from the CSS *Nashville*, a luxury liner reoutfitted by the Confederate army as a supply ship. Free brochures are available for self-guided tours.

ILLINOIS

Many of the Civil War places in Illinois center around its distinguished resident, Abraham Lincoln. The Lincoln Home National Historic Site in Springfield contains many of the family's personal belongings. The sixteenth president, his wife, and three of their sons are buried at nearby Oak Ridge Cemetery. On the steps of the nearby Old State Capitol, Lincoln delivered the immortal lines, "A house divided against itself cannot stand." Fewer than three years later, the first shots of the Civil War would tear the country in two. Even Lincoln's own family would not be immune from the division.

Illinois served as a strategic point, guarding the gateway to the Great Plains and its store of agricultural resources. Its position on the Mississippi River also proved helpful in moving supplies to southbound Union forces. Cairo, at the confluence of the Mississippi and Ohio Rivers, served as a major Union supply depot during the war. Upstream lies Galena and General Grant's home. Still further upstream, a prisoner of war camp was located at Rock Island Arsenal.

At a cemetery in Carbondale, Illinois, General John A. Logan began Decoration Day on May 30, 1868, to commemorate the Civil War dead. This holiday is now officially recognized as Memorial Day and serves as a tribute to all Americans who have sacrificed for their country.

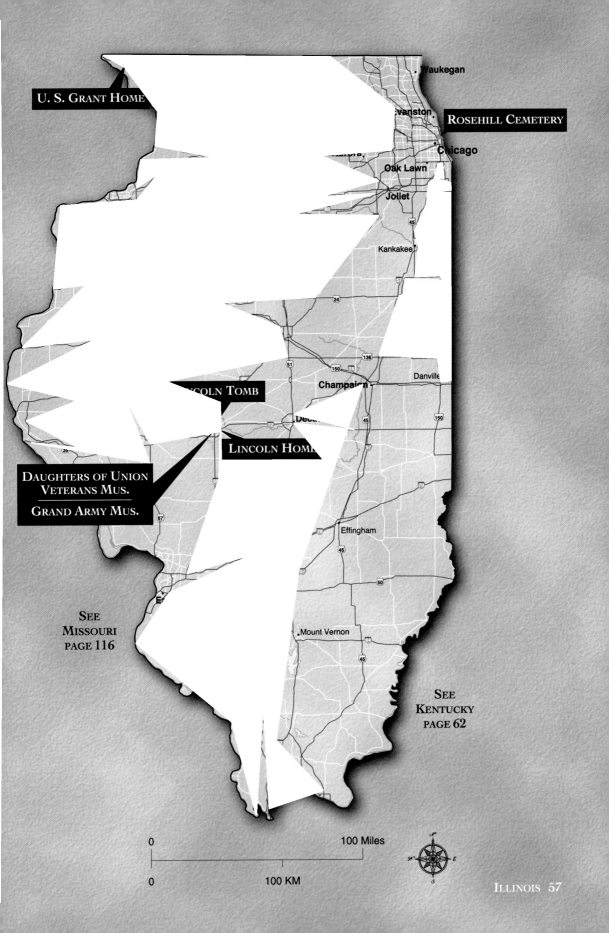

U. S. GRANT HOME

ROSEHILL CEMETERY

Waukegan

Evanston

Chicago

Aurora

Oak Lawn

Joliet

Kankakee

LINCOLN TOMB

Champaign

Danville

Decatur

LINCOLN HOME

DAUGHTERS OF UNION
VETERANS MUS.

GRAND ARMY MUS.

Effingham

SEE
MISSOURI
PAGE 116

Mount Vernon

SEE
KENTUCKY
PAGE 62

0   100 Miles

0   100 KM

U. S. GRANT HOME STATE HISTORIC SITE

500 Bouthillier Street, Galena, IL
PHONE: 815-777-3310
HOURS: Wednesday – Sunday; closed federal and state holidays.
ADMISSION: A donation is requested.

This home was presented to General Grant by the citizens of Galena upon his return from serving in the Civil War. Although Grant lived in the home for only a short time, he used it as his legal voting residence. Ninety percent of the furnishings are original and include Grant's cane and favorite chair. Tours are available.

U. S. Grant Home State Historic Site

ROSEHILL CEMETERY

5800 North Ravenswood Avenue, Chicago, IL
PHONE: 773-561-5940
HOURS: Open daily.
ADMISSION: Free.

The Rosehill Cemetery is the final resting spot for seventeen generals and hundreds of Civil War soldiers, including members of the Eighth Illinois Cavalry. A Civil War memorial area is located near the Ravenswood Avenue entrance. Self-guided walking tours are available, and stops on the tour include a bolder taken from the Georgia battlefield and placed on the grounds as a tribute to Gen. George Henry Thomas, the "Rock of Chickamauga." Thomas was so designated because of his glorious feat in holding the left wing against tremendous odds at the Battle of Chickamauga. Maps for the tour are available in the administration building.

DAUGHTERS OF UNION VETERANS OF THE CIVIL WAR MUSEUM

503 South Walnut Street, Springfield, IL
PHONE: 217-544-0616
HOURS: Tuesday – Saturday 9:30AM – 3:30PM.
ADMISSION: Free.

The Daughters of Union Veterans of the Civil War began in 1865 and seeks to preserve the memory of all Union veterans. The museum's collection includes Civil War medals, swords, guns, photographs, and official records. Also on exhibit are uniforms, including an African-American soldier's uniform. Civil War records of every member of the organization are also located at the museum. The Museum has opened a library and research center next door, which houses records on both Confederate and Union soldiers. Hours for the library are by appointment only.

GRAND ARMY OF THE REPUBLIC MEMORIAL MUSEUM

629 South 7th Street, Springfield, IL
PHONE: 217-522-4373
HOURS: Open Tuesday – Saturday 10AM – 4PM; closed mid-December through February.
ADMISSION: Free.

Grand Army of the Republic Memorial Museum

The Grand Army of the Republic Memorial Museum is maintained by the Women's Relief Corps, an auxiliary group to the Grand Army of the Republic. The organization was begun in 1866 and composed of Union veterans. The WRC is still active today in veterans' affairs. The museum contains collections of Civil War memorabilia, battlefield relics, weapons, official Civil War records, two Mathew Brady photographs, and one of the flags that flew at Ford's Theatre the night Lincoln was assassinated.

LINCOLN HOME NATIONAL HISTORIC SITE ──────

413 South 8th Street, Springfield, IL
Visitor Center: 426 South 7th Street, Springfield, IL
PHONE: 217- 492-4241
WEB: www.nps.gov/liho
HOURS: Open daily 8:30AM – 5PM; closed Thanksgiving Day,
Christmas Day, and New Year's Day.
ADMISSION: Free; free tour ticket needed to visit Lincoln Home available at Visitor Center.

At the park's center stands the two-story home of Abraham Lincoln, the only home he ever owned. The home was constructed in 1839 as a one-story cottage, and the Lincolns lived in the house from 1844 until his election to the Presidency in 1861. The home, which has been restored to its 1860s appearance, portrays Lincoln as husband, father, politician, and President-elect. It stands in the midst of a four-block historic neighborhood which the National Park Service

Lincoln Home National Historic Site

is restoring it to its Lincoln-era appearance. The film, *Abraham Lincoln: A Journey to Greatness*, is shown continuously at the Visitor Center.

LINCOLN TOMB STATE HISTORIC SITE

Oak Ridge Cemetery, 1500 Monument Avenue, Springfield, IL
PHONE: 217-782-2717
HOURS: Open daily Memorial Day through Labor Day, otherwise open Tuesday – Saturday 9AM – 4PM.
ADMISSION: Free.

President Abraham Lincoln's tomb is located within Oak Ridge Cemetery and includes a monument and small sculptures of Lincoln at various stages of his life. The 117-foot granite tomb contains the bodies of Lincoln and his wife, Mary, and three of their four sons: Edward, William, and Thomas (Tad). During the summer, a Civil War Retreat Ceremony is held at the tomb each Tuesday evening.

Photo right: Lincoln's Tomb, Oak Ridge Cemetery

Photo below: Grand Army of the Republic Monument, Oak Ridge Cemetery

KENTUCKY

The birthplace of both Abraham Lincoln and Jefferson Davis, Kentucky was truly divided by the Civil War: cities, towns, and families found themselves at odds— often violently—over loyalties to the North or the South. Kentucky began the war with a proclamation of neutrality and a warning to both Union and Confederate troops that the state was off limits. But neutrality proved impossible to maintain; by September of 1861 Confederate troops had moved to secure the city of Columbus and Federal soldiers had responded in an effort to drive them out. For the remainder of the war, Kentucky remained torn in its loyalties. Whereas the state never officially left the Union, a group of pro-Confederates organized a convention, voted to secede, and added a star to the Confederate flag.

The Civil War came to Kentucky most violently at Perryville, the site of a 1862 battle that helped the Union secure control of Kentucky although it did little to end fighting and internal contention. In all, 75,000 Kentuckians fought for the Union, and 30,000 fought for the Confederacy. Modern Kentucky remembers this tumultuous time in state history with a small but varied list of battlefields and other historical sites.

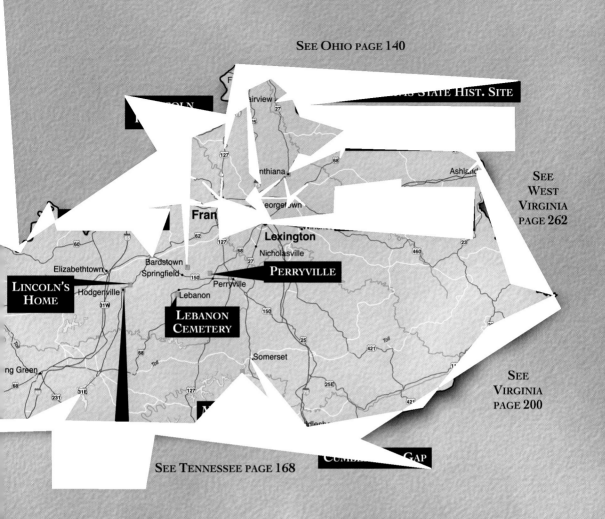

SEE OHIO PAGE 140

...S STATE HIST. SITE

LINCOLN

Fairview

27

5

127

nthiana

68

Georgetown

Ashland

SEE
WEST
VIRGINIA
PAGE 262

Fran

62

127

Lexington

68

27

Nicholasville

460

23

Winche...

Bardstown

Springfield

150

PERRYVILLE

Elizabethtown

60

Perryville

**LINCOLN'S
HOME**

Hodgenville

31W

Lebanon

**LEBANON
CEMETERY**

150

68

Toll

25

421

Toll

ng Green

68

231

31E

127

Somerset

25E

421

SEE
VIRGINIA
PAGE 200

...dlesb...

CUMB... **GAP**

SEE TENNESSEE PAGE 168

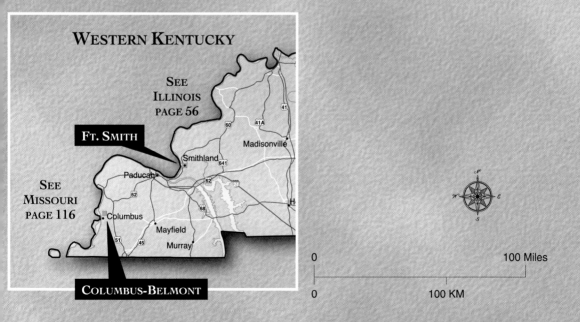

WESTERN KENTUCKY

SEE
ILLINOIS
PAGE 56

41

60

41A

FT. SMITH

Madisonville

Smithland

641

Paducah

62

SEE
MISSOURI
PAGE 116

62

68

H...

Columbus

51

45

Mayfield

Murray

0   100 Miles

0   100 KM

COLUMBUS-BELMONT

NORTHERN COMMANDER:
Maj. Gen. D. C. Buell

STRENGTH: 55,000

CASUALTIES: 4,211

THE BATTLE OF PERRYVILLE

October 8, 1862

One of the bloodiest battles of the Civil War for its size, Perryville ensured that Kentucky would be controlled by the Union.

At the beginning of the Civil War, Kentucky declared its neutrality and warned both Union and Confederate soldiers not to cross its borders. The peace did not last long, however, as both sides saw strategic benefit to controlling Kentucky. In 1862 Confederate Generals Braxton Bragg and Edmund Smith fought their way into Kentucky. Union Major General Don Carlos Buell followed. The two sides met before daylight at Perryville on October 8. By dawn, the fighting had ceased. The battle resumed at 2:00PM and fighting escalated as the afternoon wore on.

Monument on the Perryville Battlefield

Perryville Battlefield State Historic Site

One Union general described the action as "the bloodiest battle of modern times." At the end of battle, the Confederates had fared well. Bragg, however, realized that only a portion of the Union army had seen battle, so he began a midnight retreat to Harrodsburg. There he joined Smith but disregarded the wishes of his officers to reengage the now outnumbered Union troops. Buell permitted the Confederates to withdraw unmolested, an action that resulted in his being dismissed as Union commander.

The victory left Kentucky in Federal hands for the remainder of the war. The Battle of Perryville was the most important Civil War engagement fought in Kentucky. Some historians believe that this battle was as decisive as any other during the entire four-year conflict, for it marked a fatal loss of initiative for the South.

Cannon on the Perryville Battlefield

"We have so far received no accession to this army. . . . Enthusiasm runs high but exhausts itself in word. . . . Unless a change occurs soon we must abandon the garden spot of Kentucky."

Gen. B. Bragg

COLUMBUS-BELMONT STATE PARK

350 Park Road, Junction of Kentucky Highways 80 and 58, Columbus, KY
PHONE: 270-677-2327
WEB: parks.ky.gov
HOURS: 8AM – 9PM, April 1 – October 31; 8AM – 3PM, November 1 – March 31.
ADMISSION: A fee is charged.

On this site, Confederate troops used a massive anchor and chain to block Union gunboats from traveling up the Mississippi River. Self-guided hiking trails encompass two-and-a-half miles of trenches from the Battle of Columbus. A museum, which was once used as a hospital, displays Civil War artifacts; a video presentation describes the Battle of Belmont. Each October the site hosts "Civil War Days," which features a reenactment of the Battle of Belmont.

Photo right: Anchor from the Battle of Columbus

Photo below: Columbus-Belmont State Park Museum

FORT SMITH

Kentucky Highway 60 to Level Street, Smithland Cemetery, Smithland, KY
PHONE: 502-928-2446 (Smithland City Hall)
HOURS: Open daily.
ADMISSION: Free.

Fort Smith served as the Union protection of the Cumberland River. The Battle of Fort Smith launched the offensive to Fort Donelson, Tennessee. The original earthworks of the fort are well-preserved. The fort is located above the Smithland Cemetery. Brochures on the fort and booklets on other historic Civil War sites in Smithland are available from the City Hall.

ABRAHAM LINCOLN BIRTHPLACE NATIONAL HISTORICAL PARK

2995 Lincoln Farm Road, Hodgenville, KY
PHONE: 270-358-3137
WEB: www.nps.gov/abli
HOURS: Open daily 8AM – 4:45PM; closed
Thanksgiving, Christmas, and New Year's.
ADMISSION: Free.

This site of Lincoln's birth contains 116 acres
of the original Thomas Lincoln Farm. It features a symbolic birthplace cabin, a picnic
area, a sinking spring where the family drew
its drinking water, and hiking trails. The Visitor Center contains exhibits and a film. The

Abraham Lincoln Birthplace National Historical Park

site features a 100-year-old granite and marble Birthplace Memorial Building housing a symbolic birthplace cabin to honor Lincoln and mark the site of his birth.

THE LINCOLN MUSEUM

66 Lincoln Square, Hodgenville, KY
PHONE: 270-358-3163
E-MAIL: abe@lincolnmuseum-ky.org
WEB: www.lincolnmuseum-ky.org
HOURS: Open daily; closed
Christmas and Thanksgiving.
ADMISSION: A fee is charged.

Listed in the National Register of Historic
Places, this museum features twelve rooms
which interpret different stages of Lincoln's
life as well as American history. Art collections, memorabilia, a film, and changing
exhibits are included in the museum.

The Lincoln Museum

LINCOLN'S BOYHOOD HOME

U.S. Highway 31 E, 7 miles northeast of Hodgenville, KY
PHONE: 270-358-3137
WEB: www.nps.gov/abli
HOURS: Open daily 8AM – 4:45PM; park rangers on duty Memorial Day – Labor Day only;
closed Thanksgiving, Christmas, and New Year's Day.
ADMISSION: Free.

The Lincolns lived here, at what is called Knob Creek, from 1811 to 1816. A facsimile of the Lincoln cabin rests on its original site. Guided tours are provided Memorial Day through Labor Day. A small gift shop is available during the summer months, and a picnic area and interpretive garden are open to the public.

Lincoln's Boyhood Home at Knob Creek

CIVIL WAR MUSEUM AT OLD BARDSTOWN VILLAGE

310 East Broadway, Bardstown, KY
PHONE: 502-349-0291
HOURS: Open daily 10AM – 5PM; closed December 15 – end of February.
ADMISSION: A fee is charged.

The museum houses a large collection of Civil War artifacts, including collections of authentic uniforms, battle flags, and weaponry.

Civil War Museum at Old Bardstown Village

LEBANON NATIONAL CEMETERY

Kentucky Highway 208, Lebanon, KY
PHONE: 502-893-3852
HOURS: Open daily.
ADMISSION: Free.

This still-active cemetery covers 14.8 acres and is the final resting place of many Union soldiers who fell at the Battle of Perryville in 1862.

LINCOLN HOMESTEAD STATE PARK

5079 Lincoln Park Road, Springfield, KY
PHONE: 859-336-7461
WEB: parks.ky.gov
HOURS: Cabins open daily May–September and weekends in October. Golf course open year round.
ADMISSION: Free; $2 adult, $1.50 children to visit cabins.

This park preserves the pioneer heritage of the president's parents, Thomas Lincoln and Nancy Hanks. Featured are a reproduction of the cabin that was the boyhood home of Lincoln's father and the actual house in which the President's mother lived during her courtship by Thomas Lincoln. Split-rail fences and pioneer furniture made by Thomas Lincoln and his contemporaries complete the picture of life in the rugged Lincoln home. The park also features a blacksmith shop.

Photo right: Interior view of Berry House, Lincoln Homestead State Park

Photo below: Lincoln Homestead State Park

PERRYVILLE BATTLEFIELD STATE HISTORIC SITE

1825 Battlefield Road, Perryville, KY
PHONE: 859-332-8631
WEB: www.perryvillebattlefield.org
HOURS: Grounds open year-round; check website for museum hours.
ADMISSION: A fee is charged; children and groups are discounted.

Perryville Battlefield State Historic Site contains 745 acres of the original battleground. The site features over 10 miles of interpretive trails, with about 70 informational signs dispersed throughout. The Civil War comes to life in the newly redesigned Perryville Battlefield Museum. Examine actual battle artifacts, a Civil War display, and a map with the layout of the battle. Several states have erected monuments which honor their fallen dead from the Perryville Battle; these dot the battlefield site. In 1902 a Confederate monument was erected; in 1931 a Union monument was built. The entire town of Perryville is on the National Register of Historic Homes.

Perryville Battlefield Museum

JEFFERSON DAVIS STATE HISTORIC SITE

258 Pembroke-Fairview Road, Fairview, KY
PHONE: 270-889-6100
WEB: parks.ky.gov
HOURS: Open daily May– October.
ADMISSION: $5 adults; $3 children.

The nineteen-acre Jefferson Davis State Historic Site contains a 351-foot limestone obelisk dedicated to Jefferson Davis, president of the Confederacy. Davis was born on this site on June

3, 1808. Walls of the obelisk are nine-feet thick at the base and taper to two-feet thick where the point inclines. The monument's elevator takes visitors to the observation room high atop the structure which offers a panoramic view of the countryside. On the first weekend in June, a Jefferson Davis Birthday Celebration is held at the site.

Ironically, just eight months after the birth of Davis and fewer than 100 miles away, another Kentuckian was born—Abraham Lincoln. The two were destined to become Civil War adversaries.

Photo right: Jefferson Davis State Historic Site

CYNTHIANA BATTLES TOUR

201 South Main Street, Cynthiana, KY
PHONE: 859-234-5236 (Cynthiana Chamber of Commerce)
HOURS: Open daily.
ADMISSION: Free.

The Cynthiana Chamber of Commerce offers a free brochure describing the battles in the Cynthiana area. The tour is not marked, but directions and a map are in the brochure. A reenactment of the battle is held every July.

CYNTHIANA HARRISON COUNTY MUSEUM

124 South Walnut Street, Cynthiana, KY
PHONE: 859-234-7179
HOURS: Open Friday and Saturday 10AM – 5PM or by appointment.
ADMISSION: Free.

The Cynthiana Harrison County Museum contains several Civil War artifacts. Information regarding a walking tour is available through the museum; the tour highlights Battle Grove Cemetery and its Confederate memorial, the second oldest such memorial in the U.S., as well as historic homes in the area.

LEXINGTON CEMETERY

833 West Main, Lexington, KY
PHONE: 859-255-5522
HOURS: Open daily.
ADMISSION: Free.

Lexington Cemetery is the burial site of Confederate Gen. John Hunt Morgan, statesman Henry Clay, and the Mary Todd Lincoln family.

THE MARY TODD LINCOLN HOUSE

578 West Main, Lexington, KY
PHONE: 859-233-9999
WEB: www.mtlhouse.org
HOURS: March 15 – November 30,
Monday – Saturday, 10AM – 4PM (last tour 3PM).
ADMISSION: A fee is charged.

In 1832 Robert Todd moved his family, including the future wife of the sixteenth president, to this late-Georgian house. Abraham Lincoln visited here in 1847. Many Lincoln and Todd family items are on display.

Photo right: Front parlor, The Mary Todd Lincoln House

Photo below: The Mary Todd Lincoln House

MILL SPRINGS BATTLEFIELD

Visitor Center and Museum: 9020 West Highway 80, Nancy, KY
PHONE: 606-636-4045
WEB: www.millsprings.net
HOURS: Open year round; closed major holidays.
ADMISSION: Free; a fee is charged for the museum.

The Mill Springs Battlefield is the site of the first major Union victory of the Civil War. The first Confederate general of the west, Felix K. Zollicoffer, was killed in this battle. An eight-mile self-guided driving tour with interpretive signs is available at the battlefield site; guided tours are offered as well. The battle is commemorated each Memorial Day. The site also features a bed and breakfast, the Historic Brown-Lanier House; reservations can be made by calling 606-340-1656.

CUMBERLAND GAP NATIONAL HISTORICAL PARK

Kentucky Highway 25 E, Middlesboro, KY
PHONE: 606-248-2817
WEB: www.nps.gov/cuga
HOURS: Visitor center: open daily except Christmas. Park: open year-round.
ADMISSION: Free.

Although this 24,000-acre park is located at the juncture of Tennessee, Kentucky, and Virginia, the visitor center is in Kentucky. No major battles were fought here, but the Cumberland Gap National Historical Park marks the gateway to the West and stands where Daniel Boone led 200,000–300,000 settlers through the gap in the Appalachian Mountains. Civil War earthwork fortifications remain. Union cannons guard Fort McCook and Fort Lyon. The cannon at Fort McCook is an example of a bronze-barreled, rifled cannon which allowed for greater accuracy.

Cannon at Fort McCook, Cumberland Gap National Historical Park

LOUISIANA

Louisiana voted to secede from the Union in January of 1861. An agricultural state with a heavy reliance on slave labor and a state where white residents were nearly outnumbered by African-Americans, Louisiana was ready and willing to take up arms to protect its citizens' right to own slaves. No state west of the Mississippi River was more important to the Confederacy than Louisiana, both for the port city of New Orleans and for the lower reaches of the Mississippi River that flowed within its borders. The Union valued Louisiana for the same reasons; thus, the state was the site of early and frequent Civil War conflict, most of it centered in the southern third of the state.

Nearly 66,000 Louisianans fought for the Confederacy; as many as 15,000 are believed to have paid the price of their lives. Commitment to the Confederate cause never wavered in Louisiana. While the Union had great success in gaining control of New Orleans and the river, the Confederate army in Louisiana did not give up fighting until many weeks after General Lee's surrender at Appomattox Court House. After the war, Louisiana held on to its uniquely southern character and has preserved its past with care.

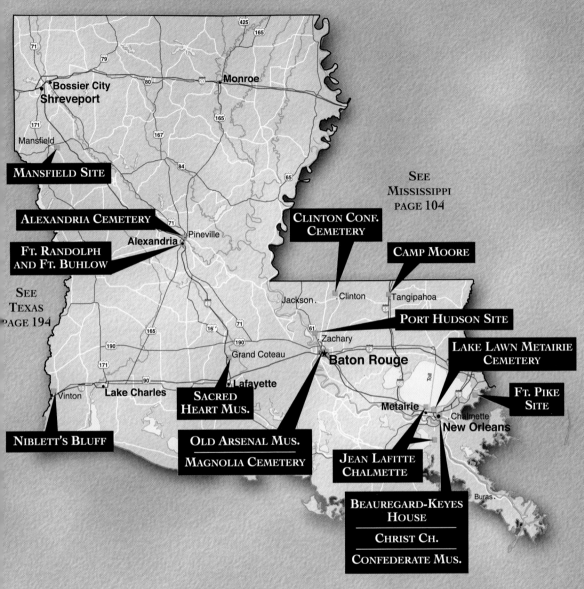

SEE ARKANSAS PAGE 20

Bossier City
Shreveport

Monroe

Mansfield

MANSFIELD SITE

ALEXANDRIA CEMETERY

Pineville

Alexandria

FT. RANDOLPH AND FT. BUHLOW

SEE TEXAS PAGE 194

SEE MISSISSIPPI PAGE 104

CLINTON CONF. CEMETERY

CAMP MOORE

Jackson

Clinton

Tangipahoa

PORT HUDSON SITE

Zachary

Baton Rouge

LAKE LAWN METAIRIE CEMETERY

Grand Coteau

Lafayette

SACRED HEART MUS.

Lake Charles

Vinton

NIBLETT'S BLUFF

OLD ARSENAL MUS.

MAGNOLIA CEMETERY

Metairie

Chalmette

New Orleans

FT. PIKE SITE

JEAN LAFITTE CHALMETTE

BEAUREGARD-KEYES HOUSE

CHRIST CH.

CONFEDERATE MUS.

Buras

0   100 Miles

0   100 KM

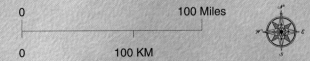

RED RIVER CAMPAIGN: BATTLES OF MANSFIELD AND PLEASANT HILL

April 8–9, 1864

The Battles of Mansfield and Pleasant Hill were the climax of the Union Red River Campaign.

The Red River runs from the northwest corner of Louisiana southeast to the Mississippi River. The Union's prime military objective in the Red River Campaign of 1863 was to capture Shreveport and break up Confederate military operations in the west. However, the political objectives—opening Louisiana and Texas to Reconstruction and capturing large quantities of cotton for Northern textile mills—actually drove the operation.

On March 11, 1864, Brigadier General Andrew J. Smith and his men captured Fort de Russy at the confluence of the Red and Mississippi Rivers. They then steamed north up the Red River to Alexandria which they occupied on March 15. Ten days later Major General Nathaniel Banks arrived by land with 20,000 infantry soldiers. Low water hampered the water

Interpretive Center, Mansfield State Historic Site

Mansfield State Historic Site

operations, and Banks left the river for Shreveport by way of Pleasant Hill and Mansfield.

In the meantime, Confederate forces under Major General Richard Taylor (the son of President Zachary Taylor) had dug in at Mansfield with 8,800 troops to wait for his chance to hit the Union force. His chance came on April 8 against General Banks's advance force of 7,000 troops. The first day ended in a Confederate victory with the Union falling back to its reinforcements of 5,000 troops at Pleasant Hill. During the night, the Confederates were also reinforced. When they met the next day, it was with comparatively equal strength of 12,000. Fighting resumed at 5:00PM, April 9 at Pleasant Hill. The Confederates were successful in the center of the Union line, but an unsuccessful Confederate flanking movement brought the battle to a draw. The Red River Campaign, although not a decisive Confederate victory, caused General Banks to withdraw to Nachitoches and give up on the capture of Shreveport.

MANSFIELD STATE HISTORIC SITE

15149 Highway 175, Mansfield, LA
PHONE: 318-872-1474
HOURS: Open daily.
ADMISSION: A fee is charged; children 12 and under and seniors 62 and over are free.

Within the forty-four acres of the remaining battlefield is a museum with maps, an audiovisual presentation, interpretive programs, exhibits, and monuments. The site also features living history events, battlefield lectures, and a picnic area. Special events throughout the year include encampments, artillery demonstrations, and a haunted night tour of the battefield in October.

Mansfield State Historic Site

ALEXANDRIA NATIONAL CEMETERY

209 East Shamrock Street, Pineville, LA
PHONE: 318-449-1793
WEB: www.cem.va.gov
HOURS: Open daily; office hours Monday – Friday 8AM – 4:30PM.
ADMISSION: Free.

Alexandria National Cemetery was established in 1867. More than 1,500 Union soldiers are buried at this cemetery; a monument commemorates their valor. The cemetery also contains the graves of soldiers who fought in various American wars.

Photo right: Entrance to Alexandria National Cemetery

Photo below: Alexandria National Cemetery

FORTS RANDOLPH AND BUHLOW
STATE HISTORIC SITE

135 Riverfront Street, Pineville, LA

PHONE: 318-484-2390

HOURS: Open Wednesday – Sunday.

ADMISSION: A fee is charged; children under 13 and seniors over 61 are free.

Fort Randolph and Fort Buhlow stand 500 yards apart on the Pineville side of the Red River. These earthen forts were built as a defense against an expected third Red River Campaign, a campaign which never came. The site features a museum, elevated walkways in both forts, and an overlook on the Red River at the site of Bailey's Dam.

NIBLETT'S BLUFF

3409 Niblett's Bluff Road, Vinton, LA
PHONE: 337-589-7117
WEB: www.niblettsbluffpark.com
HOURS: Open daily.
ADMISSION: Free.

Niblett's Bluff was the site of an 1863 Confederate encampment. Slave laborers used wooden shovels to erect the fortifications. From the self-guided trails, the breastworks are still visible.

ACADEMY OF THE SACRED HEART MUSEUM

1821 Academy Road, Grand Coteau, LA
PHONE: 337-662-5275
HOURS: Open weekdays 8AM – 4PM.
ADMISSION: Free; appointments recommended.

After 3,000 Confederate and 20,000 Union troops engaged in severe fighting around the Academy of the Sacred Heart, the Mother Superior of its sister convent in New York City wrote to the wife of Gen. Nathaniel Banks, the commander of the Union forces. Banks's own daughter

Academy of the Sacred Heart Museum

attended the Convent of the Sacred Heart in New York. Banks honored the Mother Superior's request that the Grand Coteau school be cared for by issuing a safeguard. This military order, issued through Banks's wife to M. Hardey, stated that any harm done to the nuns or students would be a crime punishable by death. In addition, he ensured that the school was kept supplied with food throughout the war. The original correspondence from Banks is on display in the museum. Guided tours are also available.

CLINTON CONFEDERATE STATE CEMETERY

Marston Street, Clinton, LA
PHONE: 225-634-7155
HOURS: Open daily.
ADMISSION: Free.

Although established as a Confederate cemetery, hundreds of troops from both sides rest at the Clinton Confederate State Cemetery. Many of those interred are casualties of the Port Hudson Battle. The railroad brought many of the sick and wounded to Clinton.

CAMP MOORE

70640 Camp Moore Road, Kentwood, LA
PHONE: 985-229-2438
HOURS: Open Tuesday – Saturday 10AM – 3PM.
ADMISSION: A fee is charged;
children under 6 are free.

Camp Moore was used as a Confederate training ground at the beginning of the war. Today, over 400 Confederate soldiers are buried in the camp cemetery. A museum exhibits the camp's history and displays relics from the training camp.

Camp Moore

PORT HUDSON STATE HISTORIC SITE

U.S. Highway 61, Zachary, LA
PHONE: 225-654-3775
HOURS: Open daily; closed
Thanksgiving, Christmas,
and New Year's Day.
ADMISSION: A fee is charged;
children under 13 and seniors
are free.

Photo right: Fort Desperate,
Port Hudson State Historic Site

The Port Hudson State Historic Site encompasses 640 acres of the historic battlefield. Earthwork fortifications survive and may be viewed from one of the walking trails. Exhibits at the Interpretive Center give an overview of Port Hudson's significance during the war and provide information concerning the forty-eight-day siege. The Battle of Port Hudson was one of the first battles in which free African-American soldiers engaged in combat on the side of the Union. Port Hudson National Cemetery, located about four miles south of the battlefield on Highway 61, includes more than 3,000 Union soldiers, most of whom are unknown.

MAGNOLIA CEMETERY

North 19th Street at Florida Boulevard, Baton Rouge, LA
PHONE: 225-387-2464 (Foundation for Historical Louisiana)
HOURS: Open daily.
ADMISSION: Free.

Established in 1854, Magnolia Cemetery rests on the site of the heaviest fighting of the Battle of Baton Rouge; it is also the only area of the battlefield totally intact. During the battle, tombstones provided soldiers much needed cover. Confederate soldiers who died during the battle are buried in a mass grave. Southerner Alexander Todd, half-brother of Mary Todd Lincoln, died in the battle. Each August a commemorative ceremony is held at the cemetery.

The Union soldiers who died in the Battle of Baton Rouge are interred across the street at National Cemetery.

Magnolia Cemetery

OLD ARSENAL MUSEUM

East Side State Capitol Grounds, Baton Rouge, LA

PHONE: 225-342-0401

WEB: www.sos.louisiana.gov/oam

HOURS: Tuesday – Saturday 9AM – 4PM; closed major holidays.

ADMISSION: Free.

When Louisiana seceded from the Union, the governor ordered the arsenal seized and the weapons, ammunition, and powder given to Southern armies. Union forces occupied the arsenal in May 1862 after Baton Rouge was captured. In August a Confederate army under General Breckinridge unsuccessfully tried to drive the Union soldiers into the Mississippi River. A self-guided tour through the museum and grounds is available.

Old Arsenal Museum

EXPEDITION TO CAPTURE NEW ORLEANS

April 15–28, 1862

Union victory at New Orleans opened the Mississippi River to Northern ships from the Gulf of Mexico and split the Confederacy in half, east and west.

Despite its immense commercial and strategic importance as the gateway to the Mississippi Valley, a campaign to take New Orleans was not approved until November 15, 1861. Federal authorities devised a joint army-navy operation to capture New Orleans. The port was guarded at the mouth of the Mississippi River by two Confederate forts on either side of the river, Fort St. Phillip and Fort Jackson. In addition, the river had been barricaded by a chain floated on barges and hulks. The ram *Manassas*, the unpowered *Louisiana*, and the unfinished *Mississippi*, along with an assortment of other ships and firebarges, were part of the Confederate's river defenses. The forts were manned by about 500 men and eighty guns—all designed to block any Union advance on New Orleans.

Union Commodore David D. Porter countered these defenses by towing mortar boats just below the forts where they barraged the forts with thirteen-inch shells. Much damage was inflicted, but the forts held out for six days, longer than

Chalmette Battlefield

Cannon in foreground, Beauregard House in background, Chalmette Battlefield

Admiral David G. Farragut had anticipated. An impatient Farragut ordered Union ships through the gap in a Confederate boom laid across the river. Under continual mortar fire, Union ships advanced, one by one, upstream. Five days late, a makeshift Confederate naval defense met the Union navy. Farragut sank six of the eight ships, then dropped anchor in the New Orleans port, capturing it without any further conflict.

With New Orleans captured, the demoralized troops in Forts Jackson and St. Phillip mutinied and forced a surrender from their commanders. Union forces led by General Benjamin F. Butler garrisoned the forts and occupied the city. General Butler's harsh treatment of the citizens of New Orleans prompted a court of inquiry to be held and earned him the nickname "Beast" Butler.

CHRIST CHURCH CATHEDRAL

2919 St. Charles Avenue, New Orleans, LA
PHONE: 504-895-6602
WEB: www.cccnola.org
HOURS: Office: Monday – Friday 9AM – 5PM;
Saturday 9AM – 12PM; closed major holidays. Services:
Monday – Friday 12:15PM; Saturday 9:30AM;
Sunday 7:30AM, 10AM, and 6PM.
ADMISSION: Free.

Christ Church Cathedral contains the grave of the "Fighting Bishop," Leonidas Polk. The West Point educated Polk became an Episcopal minister and eventually was named Bishop of Louisiana in 1841. In 1861 his friend and former classmate Jefferson Davis urged Polk to accept a commission in the Confederate army. Polk was killed in 1864 during the Atlanta Campaign.

Guided tours of the Cathedral are led on Sundays after the 10AM service. The Cathedral can be viewed during all open office hours except when services are being held.

Photo above: Leonidas Polk's grave, Christ Church Cathedral

Photo left: Christ Church Cathedral

LAKE LAWN METAIRIE CEMETERY

5100 Pontchartrain Boulevard, New Orleans, LA
PHONE: 504-486-6331
WEB: www.lakelawnmetairie.com
HOURS: Open daily.
ADMISSION: Free.

Confederate Generals P. G. T. Beauregard and Richard Taylor are buried here. Monuments to the Louisiana Division of the Army of Tennessee, the Louisiana Division of the Army of Northern Virginia, and the Washington Artillery Unit can also be viewed. A self-guided audio tour is available at the funeral home inside the cemetery.

FORT PIKE STATE HISTORIC SITE

27100 Chef Menteur Highway, New Orleans, LA
PHONE: 504-255-9171
HOURS: Open daily 9AM – 5PM; closed major holidays.
ADMISSION: A fee is charged; children and seniors are discounted.

During the Civil War, Fort Pike switched hands twice without any guns from the fort being fired. The fort was first captured by Confederates before the start of the war. In 1862 the North recaptured the fort and used it as a base for raids along the gulf. There is a museum at Fort Pike State Historic Site, and tours of the fort are available.

CONFEDERATE MUSEUM

929 Camp Street, New Orleans, LA
PHONE: 504-523-4522
WEB: www.confederatemuseum.com
HOURS: Open Tuesday – Saturday; closed major holidays.
ADMISSION: A fee is charged; children and seniors are discounted.

Confederate veterans of Louisiana founded the museum in 1891 as a repository of their memorabilia from the war. The collection includes more than 125 original Southern battle flags, rifles, guns, swords, more than 500 rare photographs, and uniforms of Confederate officers and soldiers, including the frock coats of Generals P. G. T. Beauregard and Braxton Bragg.

BEAUREGARD-KEYES HOUSE

1113 Chartres Street, New Orleans, LA
PHONE: 504-523-7257
WEB: www.bkhouse.org
HOURS: Open daily except Sunday.
ADMISSION: A fee is charged; children and seniors are discounted.

Confederate General P. G. T. Beauregard lived at this late Federal home from 1866

Photo right: The courtyard area of the Beauregard-Keyes House

to 1868. Novelist Frances Parkinson Keyes also lived here from the 1940s to the 1970s. The home contains many of the general's personal belongings. Each hour from 10AM to 3PM, costumed interpreters lead tours of the house and its beautiful and peaceful walled garden.

Beauregard-Keyes House

 # JEAN LAFITTE NATIONAL HISTORICAL PARK AND PRESERVE — CHALMETTE BATTLEFIELD AND NATIONAL CEMETERY

8606 West St. Bernard Highway, Chalmette, LA

PHONE: 504-281-0510
WEB: www.nps.gov/jela
HOURS: Open daily; closed Christmas.
ADMISSION: Free.

Judge René Beauregard, son of Confederate General P.G.T. Beauregard, was the last private owner of the Malus-

Photo right: Chalmette National Cemetery

Beauregard House. It was built in the early 1830s on the site of 1815's Battle of New Orleans, now Chalmette Battlefield. In 1862, Confederate forces defended the same ground with earthworks that are no longer visible. Chalmette National Cemetery was established in 1864 for Union troops who died in Louisiana; it is now the final resting place for nearly 16,000 veterans of all major U.S. wars from the War of 1812 to Vietnam.

Malus-Beauregard House, Chalmette Battlefield

MARYLAND

Maryland, despite its ties to Southern culture, remained loyal to the Union throughout the Civil War and served as a bloody buffer between the North and South. Death came early to Maryland; it boasts the auspicious honor of having the first casualties of the Civil War. President Street Station commemorates four militiamen and twelve civilians who were killed by secessionist sympathizers in the Baltimore Riot of 1861.

A little over a year later, the now-quiet battlefield of Antietam was covered with bodies. More men died on September 17, 1862, than on any other day during the Civil War; the Battle of Antietam was the bloodiest day of the war. Over 350 monuments stand in tribute to those Confederate and Union soldiers who paid the ultimate price of battle. Many are buried at the Antietam Union Cemetery and at Washington Confederate Cemetery in nearby Hagerstown.

Less than two years after the Battle of Antietam, Union victory at the Battle of Monocacy helped secure the nation's capital from Confederate advance. The Monocacy National Battlefield Park contains monuments and self-guided tours that help interpret this pivotal battle.

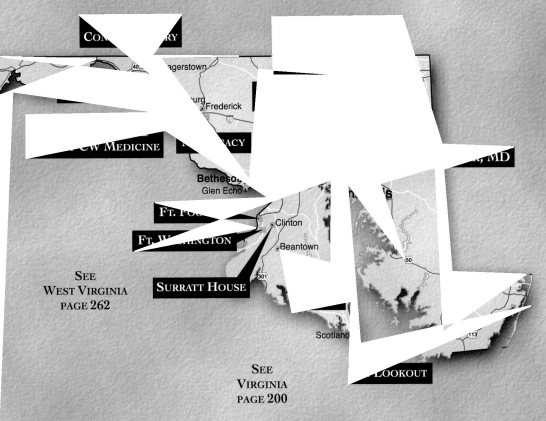

SEE PENNSYLVANIA PAGE 152

COL... ...RY

...gerstown

...urg Frederick

...CW MEDICINE ...ACY ..., MD

Bethesda
Glen Echo

FT. FO...

FT. W...HINGTON

Clinton

Beantown

SEE
WEST VIRGINIA
PAGE 262

SURRATT HOUSE

301

Scotland

SEE
VIRGINIA
PAGE 200

...LOOKOUT

113

0   100 Miles

0   100 KM

THE BATTLE OF ANTIETAM (SHARPSBURG)

September 17, 1862

This battle marked the bloodiest day of the Civil War and the end of the Confederate invasion of the North.

On September 4, 1862, General Robert E. Lee crossed the Potomac River and brought his Confederate army into Northern territory. His plan was to take the fighting out of his beloved Virginia and force a showdown with Union Major General George B. McClellan at Harrisburg, Pennsylvania. En route north, however, Lee divided his army to allow General Thomas Jackson to capture the Federal garrison at Harpers Ferry, West Virginia.

McClellan learned of Lee's movements and decided to move southward to meet the Confederate troops. On September 6, McClellan began marching toward the Army of Virginia, which was concentrated at Frederick, Maryland. Cautious by nature, McClellan was slow in advancing; he was convinced that Lee's army outnumbered his own. Even when he learned the details of Lee's entire operational plan, McClellan did not act immediately. He made the additional mistake of allowing a Confederate sympathizer to be present as Lee's order was

Artist's rendering of Burnside Bridge at the Battle of Antietam

discussed. When McClellan finally acted on the order, Lee had been warned.

After preliminary skirmishing, Lee positioned his army behind Antietam Creek on rising, rocky terrain, with his back to the city of Sharpsburg and waited for McClellan. On September 17, the battle began at daybreak on Lee's left flank. This section of the battle surged back and forth across a cornfield. After only four hours, the cornstalks were sheared off, and 13,000 soldiers lay dead or wounded. The center of the lines fared even worse. Confederate General Daniel H. Hill's division was forced into a sunken road. Dead men were piled on top of one another in the trench-like road, now called Bloody Lane.

After four hours of savage fighting, the Confederates were driven back. Lee's right flank fought Federals who attempted to cross a narrow bridge. Two attempts were made to cross the bridge; both times 400 Confederates from Georgia blocked the crossing. A third attempt proved successful. By 4:00PM, the Union had gained almost all of the high ground east and south of Sharpsburg when an unexpected Confederate attack created confusion. The South pushed the Union's left flank back to Antietam Creek, and there the fighting ended. McClellan chose not to continue fighting the next day, and Lee began withdrawing his army back across the Potomac the evening of September 18.

More men were killed at Antietam than in any other battle of the Civil War. The battle's combined total casualties remain as the single bloodiest day in U.S. history. Antietam was also a turning point in the war. Never again would the Confederates have such strength and opportunity. Shortly after Antietam, President Lincoln issued his preliminary Emancipation Proclamation, which paved the way for the official proclamation on January 1, 1863. This act changed the nature of the war by making it as much a fight against slavery as a fight against the disruption of the Union.

"I have always had a high opinion of General McClellan, and have no reason to suppose that he failed to accomplish anything that he was able to do."

Gen. R. E. Lee

WASHINGTON CONFEDERATE CEMETERY
(INSIDE ROSE HILL CEMETERY)

600 South Potomac Street, Hagerstown, MD
PHONE: 301-739-3630
HOURS: Open daily.
ADMISSION: Free.

Two thousand four hundred and sixty-eight Confederate soldiers from the battles of Antietam and South Mountain have been reburied at the Washington Confederate Cemetery. Of the soldiers interred, the identities of only 346 are known. Originally buried on the field at Antietam, these Confederates were disinterred around 1871 and moved to Washington Confederate Cemetery.

ANTIETAM NATIONAL BATTLEFIELD PARK

Visitor Center: 5831 Dunker Church Road, Sharpsburg, MD
PHONE: 301-432-5124
WEB: www.nps.gov/anti
HOURS: Open daily; closed Thanksgiving, Christmas, and New Year's Day.
ADMISSION: A fee is charged.

Antietam National Battlefield contains 3,244 acres of the original battlefield. The park features a self-guided driving tour and several walking trails. Along the tour is the rebuilt Dunker Church, around which much of the battle took place. Burnside's Bridge may also be seen along with more than 350 monuments, tablets, markers, and forty-one cannons.

The Visitor Center showcases panoramic battle paintings by a Civil War veteran and a twenty-six-minute movie entitled *Antietam Visit*. During the summer, interpretive programs are presented by rangers or costumed interpreters.

Photo left: Monument to 128th Pennsylvania Volunteer Infantry, Antietam National Battlefield

Antietam National Cemetery is located within the confines of the National Park. Nearly 5,000 Union soldiers, of whom 1,836 remain unknown, rest on this hilltop. Most of the fallen Confederates from this battle are buried in Hagerstown and Frederick, Maryland, and in Shepherdstown, West Virginia.

Photo right: Sunken Road Monument, Antietam National Battlefield

Photo below: Cannon, Antietam National Battlefield

THE BATTLE OF MONOCACY

July 9, 1864

*Union victory at Monocacy saved Washington, D.C., from
Confederate invasion.*

In 1864, acting upon orders from General Robert E. Lee, Confederate Lieutenant General Jubal Early cleared the Shenandoah Valley of Union troops and moved across the mountains to threaten Baltimore and Washington, D.C.; Confederate commanders hoped that Early's movement would draw Union troops away from General Ulysses S. Grant's siege of Petersburg.

Major General Lewis Wallace, with a small force of Union home-front guards and second-line troops, waited on the Monocacy Junction. Here, the Georgetown Pike to Washington and the National Road to Baltimore crossed the Monocacy River, as did the Baltimore & Ohio Railroad. Wallace did not know which city was the target, but he was determined to delay Early until Grant could send reinforcements.

Because Confederate forces significantly outnumbered Union, Wallace took up defensive positions behind railroad embankments, blockhouses, and the higher riverbank on the east side. For eight hours, fighting raged up and down the Union lines. It became clear that Southern numbers were

Gambrill Mill, Monocacy National Battlefield

New Jersey Monument, Monocacy National Battlefield

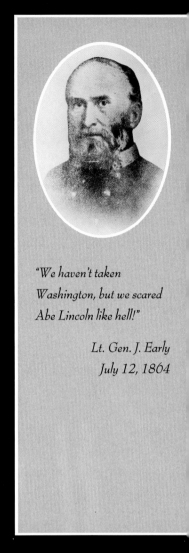

SOUTHERN COMMANDER:
Lt. Gen. J. Early

STRENGTH: 18,000

CASUALTIES: 800

overwhelming; even with the reinforcements of two of Grant's corps. At about 4:30PM, Wallace ordered a withdrawal. A Confederate troop harried the retreating forces until Early called it off and moved back into the valley. Early had achieved his objective of weakening Grant's Richmond and Petersburg forces.

Although the Battle of Monocacy was a tactical victory for the Confederacy, it was a moral victory for the Union. The battle delayed Early's ability to enter Washington and made a future invasion of the Union capital unlikely.

MONOCACY NATIONAL BATTLEFIELD PARK

5201 Urbana Pike, Frederick, MD
PHONE: 301-662-3515
WEB: www.nps.gov/mono
HOURS: Open daily 8:30AM – 5:00PM; closed Thanksgiving Day, Christmas Day, and New Year's Day.
ADMISSION: Free.

The Visitor Center features engaging interpretive exhibits, artifacts, a fiber optic map, and a museum shop. A self-guided auto tour and walking trails help visitors experience the battlefield where Union forces under Gen. Lew Wallace were defeated by Gen. Jubal Early who was delayed in his efforts to threaten Washington, D.C.

Photo right: Visitor Center,
Monocacy National Battlefield Park

The Worthington House at Monocacy National Battlefield

MOUNT OLIVET CEMETERY

515 Market Street, Frederick MD
PHONE: 301-662-1164
WEB: www.mountolivetcemeteryinc.com
HOURS: Open daily.
ADMISSION: Free.

Four-hundred-eight unknown soldiers from the Battle of Monocacy are buried at Mount Olivet Cemetery in a mass Confederate grave. In Confederate Row, there are 303 soldiers interred, about twenty of whom are listed as unknown. Also buried at Mount Olivet is Barbara Fritchie, Union loyalist and heroine of Frederick, Maryland, whom the poet Henry Wadsworth Longfellow memorialized in his poem. From another era, but also buried here, is Francis Scott Key, author of *The Star-Spangled Banner*.

NATIONAL MUSEUM OF CIVIL WAR MEDICINE

48 East Patrick Street, Frederick, MD
PHONE: 301-695-1864
WEB: www.civilwarmed.org
HOURS: Open daily year round;
closed major holidays.
ADMISSION: A fee is charged.

The National Museum of Civil War Medicine uses its extensive collection of artifacts and illustrations to describe the care of the sick and wounded during the Civil War.

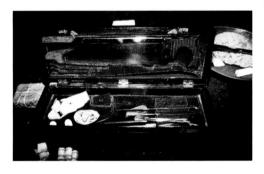

Photo above: Field dressing station exhibit, National Museum of Civil War Medicine

Photo left: Civil War-era medical tools, Museum of Civil War Medicine

PRESIDENT STREET STATION

601 President Street Station, Baltimore, MD
PHONE: 410-461-9377
WEB: www.angelfire.com/biz/presidentststation
HOURS: Open weekends 10AM – 5PM or by appointment; call for details.
ADMISSION: Free.

This 1849-50 train depot, reopened as a museum by volunteers from the Friends of President Street Station, is devoted to Baltimore's role in the Civil War, specifically a riot which occurred on April 19, 1861. On their way to Camden Station, Union troops were stoned by Confederate sympathizers. The first death of the Civil War occurred in the ensuing melee. The museum also features information on railroad history and Underground Railroad history.

FORT MCHENRY NATIONAL MONUMENT AND HISTORIC SHRINE

2400 East Fort Avenue, Baltimore, MD
PHONE: 410-962-4290
WEB: www.nps.gov/fomc
HOURS: Open daily; closed Thanksgiving, Christmas, and New Year's Day.
ADMISSION: A fee is charged; children under 16 are free.

This late 18th-century star-shaped fort is world famous as the birthplace of the American national anthem. This historic

Fort McHenry National Monument and Historic Site

fort, whose flag inspired Francis Scott Key to write the *The Star-Spangled Banner*, was used as a prison for Confederate soldiers and sympathizers during the Civil War. A Civil War Weekend reenactment is held each spring, usually in April.

CLARA BARTON NATIONAL HISTORIC SITE

5801 Oxford Road, Glen Echo, MD
PHONE: 301-320-1410
WEB: www.nps.gov/clba
HOURS: Open daily; closed Thanksgiving, Christmas, and New Year's Day.
ADMISSION: Free.

Clara Barton served with distinction during the Civil War and was the founder of the American Red Cross. This site was built in 1891 and used as a warehouse for disaster relief supplies until 1897. At that time,

Clara Barton National Historic Site

Barton remodeled the interior and used the building as her home and as the headquarters for the American Red Cross. Barton lived here until her death in 1912. Army surgeon Dr. James I. Dunn wrote to his wife about Barton, "At a time when we were entirely out of dressings of every kind, she supplied us with everything, and while the shells were bursting in every direction . . . she staid [sic] dealing out shirts . . . and preparing soup. . . . I thought that night that if heaven ever sent out a homely angel, she must be one."

NATIONAL ARCHIVES AT COLLEGE PARK, MD

8601 Adelphi Road, College Park, MD
PHONE: 301-837-3002
WEB: www.archives.gov/dc-metro/college-park
HOURS: Open daily except Sunday; closed major holidays; reservations required for tours.
ADMISSION: Free.

Free tours are available. The Still Picture Branch houses Mathew Brady's photographs of the Civil War.

SURRATT HOUSE MUSEUM

9118 Brandywine Road, Clinton, MD
PHONE: 301-868-1121
WEB: www.surratt.org
HOURS: Open mid-January – mid-December, closed major holidays and Easter Sunday.
ADMISSION: A fee is charged.

Built in 1852 as a middle-class plantation home, historic Surratt House also served as a tavern and hostelry, a post office, and a polling place during the crucial decade before the Civil War. During the war, it was a safe house for the Confederate underground which

Surratt House Museum

flourished in southern Maryland. It was also the country home of Mary Surratt, the first woman to be executed by the United States government. Surratt was found guilty of conspiring with John Wilkes Booth to assassinate Abraham Lincoln. After the assassination, Booth stopped at the Surratt House to retrieve guns and ammunition; he then went on to Dr. Samuel A. Mudd's house. Each spring and fall the Surratt Society sponsors bus tours along Booth's escape route.

FORT WASHINGTON PARK

13551 Fort Washington Road, Fort Washington, MD
PHONE: 301-763-4600
WEB: www.nps.gov/fowa
HOURS: Open daily; closed Thanksgiving, Christmas, and New Year's Day.
ADMISSION: November – March: free; April – October: a fee is charged.

The historic fort was built from 1814 to 1824 to replace Fort Warburton, which was destroyed during the War of 1812. Under the command of Capt. Joseph Haskins, Fort Washington was held by the Union forces throughout the Civil War. Labeled obsolete in 1872, the garrison was withdrawn and Fort Washington closed. Fort Washington was part of the Coast Defense System during the 1890s through World War I; eight concrete and steel (Endicotte) gun batteries were constructed for defense of Washington, DC. After 1921, Fort Washington was used for housing and training; during World War II, the Adjutant General/Officer's Candidate School was here. Today, as part of the National Park Service, a Visitor Center and tours of the old fort are offered.

Fort Washington Park

FORT FOOTE PARK

Fort Foote Road, Fort Washington, MD
PHONE: 301-763-4600
WEB: www.nps.gov/fofo
HOURS: Open daily.
ADMISSION: Free.

The fort's outline is marked by trees, and the earthworks are still intact. Fort Foote contains the largest smooth-bore cannons used in the Civil War, 15-inch Rodmans. Each gun barrel weighs over twenty-five tons. There is no Visitor's Center.

Photo right: Fort Foote

Dr. Samuel A. Mudd House

3725 Dr. Samuel Mudd Road, Waldorf, MD
PHONE: 301-274-9358
HOURS: Open Saturday, Sunday, and Wednesday, April – November.
ADMISSION: A fee is charged.

The buildings and surrounding grounds have remained in the Mudd family and retain much of their original ambiance. After killing President Lincoln, John Wilkes Booth needed medical assistance for a broken leg. Doctor Mudd set Booth's leg and was later tried and convicted of conspiracy for the act. He was sentenced to life in prison, but the sentence was commuted in 1869 by President Andrew Johnson after Mudd heroically treated victims during an outbreak of yellow fever.

Dr. Samuel A. Mudd House

Point Lookout State Park

Maryland Highway 5, Scotland, MD
PHONE: 301-872-5688
HOURS: Museum and Visitor's Center open daily
Memorial Day – Labor Day; park open daily year round.
ADMISSION: A fee is charged; children in car seats and seniors free.

Features of the park include the remains of Hammond Hospital for the Union's Sick and Wounded and Point Lookout Prison for Confederates. By the end of the war, over 52,000 Confederates had passed through the prison, although only 20,000 were held at any one time in the twenty-acre, square prison pen. Point Lookout was the largest prisoner of war camp during the Civil War and was used mainly for enlisted men, one of whom was Confederate poet Sidney Lanier.

Today, only the earthen wall of Fort Lincoln, built by Confederate prisoners to protect the prison from an attack from Virginia, remains intact. A fishing pier stands where the prison pen once was. The park hosts Blue and Gray Days in June and the Spirits of Point Lookout in October.

MISSISSIPPI

Situated high on the bluffs overlooking the Mississippi River, Vicksburg was a key military site. At the Vicksburg National Military Park, a sixteen-mile self-guided auto tour highlights monuments, markers, and reconstructed earthworks. Of special note is the Illinois Memorial, the largest monument on the battlefield. The remains of the Cairo, a Union ironclad, are located in one corner of the park.

Nearby, Grand Gulf Military Monument commemorates the South's attempt to secure Vicksburg. A thirty-foot observation tower offers excellent views of the park and its forts, and each year a Civil War artillery demonstration is held. Port Gibson, a charming city located thirty miles from Vicksburg, was spared devastation during the Battle of Port Gibson. General Ulysses S. Grant found the city too beautiful to burn.

Overlooking the Pearl River, Mississippi's capital, Jackson, is home to a number of historic sites, including the beautiful Oaks House Museum, the Old Capitol Museum, and the Governor's Mansion. In 1863, the city developed the nickname, "Chimneyville," after Union General William T. Sherman's troops thoroughly burned the state capital, leaving only the buildings' brick chimneys as reminders of the once grand homes.

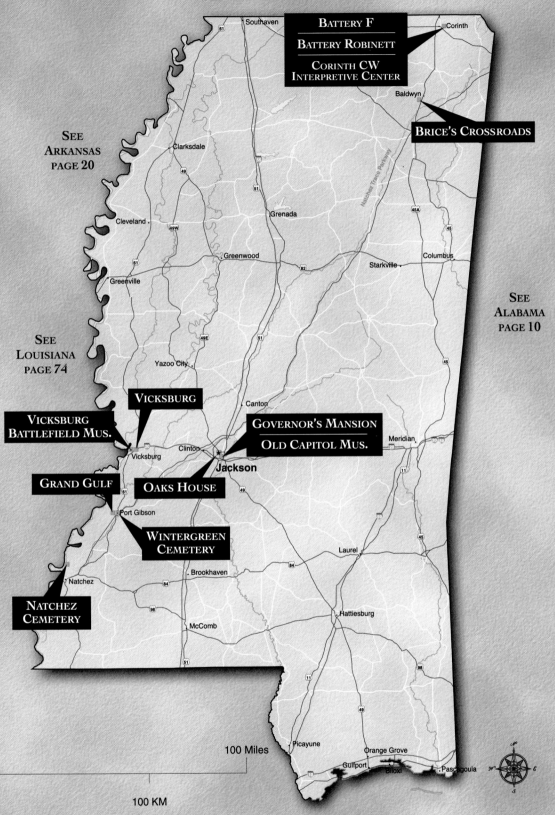

BATTERY F

BATTERY ROBINETT

CORINTH CW
INTERPRETIVE CENTER

BRICE'S CROSSROADS

SEE
ARKANSAS
PAGE 20

SEE
LOUISIANA
PAGE 74

SEE
ALABAMA
PAGE 10

VICKSBURG

VICKSBURG
BATTLEFIELD MUS.

GOVERNOR'S MANSION

OLD CAPITOL MUS.

GRAND GULF

OAKS HOUSE

WINTERGREEN
CEMETERY

NATCHEZ
CEMETERY

100 Miles

100 KM

NORTHERN COMMANDER:
Maj. Gen. H. W. Halleck

STRENGTH: 23,000

CASUALTIES: 2,350

THE SIEGE AND BATTLE OF CORINTH

April 29–30, 1862

With victory at Corinth, the Union secured a vital railroad connection to Tennessee and Virginia and opened a route into the Deep South.

In the spring of 1862, the city of Corinth, in northeastern Mississippi, became vitally important to both the Union and the Confederacy. The Union had just won significant victories in Kentucky and Tennessee and looked to the major railroad junction at Corinth as a launching point for further advances into Confederate territory. For the Confederates, Corinth was equally vital; Southern forces needed a place to consolidate and organize

Jacinto Courthouse in Corinth

Corinth Depot

their defenses as they prepared to keep Union forces out of the Mississippi River Valley. In anticipation of Union advances to this very strategic town, Confederate General P. G. T. Beauregard reinforced and deepened entrenchments around the town. The first Union attempt on Corinth came in early May, when Union Major General Henry W. Halleck led a formal siege on Corinth. Recognizing that his troops were weak from illness and had few rations, Beauregard decided not to fight. He withdrew his men to Tupelo on May 29–30, leaving Corinth for the Union.

The Union army rebuilt Corinth's railroads to use as supply lines to western Tennessee. But the Confederates were not ready to give up without one last fight. In September General Earl Van Dorn ordered an attack on Corinth, hoping to win the railroad lines which would facilitate Confederate advance into Tennessee. Although the assault was costly to the Union, after a day and a half of fighting, it also proved ineffective. The Confederates withdrew on October 4, leaving Corinth to the Union.

CORINTH CIVIL WAR INTERPRETIVE CENTER/ BATTERY ROBINETT

501 West Linden Street, Corinth, MS

PHONE: 662-287-9273
WEB: www.nps.gov/shil
HOURS: Open daily 8:30AM–4:30PM; closed Christmas Day.
ADMISSION: Free.

Reconstructed fort on the site of Battery Robinett outside the Corinth Civil War Interpretive Center

A unit of Shiloh National Military Park, this interpretive center traces the story of the key role Corinth played throughout the Civil War. Built on the site of Battery Robinett, its grounds were once the site of intense fighting. A reconstructed battery awaits visitors, as does an exhibit on how the soldiers would have built the earthworks. The center also features additional interactive exhibits and two films, on the Battle of Corinth and the Battle of Shiloh. The path into the center is strewn with bronze replicas reflecting the aftermath of battle, and at the entrance, visitors pass six bronze marching Civil War soldiers. Available at the center are informative maps and brochures on the Siege and Battle of Corinth.

BATTERY F

Bitner and Davis Streets, Corinth, MS

Battery F is one of six outer batteries built by the Union army and captured by the Confederates on October 3, 1862. This well-preserved battery protected the Memphis & Charleston Railroad.

CORINTH NATIONAL CEMETERY

1551 Horton Street, Corinth, MS
PHONE: 901-386-8311
(Memphis National Cemetery)
WEB: www.cem.va.gov
HOURS: Open weekdays.
ADMISSION: Free.

In 1866, Corinth National Cemetery was authorized to honor those who died in the Civil War in and around Corinth. Within the twenty acres rest 1,793 known and 3,895 unknown Union soldiers.

Corinth National Cemetery

BRICE'S CROSSROADS NATIONAL BATTLEFIELD SITE

Mississippi Highway 370, Visitor's Center at 607 Grisham Street, Baldwyn, MS
PHONE: 662-365-3969
HOURS: Open daily except Sunday and Monday.
ADMISSION: A fee is charged; children and groups are discounted.

The visitor's center of Brice's Crossroads National Battlefield Site and Old Town Creek Battlefield is located in Baldwyn. The visitor's center offers a video that interprets the battles of Tupelo/Harrisburg and Brice's Crossroads and displays a permanent exhibit and temporary exhibits. Outside is a flag exhibit with fifteen present-day state flags that represent soldiers who fought at Brice's Crossroads. The 1,500-acre Brice's battlefield site has four trails and a reproduction of the Tishomingo Creek bridge where the Union rout occurred on June 10, 1864, when 7,800 Union soldiers under General Samuel Sturgis were defeated by half as many Confederate soldiers under the command of General Nathan Bedford Forrest. The Battle of Tupelo/Harrisburg is interpreted at a 12-acre site at Old Town Creek in Tupelo where the Union troops under A. J. Smith met Forrest and Gen. Lee, and a guided driving tour between the two fields is provided. The center interprets the two last stands of the Confederacy in the summer of 1864.

Visitor's Center for the battles of Brice's Crossroads and Tupelo/Harrisburg

THE BATTLE AND SIEGE OF VICKSBURG

March 29–July 4, 1863

Vicksburg was the last western theater stronghold to fall to the Union. This siege established Ulysses S. Grant's reputation as a brilliant field commander.

The Union considered winning Vicksburg, Mississippi, essential to winning the war. With Vicksburg in hand, the Union would control the Mississippi River and would also effectively split the Confederacy in two, cutting off western forces from those in the east. The campaign of Vicksburg encompassed the area from Vicksburg east to Jackson and south to Port Gibson.

The Union's first attempt at Vicksburg occurred in April 1862 when, after capturing New Orleans, Admiral David G. Farragut moved upstream. Then in June of the same year, Farragut's attempts failed because of a lack of troops to back up the gunship barrages. By July Farragut had returned to New Orleans, and Vicksburg was reinforced heavily by the Con-

Vicksburg National Military Park Visitor's Center

Thayer's Approach, Vicksburg National Military Park

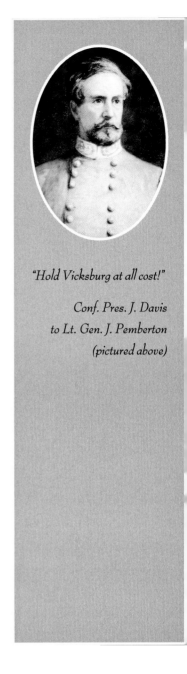

federates. Future attempts on the town would require a major Union offensive.

In the fall of 1862, Major General Ulysses S. Grant received permission to take Vicksburg. Several early assaults in November and December were effectively repulsed, however, and it was not until the spring of the following year that Grant again attacked.

In late April, Grant landed his troops at Bruinsburg, south of Vicksburg, then maneuvered east to stand between Vicksburg and Jackson. He defeated the Confederate forces led by General Joseph E. Johnston at Champion's Hill. Lieutenant General John C. Pemberton then withdrew his forces to nearby Crystal Springs.

Grant then moved onto Vicksburg itself in mid-May first attempting a direct assault. He realized, however, that siege tactics would be more effective. The siege lasted until July 4 when Pemberton, whose Confederate forces were weakened, demoralized, and starving, surrendered the city. The victory, which followed Union success at Gettysburg by one day, is seen by historians as the beginning of the end for the Confederacy.

VICKSBURG NATIONAL MILITARY PARK

3201 Clay Street, Vicksburg, MS
PHONE: 601-636-0583
HOURS: Open daily; closed Thanksgiving, Christmas, and New Year's Day (driving tour open every day).
ADMISSION: A fee is charged.

Vicksburg National Cemetery

Vicksburg National Military Park was established in 1899 to commemorate the campaign, siege, and defense of Vicksburg. Included in the park are 1,620 acres of the original battlefield, over 1,300 monuments and markers, reconstructed trenches and earthworks, one antebellum structure, and the Vicksburg National Cemetery, where more than 18,000 soldiers lie, 12,000 of whom are unknown.

The Visitor's Center runs a twenty-minute film which gives the history of the battles and siege. There is a sixteen-mile driving tour available that passes through the siege lines and includes Big Black Battlefield, Champion Hill Battlefield, the Confederate Cemetery at Raymond, Raymond Battlefield, Grand Gulf Military Monument Park, Jackson Battlefield, Port Gibson Battlefield, and Windsor Ruins.

Model of the Cairo, *Vicksburg National Military Park*

VICKSBURG BATTLEFIELD MUSEUM

4139 North Frontage Road, Vicksburg, MS
PHONE: 601-638-6500
HOURS: Open daily except Sunday; closed Thanksgiving, Christmas, and New Year's Day.
ADMISSION: A fee is charged; students and children are discounted.

The Vicksburg Battlefield Museum boasts the largest collection of Civil War gunboat models, as well as paintings, reference files, and artifacts pertaining to warships. It also features a 250-foot diorama which contains a miniature layout of Vicksburg Battlefield with 2,500 miniature soldiers. A miniature city of Vicksburg is in the planning stage.

MISSISSIPPI GOVERNOR'S MANSION

300 East Capitol Street, Jackson, MS
PHONE: 601-359-6421
HOURS: Tuesday – Friday, 9:30AM – 11AM, tours on the half hour; closed last two weeks of December.
Note: The Mansion may also be closed to visitors for official state functions. Call ahead to confirm availability. Reservations required for groups of 10 or more.
ADMISSION: Free.

The 1841 Mississippi Governor's Mansion is an outstanding example of Greek Revival architecture and hosts a fine collection of nineteenth-century furniture and decorative arts. Governor John Pettus evacuated the Mansion during the Union occupations of Jackson before and after the July 4, 1863 fall of Vicksburg. The state capital was moved from Jackson to other towns and the Governor's Mansion was used to house wounded and ill Confederate soldiers. On July 18, 1863, Union General William Sherman and other Union officers enjoyed a dinner at the Mansion.

Mississippi Governor's Mansion

THE OAKS HOUSE MUSEUM

823 North Jefferson Street, Jackson, MS

PHONE: 601-353-9339

WEB: www.theoakshousemuseum.org

HOURS: Open Tuesday – Saturday 10AM – 3PM.

ADMISSION: A fee is charged; children are discounted.

The Oaks House Museum, the Boyd House, was built in 1853 on four acres of urban farmstead. The house survived the Civil War unscathed, although the siege of Jackson raged all about it. The owner, J. H. Boyd, was alderman when the City surrendered to Union forces in 1863. Perhaps it was because Mr. Boyd was a Freemason that General Sherman, also a Mason, spared this house in what was later called "Chimneyville."

Photo above left: Bedroom of The Oaks House Museum

Photo below left: The Oaks House Museum

OLD CAPITOL MUSEUM

100 South State Street, Jackson, MS
PHONE: 601-576-6920
WEB: www.oldcapitolmuseum.com
HOURS: Tuesday – Saturday
9AM – 5PM; Sunday 1PM – 5PM;
closed major holidays.
ADMISSION: Free.

The Old Capitol Museum of Mississippi History was the site of Mississippi's Secession Convention in January 1861 and was also the seat of state government until May 1863. In October 1864, the building became the Confederate military headquarters.

Photo above: Civil War and Reconstruction Room, Old Capitol Museum

Photo left: House of Representatives Chamber, Old Capitol Museum

WINTERGREEN CEMETERY

Greenwood Street, Port Gibson, MS
PHONE: 601-437-4351 (Chamber of Commerce Tourist Information Center)
HOURS: Open daily.
ADMISSION: Free.

Established in 1807, Wintergreen Cemetery is the final resting place for many of the Confederate soldiers killed in the battle of Port Gibson. Shortly after the battle, the townspeople removed the Confederate dead from the battlefield and interred them here in Soldiers' Row. Small foot-stones marked "C.S.A." were placed by the United Daughters of the Confederacy. Elsewhere in the cemetery, Confederate Generals Earl Van Dorn and Benjamin Grubb Humphreys are also interred. General Van Dorn was born near Port Gibson on September 17, 1820.

GRAND GULF MILITARY PARK
PORT GIBSON BATTLEFIELD

12006 Grand Gulf Road, Port Gibson, MS
PHONE: 601-437-5911
WEB: www.grandgulfpark.state.ms.us
HOURS: Open daily; closed major holidays.
ADMISSION: A fee is charged.

After General Grant failed to capture Vicksburg in 1862, Union troops moved south along the Mississippi River toward Grand Gulf. On April 29, 1863, Union Admiral David D. Porter's ironclads opened fire on Forts Cobun and Wade. Although Porter destroyed the guns at Wade after a five-hour bombardment, the Union was unable to silence the big guns at Fort Cobun; Porter called off the attack. After dark, the Union troops simply bypassed Grand Gulf and crossed the river at Bruinsburg, 12 miles south of Grand Gulf. Admiral Porter later called Grand Gulf "the strongest place on the Mississippi." Forts Wade and Cobun still retain their original earthworks and ammunition magazines. The museum contains exhibits of Civil War artifacts, including Union and Confederate uniforms, cannonballs, and muskets.

NATCHEZ NATIONAL CEMETERY

41 Cemetery Road, Natchez, MS
PHONE: 601-445-4981
HOURS: Open daily.
ADMISSION: Free.

Over 3,000 Union soldiers are interred at the Natchez National Cemetery. Soldiers who had been buried in the levees were disinterred and brought to this national cemetery in 1863, where they now rest in dignity. In addition, seven Buffalo Soldiers—African-American soldiers from Louisiana and Mississippi who served in the West during the late nineteenth century—are interred here.

Photo right: Natchez National Cemetery

MISSOURI

Missouri's status during the Civil War is best symbolized by the fact that whereas the Confederate flag featured a star for Missouri, the state itself never officially left the Union. Torn apart over the issue of slavery before the war, Missouri found no respite from internal strife during the conflict: more incidents of guerrilla warfare occurred in Missouri than in any other state. And while 100,000 Missouri citizens fought for the Union, 40,000 of their neighbors fought for the Confederacy. Militarily, the Confederacy never got a secure foothold in Missouri, and the Union controlled the state for most of the war; nonetheless, life in Missouri was disrupted and devastated by Civil War fighting, and the internal divisiveness that marked the state before and during the war was destined to last long after.

In the southwestern corner of Missouri is a National Battlefield Site commemorating the Battle of Wilson's Creek, which took place in August of 1861. Although the Confederates won this battle, they suffered heavy losses and damage and thereafter were unable to make any significant move to control Missouri. Whereas Wilson's Creek was the largest and most important battle, Missouri was the site of more than 1,100 Civil War battles or skirmishes, and points of historic interest exist in almost every corner of the state.

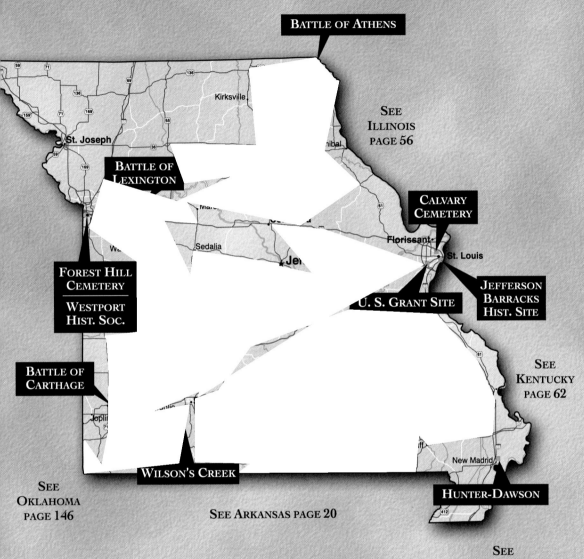

BATTLE OF ATHENS

SEE
ILLINOIS
PAGE 56

**BATTLE OF
LEXINGTON**

**CALVARY
CEMETERY**

Florissant

St. Louis

**FOREST HILL
CEMETERY**

**WESTPORT
HIST. SOC.**

Sedalia

**JEFFERSON
BARRACKS
HIST. SITE**

U. S. GRANT SITE

SEE
KENTUCKY
PAGE 62

**BATTLE OF
CARTHAGE**

Joplin

New Madrid

WILSON'S CREEK

HUNTER-DAWSON

SEE
OKLAHOMA
PAGE 146

SEE ARKANSAS PAGE 20

SEE
TENNESSEE
PAGE 168

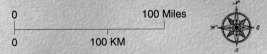

0   100 Miles

0   100 KM

"Fire low—don't aim higher than their knees; wait until they get close; don't get scared; it's no part of a soldier's duty to get scared."

Brig. Gen. N. Lyon
to his men

THE BATTLE OF WILSON'S CREEK (OAK HILLS)

August 10, 1861

The first Civil War battle west of the Mississippi River.

Missouri included the major trails west (California, Oregon, Santa Fe, and Pony Express) as well as the three major shipping rivers of the Missouri, Mississippi, and the Ohio. Because of this strategic importance, President Lincoln gave special attention to Missouri.

In July of 1861, Union soldiers under Brigadier General Nathaniel Lyon began a march southward through Missouri to confront pro-Confederate forces organizing near Springfield. By July Lyon's Union forces were camped at Springfield, while the Confederate army, under Brigadier General Benjamin McCulloch and joined by the Missouri State Guard under Major General Sterling Price, encamped near Wilson's Creek, just south of Springfield.

Initially, McCulloch planned to attack the Union army the morning of August 10, but a light rain caused him to delay.

The Ray House, Wilson's Creek National Battlefield

General Lyon's Marker at Bloody Hill, Wilson's Creek National Battlefield

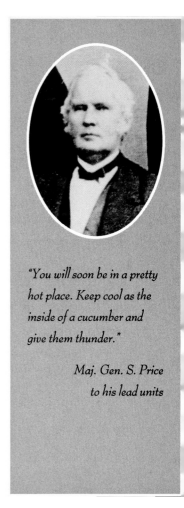

Confederate pickets, however, who had been recalled in order to prepare for battle, did not reposition themselves when the order was rescinded. Lyon realized that if he did not attack, he would be attacked by a force significantly greater in size than his own. Accordingly, he called for an attack at dawn, and on August 10, split his army into three units and attacked.

Because the pickets had not been set up, the Confederates were caught completely by surprise in the south. In the north, the Confederate cavalry stalled Lyon long enough for Price to reorganize and launch a counterattack. By midday, the Federals were nearly out of ammunition and clearly overmatched. They retreated and marched toward Springfield, without General Lyon, who had been killed during heavy hand-to-hand combat on a section of the battlefield known as "Bloody Hill."

Thirty future major and brigadier generals fought at Wilson's Creek. The Confederates won the battle, and a temporary advantage in the fight to gain control of Missouri, but they also suffered heavy losses. As a result, the South saw its plans to take Missouri stalled and eventually defeated. Additionally, two state governments were formed so that Missouri became the only state to have both seceded to the Confederacy and been reinforced by the Union.

WESTPORT HISTORICAL SOCIETY

4000 Baltimore Street, Kansas City, MO
PHONE: 816-561-1821
WEB: www.westporthistorical.com
HOURS: Open Wednesday – Saturday 1PM – 5PM; closed major holidays.
ADMISSION: A fee is charged; students are discounted; children under 5 are free.

The Westport Historical Society offers free brochures detailing the Battle of Westport, the largest Civil War engagement west of the Mississippi River. At Westport, Union forces repulsed Confederate forces, thus ending Price's Raid throughout Missouri. The thirty-two-mile, self-guided automobile tour follows thirty interpretive markers which explain the 1864 battle. Self-guided walking tours are marked through Byram's Ford and the Big Blue Battlefield, and a walking tour of Westport is also offered. The 1855 Harris-Kearney House Museum, the headquarters of the Westport Historical Society, is a certified site on the Santa Fe National Historic Trail.

The Battle of Westport Visitor Center and Museum, located at 6601 Swope Parkway in Kansas City, overlooks the Big Blue River valley and nearby historic Byram's Ford crossing and tells the story of the events of the Battle of Westport. This museum can be reached at 913-345-2000 or battleofwestport.org.

FOREST HILL CEMETERY

6901 Troost Avenue, Kansas City, MO
PHONE: 816-523-2114
HOURS: Open daily 7AM – 7PM.
ADMISSION: Free.

Forest Hill Cemetery sits on the site where the Battle of Westport took place and is the resting place for many Confederate soldiers. Also buried at Forest Hill is the leader of the "Iron Brigade," Confederate Gen. Joseph O. Shelby, who fought at the Battle of Westport. After the war, Shelby's career continued; he took his troops to Mexico to support the Emperor Maximilian and, upon his return to the U.S., became a U.S. Marshal.

BATTLE OF LEXINGTON STATE HISTORIC SITE

1101 Delaware Street, Lexington, MO
PHONE: 660-259-4654
WEB: www.mostateparks.com
HOURS: Open daily except Monday;
November – February: open
Wednesday – Sunday and tours
are by appointment only.
ADMISSION: No charge for the Visitor's Center
and battlefield; fee charged for Anderson House;
children under 6 free; groups discounted.

Anderson House, Battle of Lexington State Historic Site

Built in 1853, Anderson House was used as a hospital by both Union and Confederate forces during the Battle of Lexington. Battle damage from the September 1861 engagement is still visible in the house. The Battle of Lexington State Historic Site occasionally hosts reenactments; call for details.

BATTLE OF CARTHAGE STATE HISTORIC SITE

North side of East Chestnut Street, next to Carter Park, Carthage, MO
PHONE: 417-682-2279
WEB: www.mostateparks.com
HOURS: Open daily.
ADMISSION: Free.

The Battle of Carthage was one of the earliest engagements in the Civil War. Union Col. Franz Sigel and his 1,100 well-trained, fully armed men were sent to southeast Missouri to prevent Gov. Claiborne Jackson's army of 4,000 armed and 2,000 unarmed men from banding up with Confederate troops in Arkansas. On the morning of July 5, 1861, the troops met nine miles north of Carthage. The day's skirmishes spread out over 10 miles. The Confederate Missouri State Guard were victorious; however, the Union troops escaped with minimal losses. The State Historic Site encompasses the Carter Spring area, the campsite of the Union the night before the battle and the Confederate troops following the battle.

Battle of Carthage State Historic Site

WILSON'S CREEK NATIONAL BATTLEFIELD

6424 West Farm Road 182, Republic, MO
PHONE: 417-732-2662, ext. 227

WEB: www.nps.gov/wicr
HOURS: Open daily; closed Thanksgiving, Christmas and New Year's Day; museum closed December – March.
ADMISSION: A fee is charged; children under 16 are free.

Wilson's Creek National Battlefield covers 1,940 acres and features a marked, five-mile, self-guided driving tour that features eight interpretive stops detailing the progress and action of the

Cannon at Sharp Farm, Wilson's Creek National Battlefield

battle. Included are Gibson's House and Mill sites; the Ray House that was used as a Confederate field hospital; Pulaski Arkansas Battery and Price's Headquarters; Sigel's Second Position, where Union forces routed 2,300 Southern cavalry; Sigel's Final Position, where the general committed the fatal error that gave the battle victory to the Confederates; and Bloody Hill, a site where over 1,700 Union and Confederate soldiers, including Gen. Nathaniel Lyon, were slain. The bed on which the body of General Lyon was laid is part of the exhibit at the Ray House. Five walking trails, ranging from a quarter-mile to three-quarters-of-a-mile each, provide further exploration. A picnic area and hiking trails also are available.

BATTLE OF ATHENS STATE HISTORIC SITE

Missouri Highway 81, County Blacktop Road CC, Revere, MO
PHONE: 660-877-3871
WEB: www.mostateparks.com
HOURS: Open daily.
ADMISSION: Free.

The Civil War caused bitter feelings between many of the residents of Athens. As a result of the animosity, the town of Athens was deserted during the early twentieth century. The Battle of Athens State Historic Site serves as museum both for the town's culture as well as its significance in the war. The Battle of Athens was the northernmost battle fought in Missouri during the Civil War and contributed in keeping Missouri in the Union. The battle was the clash of Confederate guardsmen pitted against Col. David Moore and his Union home guard. The Thome-Benning House, locally known as the "Cannonball House," functions as a museum and a Visitor's Center. Also on the site is the McKee House which was used by Colonel Moore as his headquarters during the Union occupation of Athens. Trails and self-guided tours are available. Battle reenactments are held occasionally; call for details.

Battle of Athens State Historic Site

CALVARY CEMETERY

5239 West Florissant, St. Louis, MO
PHONE: 314-381-1313
WEB: archstl.org/cemeteries
HOURS: Open daily 8AM – 5PM.
ADMISSION: Free.

Union Gen. William T. Sherman, Confederate Gov. Thomas Reynolds, and other Civil War individuals are interred in Calvary Cemetery.

JEFFERSON BARRACKS HISTORIC SITE

South Broadway at Kingston Dr., St. Louis, MO
PHONE: 314-544-5714
WEB: www.friendsofjeffersonbarracks.com
HOURS: Wednesday – Sunday, 12 noon – 4PM.
ADMISSION: Free; donations accepted.

Jefferson Barracks, founded in 1826, was the site of the country's first Infantry School of Practice. By the time of the Civil War, it was one of the major military installations devoted to recruiting and training. Many officers from both sides served at the Barracks at some point in their careers, including Ulysses S. Grant, Robert E. Lee, Jefferson Davis, William T. Sherman, and Braxton Bragg, among others. The most important function that Jefferson Barracks served during the Civil War was that of hospital facility, caring for more than 26,000 patients by April 30, 1865. The National Cemetery, which grew from the Old Post Cemetery at Jefferson Barracks, is the final resting place of many soldiers from the Civil War, including 1,140 Confederates. Jefferson Barracks was de-activated in 1946. Today the original 1,700 acres are home to the National Cemetery, a Missouri National Guard base, a Veterans Administration Hospital complex, a St. Louis County Park, and a Historic Area where museums are housed in two stone Powder Magazines from the 1850s. Trails are available, and tours can be arranged; there is also a Visitor's Center. Jefferson Barracks also hosts events such as Historic Hayrides and reenactments periodically.

ULYSSES S. GRANT NATIONAL HISTORIC SITE

7400 Grant Road, St. Louis, MO
PHONE: 314-842-3298
WEB: www.nps.gov/ulsg
HOURS: Open daily; closed major holidays.
ADMISSION: Free.

The Ulysses S. Grant National Historic Site contains five historic structures from the

Photo right: 1860 photograph of Ulysses S. Grant's home

Ulysses S. Grant National Historic Site

original 850-acre plantation owned by General Grant. An introductory film, ranger-guided tours, and museum information are available. Check the website for special events.

FORT DAVIDSON STATE HISTORIC SITE

Missouri Highway 221, Pilot Knob, MO
PHONE: 573-546-3454
WEB: www.mostateparks.com
HOURS: Open daily.
ADMISSION: Free.

Fort Davidson Historic Site features the preserved remains of the earthworks of Fort Davidson. The fort was built to guard the railroad line linking Pilot Knob with St. Louis. After only about an hour, the Battle of Pilot Knob in September 1864 left 1,200 dead, wounded, and missing. Union troops were forced to

Fort Davidson Historic Site Visitor's Center

abandon the fort to Southern forces. Federal troops, however, left little for the Confederate army; before evacuating, they destroyed the guns and powder magazine.

A museum and a Visitor's Center are also located at the site. The museum features two twenty-four-pound cannons. Additionally, an audiovisual presentation, brochures, and maps are available at the Visitor's Center. A self-guided driving tour of the valley features thirteen historic markers, one of which commemorates the spot where General Grant received word of his commission on August 8, 1861, in Irontown, Missouri. The courthouse in Irontown looks over two cannons on its grounds, and the building itself still bears battle scars.

THE HUNTER-DAWSON STATE HISTORIC SITE

312 Dawson Road, New Madrid, MO
PHONE: 573-748-5340
WEB: www.mostateparks.com
HOURS: Open daily; closed major holidays.
ADMISSION: A fee is charged; children are discounted.

The Hunter-Dawson State Historic Site contains an antebellum mansion that was built by the Hunter family. Originally from Virginia, the Hunter family had a son in the Confederate army. Legend has it that General John Pope used the house as his headquarters after New Madrid was occupied by Union forces. Tours of the fifteen-room house feature original furnishings.

The Hunter-Dawson State Historic Site

NEW MEXICO

During the Civil War, the Territory of New Mexico—comprising what is today the states of Arizona, New Mexico, and part of Nevada—was a thinly-populated wilderness. By 1861 the southern region of the territory was so pro-Southern, that conventions held in Mesilla and Tucson voted for secession from the Union and annexation to the Confederacy. This secessionist stance was, ironically, taken one month before the secession of Tennessee, North Carolina, Arkansas, and the Confederate capital state of Virginia.

The South sent out a military expedition to occupy and hold the territory, not for New Mexico alone, but because the territory was a steppingstone to California with its Pacific ports. With its proximity to Texas, the battle for New Mexico became a battle for the Western ambitions of Texas itself.

The Confederate venture into New Mexico ultimately ended in failure. The Union victory at the Battle of Glorieta Pass effectively halted the Confederacy's, and Texas's, movement into the West.

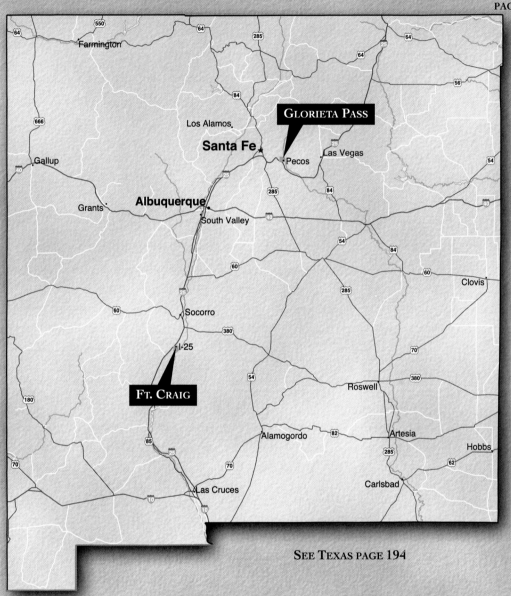

Farmington

550

64

64

285

64

25

64

56

Los Alamos

84

GLORIETA PASS

Santa Fe

Pecos

Las Vegas

Gallup

40

666

25

54

285

84

Grants

Albuquerque

South Valley

60

40

54

84

60

Clovis

60

285

285

Socorro

380

70

I-25

70

54

380

Roswell

FT. CRAIG

180

54

Alamogordo

82

Artesia

Hobbs

85

285

25

62

70

70

Las Cruces

Carlsbad

10

10

SEE TEXAS PAGE 194

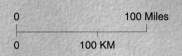

0   100 Miles

0   100 KM

THE BATTLE OF GLORIETA PASS

March 26 and 28, 1862

Victory in New Mexico saved the Far West for the Union.

In the summer of 1861, Confederate President Jefferson Davis ordered Brigadier General Henry Hopkins Sibley to recruit a force of Texans to move into New Mexico territory and secure that territory for the Confederacy, thus opening the way into Colorado and California.

The Battle of Glorieta Pass was the climax of this Confederate thrust, which began in January of 1862. The Texans, under Sibley, had marched into New Mexico, first taking the southernmost Federal post, Fort Fillmore, and then defeating the Union at the Battle of Valverde. They then stopped for provisions about 100 miles northeast of Santa Fe on the Santa Fe Trail. Meanwhile, the Union was gathering its forces at Fort Craig. On March 22, Union Colonel John P. Slough, with 1,340 troops, set out to confront the Texans and put an end to their movement through New Mexico. The two sides met on the morning of March 26 on the Santa Fe Trail when a Confederate force of 200–300 Texans under the command of Major Charles L. Pyron encamped at Johnson's Ranch, at one end of Glorieta Pass. Union Major John M. Chivington led more

Base of Sharpshooters Ridge, Glorieta Pass Battlefield, Pecos National Historical Park

Glorieta Pass, Pecos National Historical Park

than 400 soldiers to the pass and, on the morning of March 26, moved out to attack. After heavy fighting all afternoon, Chivington went into camp at Kozlowski's Ranch. No fighting occurred the next day as reinforcements arrived for both sides.

Lieutenant Colonel William R. Scurry's troops swelled the Rebel ranks to about 1,100 while Union Colonel John P. Slough arrived with about 900 men. Both Slough and Scurry decided to attack and set out early on March 28 to do so. The Confederates held their ground and then attacked and counterattacked throughout the afternoon. The fighting then ended as Slough retired first to Pigeon's Ranch and then to Kozlowski's Ranch. Scurry soon left the field also, thinking he had won the battle. Chivington's men, however, had destroyed all Scurry's supplies and animals at Johnson's Ranch. Both sides claimed victory, the Confederates because they stayed on the field, and the Union because they stopped the Confederates from continuing west.

GLORIETA PASS BATTLEFIELD ━━━━━━

Pecos National Historical Park, New Mexico Highway 63
2 miles north of the village of Pecos, NM
PHONE: 505-757-7200
WEB: www.nps.gov/peco
HOURS: Open daily; closed Thanksgiving, Christmas, and New Year's Day.
ADMISSION: A fee is charged; children under 16 free.

The Glorieta Pass Battlefield is located in the Pecos National Historical Park. The pass was a strategic location during the Civil War because it was situated at the southern tip of the Sangre de Cristo Mountains, southeast of Santa Fe and on the Santa Fe Trail. In March 1862, a battle ensued for control of the pass which the Union troops won, thereby stopping Confederate incursions into the Southwest. Glorieta Pass was the turning point of the war in the New Mexico Territory. A 2.25-mile self-guiding hiking trail of the Battle of Glorieta is open to the public. Ranger-led van tours are offered year-round. The Visitor Center at Pecos National Historical Park contains exhibits and information relating to the battle.

Photo right:
Looking towards
Sharpshooters Ridge,
from New Mexico
Highway 50, Glorieta
Pass Battlefield,
Pecos National
Historical Park

FORT CRAIG ━━━━━━

Socorro Field Office, Bureau of Land Management, exit 115 or 124 off Interstate 25
PHONE: 575-835-0412
HOURS: Open daily during daylight hours.
ADMISSION: Free (subject to change).

Founded in 1854, Fort Craig was one of the largest frontier forts in the West. It was established to control Apache and Navajo raiding and to protect the central portion of the Camino Real de Tierra Adentro, the main north-south route in New Mexico at the time. Military excursions from the fort pursued such notable Apache leaders as Geronimo, Victorio, and Nana. The fort has a rich multicultural history of courage, honor, and sacrifice. The fort was home to the predominantly Hispanic New Mexico Volunteers and New Mexico Militia; Black Regulars (also known as Buffalo Soldiers) of the 9th Cavalry and 38th and 125th Infantry; and household names such as Kit Carson, Raphael Chacon, and Captain Jack Crawford.

Fort Craig is perhaps most famous for the bloody Civil War Batle of ValVerde, which occurred just north of the fort. The battle occurred in February of 1862 as thousands of Confederate soldiers clashed with Union troops stationed at Fort Craig. Confederate forces eventually bypassed the fort and went on to capture Albuquerque and Santa Fe before being turned back at Glorieta in March of 1862.

Fort Craig offers self-guided tours, modern restroom and picnic facilities, a modest visitor center, and interpretive signs. Fort Craig is approximately 125 miles north of Las Cruces or 35 miles south of Socorro, New Mexico.

Ruins of Commanding Officer's Quarters, Fort Craig

NORTH CAROLINA

Many of North Carolina's Civil War battles occurred along its Atlantic coastline. Barrier islands and sandbars provided natural protection for small blockade-running ships. These ships were important in providing troops and civilians with supplies and weapons. The most significant maritime battle took place just outside Wilmington. Fort Fisher guarded the city from Union attack and provided a port for Confederate blockade runners. Many of these supply ships were destroyed by members of the Union blockade. Items, including supplies and arms, from sunken blockade runners are exhibited in Fort Fisher's Museum. Nearby, earthworks at the Brunswick Town/Fort Anderson State Historic Site further illustrate North Carolina's Cape Fear defense system.

Inland, North Carolina's largest battle took place at Bentonville. Union General William T. Sherman's army defeated Confederate General Joseph E. Johnston's army at the Battle of Bentonville. This last major battle of the Civil War is commemorated at living history exhibits held during the summer. Every five years, a reenactment of the battle takes place at Bentonville Battleground State Historic Site in Newton Grove.

See
Tennessee
page 168

See Virginia page 200

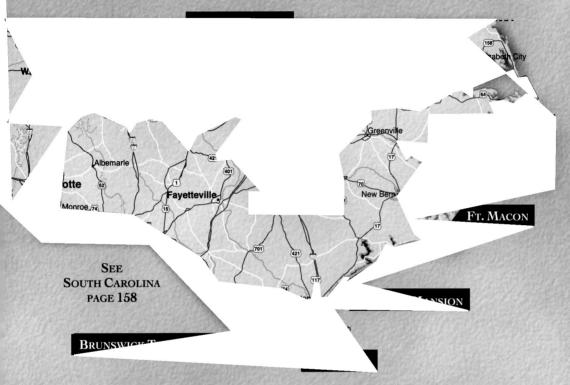

158

rabeth City

64

Greenville

17

Albemarle

421

401

1

70

New Bern

otte

52

Fayetteville

Monroe 74

15

17

Ft. Macon

701

421

40

117

74

See
South Carolina
page 158

NSION

Brunswick T

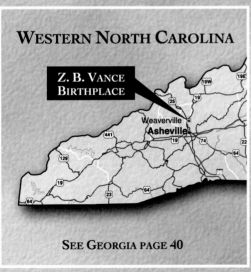

Western North Carolina

Z. B. Vance
Birthplace

19W 19E

25 19

Weaverville
Asheville

441 19

74

22

129 64

19

64

23

64

See Georgia page 40

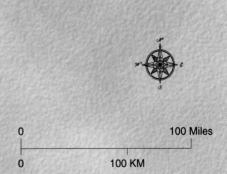

0   100 Miles

0   100 KM

THE BATTLE OF FORT FISHER

December 7–27, 1864; January 6–15, 1865

At Fort Fisher, a combined effort of Union army and navy closed the last major supply port for General Lee's Army of Northern Virginia.

Wilmington, North Carolina, was among the most important blockade-running ports in the Confederate South. With railroad connections to major cities, Wilmington was essential in supplying the Confederate army. Dangerous offshore shoals and riptides kept Union blockade ships from getting too close to shore. To defend Wilmington, the Confederates built a series of forts, one of which was Fort Fisher.

Rear Admiral David D. Porter was given orders to take Wilmington but was worried about the Confederate ship, the *Albemarle*, which had proven its ability to withstand attack. A young lieutenant, William Cushing, and fourteen others volunteered to ram the *Albemarle* with a Union torpedo boat. Only Cushing and one other crew member escaped with their lives. The *Albemarle* was sunk with a single torpedo.

With the *Albemarle* cleared, Porter agreed to General Butler's suggestion to detonate a ship of explosives next to Fort Fisher and then immediately begin shelling it. This plan would cripple the fort and make it easier for a landing party of Union army forces. The explosion, however, had little effect on the

Sheppard's Battery, Fort Fisher State Historic Site

Sheppard's Battery after the Battle of Fort Fisher, taken in January 1865 by Timothy O' Sullivan, one of Mathew Brady's traveling photographers

fort, and it was ten hours before the navy began the shelling. When the Confederates did not fire back, Union commanders erroneously concluded that their guns had been silenced. On Christmas morning, Major General Benjamin Butler landed his men at Fort Fisher; he returned them posthaste when he realized that the fort was, indeed, fully functional.

Both Union commanders blamed each other for the botched attack. General Grant relieved Butler, assigning Major General Alfred Terry in his place. Coordination between the Union army and navy improved after the change of command.

On January 15, a joint attack from both the river and land began, but the sailors and marines were ill-prepared for attacking a fort. Out of 1,200 sailors and 400 marines, 350 became casualties. Still, the attention given to the river attack allowed a group of Union troops to slip through a breach caused by naval gun fire. Seven hours of hand-to-hand combat ensued before the South surrendered Fort Fisher, its last sea stronghold. The city of Wilmington, the Confederate's last open port, surrendered five weeks later on February 22, 1865.

THE ZEBULON B. VANCE BIRTHPLACE

Zebulon B. Vance Birthplace

911 Reems Creek Road, Weaverville, NC
PHONE: 828-645-6706
WEB: www.nchistoricsites.org/vance
HOURS: Tuesday – Saturday 9AM – 5PM;
closed state holidays.
ADMISSION: Free.

This Zebulon B. Vance Birthplace commemorates the life of Zebulon B. Vance, a prominent public figure in North Carolina politics before, during, and after the Civil War. A member of the U.S. House of Representatives until North Carolina seceded, he served as colonel of the Twenty-sixth North Carolina Regiment. After the war, Vance was elected to three terms in the U.S. Senate. His birthplace is interpreted through costumed guides and includes many items authentic to the Civil War era. A springhouse, corn crib, smokehouse, loom house, slave house, and tool house are located on its grounds. Special events occur throughout the year.

BENNETT PLACE STATE HISTORIC SITE

4409 Bennett Memorial Road, Durham, NC
PHONE: 919-383-4345
WEB: www.nchistoricsites.org/bennett
HOURS: Tuesday – Saturday 9AM – 5PM; closed major holidays.
ADMISSION: Free.

On April 26, 1865, Maj. Gen. William T. Sherman and Gen. Joseph E. Johnston met at the farm of James and Nancy Bennett to negotiate the peace terms leading to the surrender of more than 89,270 Confederate soldiers, the largest surrender of the American Civil War. Today, the reconstructed farm stands along the original Hillsborough Road. Inside the main house, kitchen-house, and smokehouse, visitors

Unity Monument, Bennett Place State Historic Site

can view the life of the Bennett family and walk the hallowed ground where one of the most important events of the Civil War occurred. The Visitor's Center contains a museum gallery, gift shop, the Everett-Thissen Research Library, and theater, which shows a 17-minute movie, *Dawn of Peace.*

BENTONVILLE BATTLEFIELD STATE HISTORIC SITE

5466 Harper House Road, Four Oaks, NC
PHONE: 910-594-0789
WEB: www.nchistoricsites.org/
bentonvi/
HOURS: April – September:
Monday – Saturday 9AM – 5PM;
October – March: Tuesday – Saturday
9AM – 5PM.
ADMISSION: Free.

In March 1865, the Battle of Bentonville
marked General William T. Sherman's
last devastating march north through
the Carolinas. Despite their numerical
disadvantage, General Joseph E. Johnston's Confederate forces successfully

Reenactor at Harper House, Bentonville Battlefield State Historic Site

Goldsboro Rifles' mass grave monument, Bentonville Battlefield State Historic Site

ambushed one wing of Sherman's army on March 19, 1865; however, they were soon repulsed. For the Confederates, it was a heroic but futile effort to delay the inevitable; within a month, both Richmond and Raleigh had fallen, and Lee had surrendered.

The Harper House is located at Bentonville Battlefield State Historic Site. The downstairs room contains a functioning Civil War field hospital, while the upstairs rooms contain period domestic furnishings. A Confederate mass grave, the Harper family cemetery, and a trail leading to a section of Union earthworks are also accessible to the public. Battle relics and an audiovisual program about the battle are available at the Visitor Center. The site also features a 10-mile self-guided driving tour with four Tour Stops with interpretive signage. Tour maps are available at the Visitor Center.

THE ATTMORE-OLIVER HOUSE

511 Broad Street, New Bern, NC
PHONE: 252-638-8558
HOURS: By appointment only.
ADMISSION: $4/person.

Although the Attmore-Oliver House was
built in 1790, it contains some Civil War
memorabilia. One room exhibit includes
guns, sabers, photographs, documents,
chests, medical supplies, diaries, and
other items of interest from the Civil War
period.

The Attmore-Oliver House

New Bern Civil War Battlefield Park

Taberna Way, off U.S. Highway 70 E, New Bern, NC
Phone: 252-638-8558
Web: newbernhistorical.org
Hours: Open daily 8AM – 5PM.
Admission: Free; a fee is charged for private tours.

On March 13, 1862, 11,000 Union troops led by General Ambrose Burnside, along with thirteen heavily-armed gunboats led by Commodore Stephen Rowan, landed at Slocum's Creek to capture of the town of New Bern. Awaiting the Union forces were 4,500 inexperienced and ill-equipped Confederate troops led

New Bern Civil War Battlefield Park Entrance and Visitor Center

by General Laurence O'Bryan Branch, a politician with virtually no military experience.

The battle began at 7:30AM on March 14 and raged for six hours. Estimated casualties for the battle are 1,080. The fierce battle in the swamps and along the railroad five miles south of New Bern proved to be a major victory for the Union and led to the ensuing occupation of New Bern for the remainder of the Civil War. Although Union forces never seized and held the rail line at Goldsboro, their presence in New Bern required the Confederacy to divert troops to the railroad's defense that might have been used in critical battles in Virginia.

The New Bern Civil War Battlefield Park is in near pristine condition. Unmarked by development or agriculture, the "redans" remain as they were a century and a half ago. There is a Visitor Center and a trail and bridge system at the battlefield.

Fort Macon State Park

*North Carolina Highway 58, East Fort
Macon Road, Atlantic Beach, NC*

Phone: 252-726-3775
Hours: Open daily.
Admission: Free.

On April 26, 1862, the Union captured Fort Macon, the Confederate fort which guarded Beaufort Harbor. The well-preserved fort features a museum. Three reenactments occur annually in April, July, and September.

Fort Macon State Park

Bellamy Mansion Museum

Corner of Market and 5th Streets, Wilmington, NC
Phone: 910-251-3700
Web: www.bellamymansion.org
Hours: Tours available Tuesday – Saturday, 10AM – 5PM, and Sunday, 1PM – 5PM.
Admission: $10.

Built on the eve of the Civil War, the Bellamy Mansion was seized and used as the Union headquarters in Wilmington, NC, in 1865. Gen. Joseph Hawley and 400 troops occupied the mansion until a formal pardon was obtained from President Andrew Johnson for Dr. John D. Bellamy, restoring the home to the family.

Photo right: Bellamy Mansion Museum

BRUNSWICK TOWN/FORT ANDERSON STATE HISTORIC SITE

Fort Anderson State Historic Site

8884 St. Philips Road SE, Winabow, NC
PHONE: 910-371-6613
WEB: www.nchistoricsites.org/brunswic
HOURS: Tuesday – Saturday 9AM–5PM
ADMISSION: Free.

This 120-acre historic site contains the ruins of Brunswick, an eighteenth-century seaport, and the earthworks of Fort Anderson. Tour the site's museum to see artifacts such as the original garrison flag and learn more about the fort's fall in 1865.

FORT FISHER STATE HISTORIC SITE

1610 Fort Fisher Boulevard, Kure Beach, NC
PHONE: 910-458-5538
WEB: www.nchistoricsites.org/fisher
HOURS: April 1 – September 30: Monday – Saturday 9AM – 5PM; Sunday 1PM – 5PM. October 1 – March 31: Tuesday – Saturday 9AM – 5PM; closed most holidays.
ADMISSION: Free.

Fort Fisher State Historic Site features a reconstructed palisade, a mounted gun, interpretive trails, a fiber optic battle map of the battle of Fort Fisher, artifacts from the blockade runner *Modern Greece*, and a museum and visitor's center.

Fort Fisher State Historic Site

OHIO

Despite the fact that only one major battle, Buffington Island, took place in the state, Ohio contributed a great deal to the war effort. Among its famous native sons, Ohio boasts President Rutherford B. Hayes, General William Tecumseh Sherman, General Ulysses S. Grant, and General George Armstrong Custer. Museums honoring these Union commanders are found in Fremont, Lancaster, Point Pleasant, and New Rumley.

Ohio also numbers the "Fighting McCooks" as famous residents. The McCook House in Carrollton commemorates the fourteen McCook members who served the Union during the Civil War. General Robert McCook and General Joseph Hooker, the commander of the Army of the Cumberland, are buried in the Spring Grove Cemetery and Arboretum. Almost 1,000 other Civil War soldiers are interred on the cemetery's beautiful grounds. Statues and artwork dot the site's 733 acres.

Prisoner of war camps proliferated after Union commander Ulysses S. Grant ended prisoner exchanges and paroles on April 17, 1864, and many of the camps were located in Ohio. Over 2,000 soldiers rest at Camp Chase Cemetery in Columbus. The camp was used as a Union training center and then as a prisoner-of-war camp. To the north, the Johnson Island Cemetery in Lakeside-Marblehead was also the site of a prisoner-of-war camp and contains 206 Confederate graves.

SEE
PENNSYLVANIA
PAGE 152

JOHNSON'S IS. CEMETERY

R. B. HAYES CENTER

Toledo

Euclid

Cleveland

Lorain

Cleveland Heights

Sandusky

Fremont

Elyria

Parma

Warren

Defiance

Youngstown

Akron

Mansfield

Canton

McCOOK HOUSE

Lima

Carrollton

New Rumley

Bellefontaine

CUSTER
MON.

Columbus

Cambridge

Dayton

Springfield

Kettering

Lancaster

H. B. STOWE HOUSE

SHERMAN HOUSE MUS.

Chillicothe

Marietta

Athens

BUFFINGTON IS.

Cincinnati

Portland

SPRING
GROVE
CEMETERY

Point Pleasant

SEE
WEST VIRGINIA
PAGE 262

U. S. GRANT BIRTHPLACE

SEE
KENTUCKY
PAGE 62

0   100 Miles

0   100 KM

JOHNSON'S ISLAND CEMETERY

Off Marblehead Peninsula in Sandusky Bay, OH
WEB: www.johnsonsisland.org
HOURS: Open daily.
ADMISSION: Free.

During the war, a Union prison for Confederate officers was located on Johnson's Island. In 1865 approximately 3,000 officers were imprisoned there. More than 200 prisoners are buried in Johnson's Island Cemetery.

RUTHERFORD B. HAYES PRESIDENTIAL CENTER

Spiegel Grove, Fremont, OH
PHONE: 419-332-2081
WEB: www.rbhayes.org
HOURS: Tuesday – Saturday 9AM – 5PM;
Sundays and federal holidays, 12PM – 5PM.
ADMISSION: A fee is charged; children and seniors
are discounted.

Hayes, our nineteenth president, served in the Union army and attained the rank of brevet major general. Located on the president's former twenty-five-acre estate is the Rutherford B. Hayes Presidential Center which contains a museum, the first presidential library, the president's home, and the president's tomb. The site maintains an extensive museum that contains cannons and Civil War weaponry, personal uniforms and medals, and many other Civil War artifacts.

Photo above:
The Hayes Home,
Rutherford B. Hayes
Presidential Center

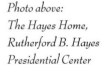

Photo left: Hayes
Museum and Library,
Rutherford B. Hayes
Presidential Center

McCook House

Public Square, Carrollton, OH
PHONE: 330-627-3345
WEB: www.carrollcountyohio.com/history
HOURS: Open Memorial Day through
Labor Day, 2nd weekend in October,
Weekend after Thanksgiving: Friday and
Saturday: 10AM – 5PM; Sunday: 1PM – 5PM.
After Labor Day through 1st weekend in
October: Saturday and Sunday only.
ADMISSION: A fee is charged for adults;
children are discounted.

McCook House

The "Fighting McCooks" were so named from their record of contributing fourteen family members to the Union army during the Civil War. In all, seven generals, one colonel, two majors, three lieutenants, and one private bore the name of McCook. Of those, four lost their lives. The McCook House has been restored and is maintained as a memorial to their name.

Custer Monument State
Memorial

Custer Monument State Memorial

State Route 646, New Rumley, OH
PHONE: 740-945-6415
WEB: ohsweb.ohiohistory.org/places/ne01
HOURS: Open daily.
ADMISSION: Free.

George Armstrong Custer, born in 1839, graduated from West Point and became one of the youngest generals of the Union. He was flamboyant and daring in his actions in the cavalry; he was involved in the battles of Manassas, Shenandoah, Waynesboro, and Appomattox. A statue of Custer stands near the site of his birth. An exhibit pavilion is also located at the site.

The Sherman House Museum

137 East Main Street, Lancaster, OH
PHONE: 740-654-9923
HOURS: Open daily except Monday April – November.
ADMISSION: A fee is charged; students, seniors,
and AAA are discounted.

The Sherman House Museum is the birthplace of Civil War Union General William T. Sherman and his brother U.S. Senator

Photo right: The Sherman House Museum

John Sherman. The museum features a Civil War collection, a *Sherman at War* exhibit, a recreation of Sherman's Civil War field tent, weapons, a veterans exhibit, Sherman family memorabilia, and seven rooms reflecting the lifestyle of the Sherman family. Special events are presented annually, and monthly meetings of the Sherman Civil War Roundtable are held at the museum.

SPRING GROVE CEMETERY AND ARBORETUM

4521 Spring Grove Avenue, Cincinnati, OH
PHONE: 513-681-7526
WEB: www.springgrove.org
HOURS: Open daily.
ADMISSION: Free.

Nearly 1,000 Civil War soldiers are buried at Spring Grove Cemetery and Arboretum. Notable Union casualties interred here include Gen. Robert McCook of the "Fighting McCooks" and Gen. Joseph Hooker. A self-guided walking tour of the arboretum and cemetery is available.

Spring Grove Cemetery and Arboretum

Spring Grove Cemetery and Arboretum

HARRIET BEECHER STOWE HOUSE

2950 Gilbert Avenue, Cincinnati, OH
PHONE: 513-751-0651
WEB: ohsweb.ohiohistory.org
HOURS: Call or see website for details.
ADMISSION: Free; a fee is charged for large groups.

Harriet Beecher Stowe inflamed public sentiment regarding slavery with her book *Uncle Tom's Cabin*. The Harriet Beecher Stowe House was actually built for her father when he moved his family from Connecticut. Each May a Memorial Day sunrise service takes place at the house.

ULYSSES S. GRANT BIRTHPLACE STATE MEMORIAL

1551 State Route 232, Point Pleasant, OH
PHONE: 800-283-8932
WEB: ohsweb.ohiohistory.org
HOURS: Wednesday – Saturday 9:30AM – 5PM (closed 12PM – 1PM); Sunday 1PM – 5PM.
ADMISSION: A fee is charged for adults; children and seniors are discounted.

Grant, our eighteenth president, served in the Civil War with distinction, rising to General of the Union army and receiving Confederate General Lee's surrender at Appomattox Court House. This small-frame house faces the Ohio River and contains items belonging to Grant's parents and period furnishings. The front room, only sixteen-and-a-half feet by nineteen feet, was the entire home when the Grants lived there. After the Grants left, two large rooms, which today serve as a museum of Civil War artifacts, were added.

Ulysses S. Grant Birthplace State Memorial

BUFFINGTON ISLAND

State Route 124, Portland, OH
PHONE: 800-686-1535
WEB: ohsweb.ohiohistory.org
HOURS: Open daily.
ADMISSION: Free.

A memorial commemorates Ohio's only major engagement. At Buffington Island, Confederate Gen. John Hunt Morgan and his cavalry were defeated by Union troops led by Gen. Edward Henry Hobson and Gen. James M. Shackelford in 1863.

Photo right: Buffington Island

OKLAHOMA

During the Civil War, Oklahoma Territory sat at a difficult crossroads; to its north were the Union states of Kansas and Missouri, and to its south and east were the Confederate states of Texas and Arkansas. The South sought to enlist many of Oklahoma's Native Americans into its army. Five tribes—the Cherokee, Chickasaw, Choctaw, Creek, and Seminole—fought for the Confederate cause. The Battle of Honey Springs, in which the Confederates were routed, marked a disillusionment for the Native Americans.

The Battle of Honey Springs is commemorated at reenactments held every three years. A newly renovated battlefield park interprets the site where Native American and African-American troops outnumbered white soldiers. The Union casualties of this battle were taken to Fort Gibson where many of the original buildings are still visible, and living history programs help interpret the site. Fort Gibson National Cemetery, one of only two national cemeteries in Oklahoma, contains the graves of over 2,000 Union soldiers.

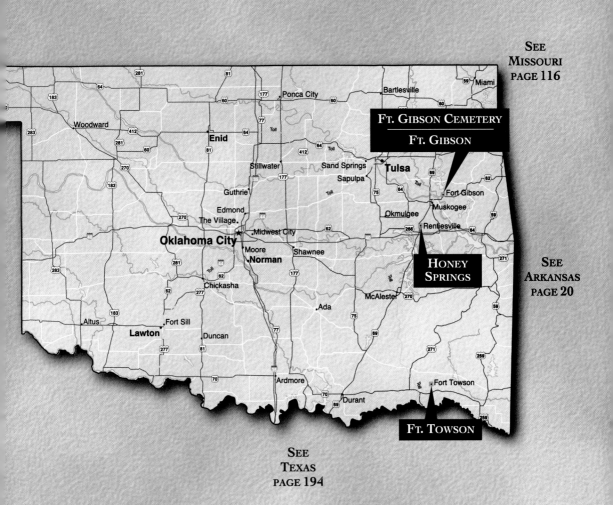

See
Missouri
page 116

Bartlesville

Miami

59

60

Ponca City

Woodward

183

281

64

281

177

60

60

412

Enid

81

64

77

Toll

412

64

Toll

Stillwater

Sand Springs

Tulsa

Ft. Gibson Cemetery

Ft. Gibson

62

270

183

177

Sapulpa

75

64

Toll

69

Fort Gibson

Guthrie

Toll

Muskogee

59

Edmond

The Village.

270

Okmulgee

Rentiesville

64

Oklahoma City

Midwest City

62

266

271

Moore

Norman

Shawnee

**Honey
Springs**

See
Arkansas
page 20

281

Toll

82

177

283

62

Chickasha

277

Toll

McAlester

270

183

Altus

Fort Sill

Ada

75

59

Lawton

Duncan

77

69

277

81

271

70

259

Ardmore

Fort Towson

70

69

Durant

Toll

Ft. Towson

259

See
Texas
page 194

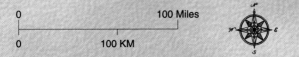

0   100 Miles

0   100 KM

THE BATTLE OF HONEY SPRINGS

July 17, 1863

The largest Civil War battle fought in Indian Territory.

The Battle of Honey Springs was the largest battle in Indian Territory, the first battle in which African-Americans fought as a unit, and the largest battle in which Native Americans fought on both sides.

Union troops, consisting of a unit of African-Americans of the First Regular Kansas Volunteers (Colored) and the Second Indian Home Guard, soundly defeated a Confederate force twice their size. The battle was the climax of the struggle over Indian Territory and was unique in the Civil War because Indian and African-American troops outnumbered white troops. The victory at Honey Springs gave the Union control over Oklahoma's vast Indian Territory.

Union and Confederate troops had frequently skirmished in the vicinity of Honey Springs Depot. The Union commander in the area, Major General James G. Blunt, correctly surmised that Confederate forces, mostly Native American troops under the command of Brigadier General Douglas H. Cooper, would attack his force at Fort Gibson. He decided to defeat the Confederates at Honey Springs Depot before they were joined by Brigadier General William Cabell's brigade which was advancing from Fort Smith, Arkansas.

Blunt began crossing the swollen Arkansas River on July 15, 1863. By midnight July 16, he had a force of 3,000

*Two African-American
Union soldiers*

UNITED STATES SOLDIERS AT CAMP "WILLIAM PENN" PHILADELPHIA, PA.

"Rally Round the Flag, boys! Rally once again,
Shouting the battle cry of FREEDOM!"

A recruiting poster of U.S. soldiers at Camp William Penn, Pennsylvania, calling for the enlistment of African-American soldiers in the Union army. Artist Unknown

white, Native American, and African-American troops marching toward Honey Springs. Early in the morning of July 17, Blunt skirmished with Rebel troops, and by mid-afternoon, full-scale fighting ensued.

The Confederates had wet powder, causing misfires, and the problem intensified when rain began. After repulsing one attack, Cooper pulled his forces back to obtain new ammunition. He then learned that Blunt was about to turn his left flank. The Confederate retreat began. Although Cooper fought a rearguard action, many of those troops counterattacked, failed, and fled. Any possibility of the Confederates taking Fort Gibson was gone. Following this battle, Union forces controlled Indian Territory north of the Arkansas River.

"Who will be in command of the Choctaws when you leave?... I do not wish it to be generally known that [they] are under my command, but prefer the enemy should think them a separate command."

From Gen. W. Steele to Brig. Gen. D. H. Cooper (pictured above) in an April 28, 1863, letter

HONEY SPRINGS BATTLEFIELD PARK
OKLAHOMA HISTORICAL SOCIETY

U.S. Highway 69 to Rentiesville Exit, park located north of Rentiesville, OK
PHONE: 918-473-5572
E-MAIL: honeysprings@okhistory.org
HOURS: Tuesday – Saturday 9AM – 5PM; Sunday 1PM – 5PM.
ADMISSION: Free.

Honey Springs Battlefield Park consists of the 1,200-acre Honey Springs Battlefield. The Oklahoma Historical Society currently administers 1,050 acres of the park. There are six self-guided trails and a driving tour that interpret the site with markers and monuments which commemorate the battle. The site has living history events and nature trails; site information is available through the Visitor's Center. The Battle of Honey Springs is reenacted every third year in mid-September. A memorial service is held every year on or near the battle's anniversary.

FORT GIBSON NATIONAL CEMETERY

1423 Cemetery Road, Fort Gibson, OK
PHONE: 918-478-2334
HOURS: Open daily.
ADMISSION: Free.

Fort Gibson National Cemetery was established in 1868 and is one of two national cemeteries in Oklahoma (the other is located in Elgin, OK). The cemetery contains 2,068 casualties of the Civil War. Most are unknown because the bodies were brought from all of the forts in the area without identification; only fifty Union soldiers are known. The cemetery is unique in that its grave markers are six-inch square markers, resembling rows of jagged teeth. Self-guided walking tours are available.

Fort Gibson National Cemetery

FORT GIBSON HISTORIC SITE

907 North Garrison, Fort Gibson, OK
PHONE: 918-478-4088
WEB: www.okhistory.org
HOURS: Open daily except Monday.
ADMISSION: A fee is charged.

Fort Gibson Historic site contains seven original buildings, entrenchments, a reconstructed log stockade, a museum, and a gift shop. Information on interpretive trails and self-guided tours are available at the Visitor's Center. Each year living history and educational programs occur at the site.

Fort Gibson Historic Site

FORT TOWSON HISTORIC SITE

U.S. Highway 70, Fort Towson, OK
PHONE: 580-873-2634
HOURS: Monday – Friday 8AM – 4:30PM; Saturday and Sunday 1PM – 5PM.
ADMISSION: Free.

Fort Towson was established in 1824 and closed in 1854. The site served as the headquarters of Confederate Maj. General Sam Bell Maxey while he served as the commander of Indian Territory. The last surrender of the Civil War took place less than a mile from the

Sutler's store, Fort Towson Historic Site

fort on June 23, 1865. A self-guided tour includes ruins of the barracks, the officers' quarters, a sutler's store, and a powder magazine. A Visitor's Center is available, and a new museum will be opened by 2013. Throughout the year, special living history and educational programs are held at the site.

PENNSYLVANIA

The first state to answer President Lincoln's call for volunteers in April of 1861, Pennsylvania provided soldiers—nearly 325,000—but also coal, iron, petroleum, and 2,500 miles of railroad lines to the Union cause. More than sixty Union generals came from Pennsylvania, and 300,000 Union soldiers trained at a camp near Harrisburg. Located on the southern edge of Northern territory, Pennsylvania saw more action than any other Northern state. The single most significant battle of the Civil War took place in the Pennsylvania town of Gettysburg in July of 1863. Gettysburg was a devastating defeat for the Confederacy and prompted a change in Southern strategy from offense to defense. Northerners, inspired both by the battle and by Lincoln's immortal Gettysburg Address, took from Gettysburg's bloody fields new dedication to winning and ending the war.

Today, Gettysburg remains the most studied military event in American history; Pennsylvania's Civil War heritage is preserved in and around the extensive, beautiful, national park site at the Gettysburg battlefield, a site which still echoes with the words of Lincoln and pays ongoing tribute to the great sacrifices made by soldiers and citizens from both North and South.

6

11

Carbondale

Dunmore

15

84

220

Kingston
Nanticoke

Williamsport

6

80

Berwick

80

11

Hazleton

209

Sunbury

Shamokin

State College

322

Pottsville

Easton

Bethlehem

209

522

22

Allentown

78

Emmaus

Toll

422

Reading

Harrisburg

Hershey

Norristown

Carlisle

76

Toll

Middletown

76

176

Toll

70

Toll

Lancaster

30

Philadelphia

Chambersburg

70

522

11

30

York

222

Gettysburg

Hanover

GETTYSBURG

SEE MARYLAND PAGE 90

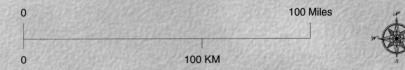

0   100 Miles

0   100 KM

THE BATTLE OF GETTYSBURG

July 1–3, 1863

A bloody, monumental battle that turned the tide of the war once and for all toward the Union.

When Robert E. Lee became the Commander of the Confederate Army of Virginia, his first priority was to defend his home state rather than his new country. Eventually, however, Lee realized that he could not ultimately win the war unless he changed his defensive stance to an offensive one; he had to take the war into the Northern states. After the Battle of Chancellorsville in June of 1863, Lee began the trek northward through Virginia, keeping the Blue Ridge Mountains between his forces and the Union army.

At this time, Major General Joseph Hooker asked Lincoln if he could be relieved after the Union defeat at Chancellorsville. Lincoln replaced him with Major General George Gordon Meade, whose orders from the overall commander, General Henry Wagner Halleck, were to "cover the capital, Baltimore, and as far as circumstances will admit."

Before leaving his command, Hooker ordered his cavalry to Emmitsburg on the Maryland-Pennsylvania border, south of Gettysburg. Meade further ordered two corps to Gettysburg. On June 30, Lee maneuvered to reach Cashtown,

Slyder Farm, Gettysburg National Military Park

just northeast of Gettysburg. All of these Northern maneuvers were unknown to Lee, who was operating without the eyes of his cavalry and believed that Meade's army was much farther south.

On July 1, Southern General Henry Heth took his division into Gettysburg to retrieve a reported store of shoes for his men. Just west of town he met with a Northern brigade. For two hours these forces fought and throughout the day, more and more Union and Confederate divisions joined the fight until Union troops retreated from Gettysburg to rally on Cemetery and Culp's Hills. Neither side had planned to fight at Gettysburg, but this unintended meeting had sparked one of the decisive battles of the war.

Fighting began the next morning with both armies at full strength. Confederate troops occupied the town and arced south on both sides, trapping the Union army inside. Meade's army formed a fishhook with Cemetery Ridge at its extreme right. Union General Sickles's corps advanced between ridges, getting caught at Devil's Den. The Confederates attacked and only quick reinforcements secured Cemetery Ridge for the Union.

July 3 dawned with both Lee and Meade determined to make a decisive stand. Lee began with a major assault on Cemetery Ridge. When this was repelled, Lee committed Major General George E. Pickett's division to the center of the line and ordered him to cross an open field and attack the center of the Union column. In what became known as Pickett's Charge, 5,000 Confederate soldiers died in an hour. Meade, content to stay on the defensive, never ordered a counterattack. On July 4, Lee began his long retreat back to Virginia. Meade let him go.

Gettysburg was a psychological turning point in the war; Union victory boosted morale and recommitted Northerners to winning the war. The battle, however, also proved negative for the Union as General Meade did not pursue Lee's Army of Northern Virginia, allowing that army to survive to fight again, thus prolonging the war.

"All this has been my fault, it is I that has lost this fight, and you must help me out the best you can."

Gen. R. E. Lee
(pictured above)
to Gen. C. Wilcox

GETTYSBURG NATIONAL MILITARY PARK ——

1105 Baltimore Pike, Suite 100, Gettysburg, PA

PHONE: 717-334-1124

WEB: www.nps.gov/gett; for advance reservations for park tours and programs, visit www.gettysburgfoundation.org

HOURS: Open daily; closed major holidays.

ADMISSION: Free; a fee is charged for some exhibits and programs, including the Cyclorama painting, film, and museum experience, and the David Wills House.

A variety of battlefield tours, self-guided auto tours, and interpretive trails are available through the park's Museum and Visitor Center. Stops along the tour include Seminary Ridge, John Burns Statue, the Eternal Peace Light Memorial, Oak Ridge, Oak Ridge Observation Tower, the North Carolina Monument, the Virginia Monument, the Eisenhower Observation Tower, Warfield Ridge, Little Round Top, Wheatfield, Trostle Farm, Peach Orchard, Forty-fourth New York Infantry

Memorial, and the Angle, the site of the last major conflict at Gettysburg. In addition, the Museum and Visitor Center offers a film about the Civil War and the battle of Gettysburg, as well as the panoramic painting of the famous "Pickett's Charge" known as the Gettysburg Cyclorama, and twelve galleries of museum exhibits showcasing one of the largest Civil War collections in existence. No visit to Gettysburg would be complete without a trip into town to understand the fighting through its streets and the battle's aftermath. The David

Tennessee Monument, Gettysburg National Military Park

Little Round Top, Gettysburg National Military Park

South Carolina Monument, Gettysburg National Military Park

Wills House is a National Park Service museum on the square in Gettysburg that tells the story of the aftermath of battle and Lincoln's visit to deliver the Gettysburg Address.

Each year a reenactment is held outside the park on the battle's anniversary. For information about the reenactment, or other area attractions and accommodations, contact the Gettysburg Convention and Visitor Bureau at www.gettysburg.travel or call 800-377-5015.

Perhaps even more memorable than the battle at Gettysburg is President Lincoln's speech. His immortal words place the battle of Gettysburg and the Civil War in perspective.

> Fourscore and seven years ago our fathers brought forth on this continent, a new nation, conceived in liberty, and dedicated to the proposition that all men are created equal.
>
> Now we are engaged in a great civil war, testing whether that nation, or any nation so conceived and so dedicated, can long endure. We are met on a great battlefield of that war. We have come to dedicate a portion of that field, as a final resting-place for those who here gave their lives that that nation might live. It is altogether fitting and proper that we should do this.
>
> But, in a larger sense, we can not dedicate—we can not consecrate—we can not hallow—this ground. The brave men, living and dead, who struggled here, have consecrated it far above our poor power to add or detract. The world will little note nor long remember what we say here, but it can never forget what they did here. It is for us, the living, rather, to be dedicated here to the unfinished work which they who fought here have thus far so nobly advanced. It is rather for us to be here dedicated to the great task remaining before us—that from these honored dead we take increased devotion to that cause for which they gave the last full measure of devotion; that we here highly resolve that these dead shall not have died in vain; that this nation, under God, shall have a new birth of freedom; and that government of the people, by the people, for the people, shall not perish from the earth.

SOUTH CAROLINA

Decades before a state convention voted unanimously to leave the Union in December of 1860, South Carolina had been steadily moving toward secession. The Southern spirit of rebellion was born in South Carolina, a state where black slaves outnumbered free whites by 100,000 and where economic and cultural life was dominated by the plantation system. South Carolinians were determined to protect their way of life from Federal intrusion.

Although South Carolina led the secessionist movement, actual combat in the state was rather limited. The Civil War brought mostly coastal fighting to South Carolina, at least until 1865, when Union troops under General William T. Sherman marched through the state bringing the terror of war to the interior. Out of the 70,000 South Carolinians who fought for the Confederacy, 13,000 gave their lives. Unlike most other Confederate states, South Carolina provided no white volunteers for the Union army.

South Carolina was transformed drastically by the war it helped begin. Civil War sites in the state today remember South Carolina's pivotal role in the rebellion, its antebellum lifestyle, and the effects of the war on its citizens.

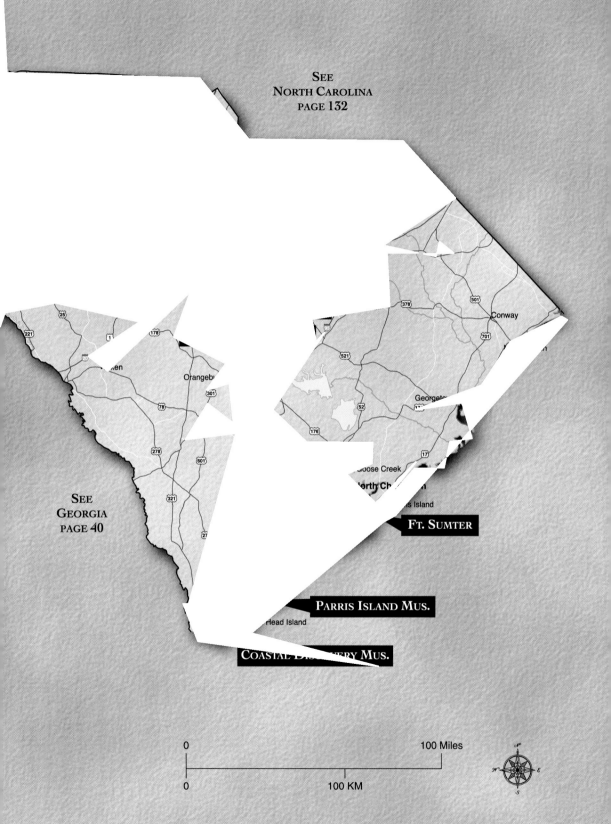

SEE
NORTH CAROLINA
PAGE 132

25
221
1
178
20
Aiken
Orangebu
301
78
278
601
321
27

378
501
Conway
701
521
Georgeto
52
176
17
Goose Creek
North Ch
s Island

FT. SUMTER

SEE
GEORGIA
PAGE 40

PARRIS ISLAND MUS.

Head Island

COASTAL DISCOVERY MUS.

0   100 Miles

0   100 KM

THE BATTLE OF FORT SUMTER

April 12–14, 1861

The opening rounds of the Civil War were fired at this small fort in Charleston Harbor.

After South Carolina voted to secede in 1860, the spirit of rebellion engulfed the state, and thousands of volunteers and militia members gathered in Charleston ready to fight. The only Union presence in the area was a force of eighty-five men at Fort Moultrie, adjacent to the mainland in Charleston Harbor. With the growing number of Confederates gathering in Charleston, these Union men were quickly transferred to nearby Fort Sumter, further out in Charleston Harbor, where better defenses were in place.

Major Robert Anderson, a Kentuckian married to a Georgian, took his Union troops from Fort Moultrie to Fort Sumter, believing the move would reduce tensions through increased distance. Southerners, however, saw the move as an act of aggression, violating sitting President James Buchanan's pledge to keep the status quo in Charleston Harbor.

Fort Sumter

The situation was ripe for conflict. The Union garrison was dangerously low on supplies, and the South had erected artillery batteries around the harbor to thwart any attempt to resupply and reinforce Fort Sumter. Both sides realized the powerful implication of possessing the fort. As long as the flag of the United States flew over Fort Sumter, the South's sovereignty would be in question. In his inaugural address, President Lincoln stated that he would use "all the powers at my disposal" to "reclaim the public property and places which have fallen: to hold, occupy, and possess these, and all other property and places belonging to the government."

The day after his inauguration, Lincoln learned that Fort Sumter had only six weeks of rations left. Time was running out for a peaceful solution. Lincoln chose to resupply his men but not reinforce them. He notified the Confederates of his intention, leaving the decision to attack a ship bringing "food for hungry men" squarely in the lap of the South.

The Confederate cabinet response was the decision to open fire on Fort Sumter prior to its resupply. The only dissenting vote came from Confederate Secretary of State Robert Toombs, who reportedly told Confederate President Jefferson Davis that the action "will lose us every friend at the North. You will wantonly strike a hornets' nest. . . . Legions now quiet will swarm out and sting us to death. It is unnecessary. It puts us in the wrong. It is fatal." He was correct. The Confederates opened fire upon Fort Sumter on April 12, 1861.

On April 14, after thirty-three hours and 5,000 rounds, the American flag was lowered and the fort surrendered. Then the Confederate flag was raised over Fort Sumter. On April 15, 1861, Lincoln called for 75,000 volunteers to help quell the Southern insurrection. The Civil War had begun.

"All proper facilities will be afforded for the removal of yourself and command, together with company arms and property, and all private property to any post in the United States which you may select. The flag which you have upheld so long and with so much fortitude . . . may be saluted by you on taking it down."

Brig. Gen. P. G. T. Beauregard to Maj. R. Anderson

SOUTH CAROLINA CONFEDERATE RELIC ROOM AND MILITARY MUSEUM

301 Gervais Street, Columbia, SC
PHONE: 803-737-8095
WEB: www.crr.sc.gov
HOURS: Tuesday – Saturday 10AM – 5PM; First Sunday of the month 1PM – 5PM.
ADMISSION: A fee is charged; youth, seniors, and military are discounted; children 12 and under and members are free.

Founded in 1896, the South Carolina Confederate Relic Room and Military Museum is the oldest history museum in the state. The museum focuses on South Carolina's military history from the Revolutionary War to the present. With evolving permanent exhibits and changing exhibit galleries, each visit is a new experience.

South Carolina Confederate Relic Room and Military Museum

THE SOUTH CAROLINA STATE HOUSE

1101 Gervais Streets, Columbia, SC
PHONE: 803-734-2430
HOURS: Open daily.
ADMISSION: Free.

The South Carolina State House

The blue granite State House shows scars from Federal fire during the Civil War. Bronze stars mark hits from General Sherman's cannon in 1865. The grounds feature a Confederate Monument and a monument to South Carolina's Confederate Gen. Wade Hampton.

RIVERBANKS ZOO AND GARDEN

500 Wildlife Parkway, Columbia, SC
PHONE: 803-779-8717
WEB: www.riverbanks.org
HOURS: Open daily 9AM – 5PM; closed Thanksgiving and Christmas.
ADMISSION: A fee is charged; children are discounted.

On the west bank of the Saluda River lies Riverbanks Zoo and Garden. The site was once the camp of Gen. William T. Sherman's troops. Because the Confederates had destroyed a covered bridge over the Saluda River leading into Columbia,

Ruins of bridge, Riverbanks Zoo and Garden

legend has it that Sherman and his men pulled up the planks of Saluda Factory, a textile mill, and made rafts to cross the river and enter Columbia. More than likely, however, they just waded across the river. Today the ruins of the factory and the original mill's small canal are joined by a new Saluda Factory Interpretive Center. The site features interpretive graphics outlining the area's Civil War history.

FIRST BAPTIST CHURCH

1306 Hampton Street, Columbia, SC
PHONE: 803-256-4251
WEB: www.fbccola.com
HOURS: Open daily; closed major holidays.
ADMISSION: Free.

The table on which the South Carolina Ordinance of Secession was drafted is exhibited at the First Baptist Church of Columbia. The secessionist convention met at the church only one day, December 17, 1860. Fear of a smallpox epidemic forced adjournment of the convention although only one case was confirmed. Later, the ordinance was signed in Charleston. Tours of the historic church are available.

First Baptist Church

THE BATTLE OF PORT ROYAL SOUND

November 7, 1861

After this battle, the Confederacy abandoned South Carolina's outlying coastal forts to concentrate on inland defenses.

Guarded on either side by Fort Walker and Fort Beauregard, Port Royal Sound, South Carolina, proved a well-guarded coastal position. Union Captain Samuel F. DuPont, the head of the Blockade Board, was given the task of capturing the sound. Contrary to conventional wisdom, he believed that a steamship, which did not have to rely on wind or tide, could successfully engage coastal fortifications without overwhelming firepower.

In preparation for attacking Port Royal, DuPont amassed 15,000 soldiers under Brigadier General Thomas W. Sherman and thirty steam warships. When the Union ships ran the gauntlet of the two Confederate forts on November 7, 1861, the ships

Bombardment and capture of Forts Walker and Beauregard, Port Royal

The bombardment of Port Royal

rained shells into the forts. Although the steamships received fire, there sustained no serious damage. Once through, the ships turned around and steamed back and forth in front of Fort Walker then Fort Beauregard. By nightfall, both forts had been abandoned. The Federal occupation of these forts established a key naval base which would aid in Scott's coastal blockade plan.

Photograph of prison, Port Royal

"Whenever [the enemy's] fleet can be brought, no opposition to his landing can be made. We have nothing to oppose its heavy guns, which sweep over the low banks of this country [South Carolina] with irresistible force."

Gen. R. E. Lee

CHARLESTON MUSEUM

360 Meeting Street, Charleston, SC
PHONE: 843-722-2996
WEB: www.charlestonmuseum.org
HOURS: Monday – Saturday 9AM – 5PM; Sunday 1PM – 5PM; closed major holidays.
ADMISSION: A fee is charged; children are discounted.

Founded in 1773, the Charleston Museum is the first and oldest museum in the United States. It features exhibits which explain South Carolina's Lowcountry heritage, as well as interpret Charleston's varied past. The museum also houses an impressive collection of Civil War-era weapons and artifacts. The museum holds various Civil War events throughout the year; call for details.

FORT SUMTER NATIONAL MONUMENT (INCLUDES FORT MOULTRIE)

1214 Middle Street, Sullivan's Island, SC
PHONE: 843-883-3123; (for transportation to island 843-722-2628)
WEB: www.nps.gov/fosu
HOURS: Open daily; closed Christmas.
ADMISSION: Fort Sumter: free; Fort Moultrie: a fee is charged; children and seniors are discounted. A fee is charged for transportation to the island.

This national historic site includes both Fort Moultrie and Fort Sumter. A highway connects Fort Moultrie to the mainland, but Fort Sumter is accessible only by boat. Transportation leaves from the Fort Sumter National Monument Visitor Education Center at Liberty Square in Charleston and Patriots Point in Mt. Pleasant.

Both forts offer brochures that include self-guided walking tours. Built in 1809, Fort Moultrie stands much as it did during the war. Passageways and ramparts offer points of interest, and the fort provides beautiful views of Fort Sumter and the city.

Fort Sumter, on which construction began in 1829, is classified as a ruins due to damage from the Civil War's heavy artillery fire. Tours provide insight into the fort's history, and the museum's exhibits cover the fort's history from 1829 through World War II.

Each fort has an exhibit area on the fort's history and a gift shop.

Photo left: Fort Moultrie

THE PARRIS ISLAND MUSEUM

111 Panama Street, Parris Island, SC
PHONE: 843-228-2951
WEB: www.parrisislandmuseum.com
HOURS: Open daily 10AM – 4:30PM;
closed Thanksgiving, Christmas, and
New Year's Day.
ADMISSION: Free.

Parris Island Museum

The Parris Island Museum contains a local history area that features an extensive exhibit on the Civil War in the Port Royal/Beaufort area. Exhibits cover the battles of Port Royal and Honey Hill, military expeditions against the Charleston and Savannah Railroad, regional military installations, raising of African-American regiments, and the reconstruction efforts that established schools for the local freedmen and helped them obtain land. Displays include maps, dioramas, photographs, cannon, artillery projectiles, firearms, and uniforms. Of note are original uniforms from Colonel Alfred Hartwell of the Fifty-fifth Massachusetts and an ornately carved Confederate Sharps carbine.

COASTAL DISCOVERY MUSEUM

100 William Hilton Parkway, Hilton Head Island, SC
PHONE: 843-689-6767
WEB: www.coastaldiscovery.org
HOURS: Monday – Saturday 9AM – 4:30PM;
Sunday 11AM – 3PM; call for holiday hours.
ADMISSION: Free.

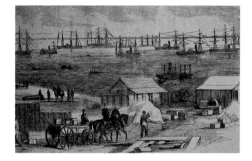

The Coastal Discovery Museum contains Civil War artifacts and offers tours of area forts including the remains of Fort Mitchel, Fort Walker, Port Royal, and Fort Howell. Fort Howell was built for the purpose of protecting Mitchelville, the nation's first Freedman's community.

Above right: Engraving of Port Royal Sound during the Union occupation of Hilton Head Island

Below right: Fort Walker

TENNESSEE

The second most populous Confederate state, Tennessee also ranked second in the number of military actions during the war. Nonetheless, Tennessee was neither eager nor unanimous in its decision to secede from the American Union, and the Confederacy never enjoyed Tennessee's full support, especially in the mountainous regions of the east. Still, the Confederacy needed Tennessee. The state's farmers supplied the Southern armies with wheat, corn, horses, mules, and meat. Tennessee was also crossed or bordered by three major rivers—the Mississippi, the Cumberland, and the Tennessee—all of them possible passageways into the Deep South. In addition, cities like Nashville and Memphis were important centers for trade and transportation for all of the Southern states. All of this made Tennessee equally attractive to the Union armies, who came in full force and fought battles all over middle and southern Tennessee.

The people of Tennessee survived four solid, bloody years of battle before Confederate surrender put an end to the Civil War and restored peace within the state's borders; today, in large battlefields, small museums, and wayside monuments, the state pays tribute to those who fought and those who lost their lives.

SEE
MISSOURI
PAGE 116

SEE
ARKANSAS
PAGE 20

Hennin

SEE
MISSISSIPP
PAGE 104

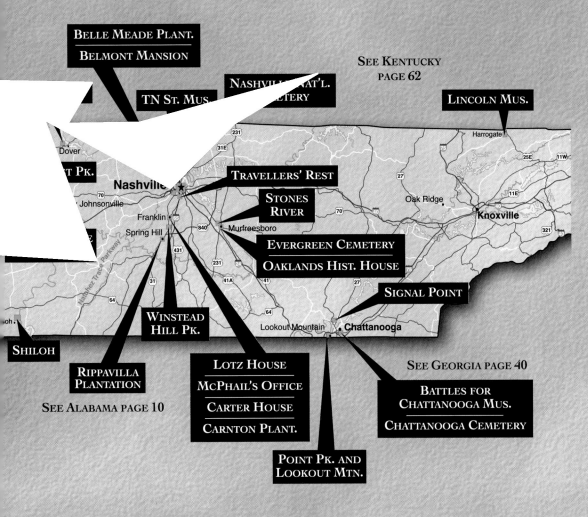

BELLE MEADE PLANT.
BELMONT MANSION

TN ST. MUS.

NASHVILLE NAT'L.
CEMETERY

SEE KENTUCKY
PAGE 62

LINCOLN MUS.

Harrogate

Dover

T PK.

Nashville

Johnsonville

Franklin

Spring Hill

Oak Ridge

Knoxville

TRAVELLERS' REST

STONES
RIVER

Murfreesboro

EVERGREEN CEMETERY
OAKLANDS HIST. HOUSE

SIGNAL POINT

WINSTEAD
HILL PK.

Lookout Mountain

Chattanooga

SHILOH

RIPPAVILLA
PLANTATION

LOTZ HOUSE

McPHAIL'S OFFICE

CARTER HOUSE

CARNTON PLANT.

SEE GEORGIA PAGE 40

BATTLES FOR
CHATTANOOGA MUS.

CHATTANOOGA CEMETERY

SEE ALABAMA PAGE 10

POINT PK. AND
LOOKOUT MTN.

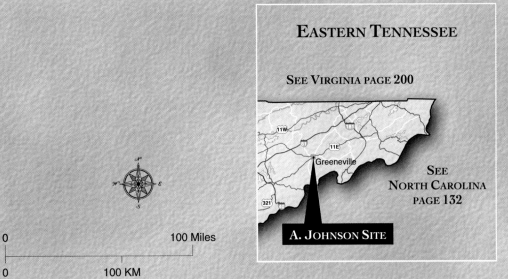

EASTERN TENNESSEE

SEE VIRGINIA PAGE 200

Greeneville

SEE
NORTH CAROLINA
PAGE 132

A. JOHNSON SITE

0   100 Miles

0   100 KM

THE BATTLE OF SHILOH

April 6–7, 1862

The Union victory at Shiloh led to the fall of Nashville. Soon, all of western Tennessee fell under Union control.

Major General Ulysses S. Grant's victory at Fort Donelson opened up the Tennessee and Cumberland Rivers to the Union. Grant, using the Tennessee River, advanced 43,000 troops toward the rail connections near Corinth, Mississippi. Forty thousand Confederate forces massed for an attack to defend this vital rail line. By March Grant and his men encamped around Shiloh Church at Pittsburg Landing, Tennessee, twenty-three miles northeast of Corinth. In early April, General P. G. T. Beauregard moved to attack Grant.

After a long hard march of three days, Beauregard set up camp within a mile of Grant, who believed the Confederates were still at Corinth, and therefore had not set out his pickets and patrols. The initial attack was a complete surprise, but after the Union's first shock, they established control and set up defensive lines. These lines, however, contained gaps, which the Confederate troops quickly used to their advantage.

Union troops took up a line from the Tennessee River bluffs to Owl Creek; this line passed directly through a place called Hornets' Nest. After eleven separate assaults on Hor-

Powell's Artillery Battery marker, Shiloh National Military Park

William Manse George Cabin, Shiloh National Military Park

nets' Nest, which lasted from 10:00AM until 5:30PM, Confederate troops finally overwhelmed Union forces. Many soldiers escaped to the rear, but 2,100 troops surrendered.

Grant's final line stretched from Dill Branch to Tilghman Branch. Union forces amassed fifty-three cannon and 20,000 troops to protect Pittsburg Landing and the Hamburg-Savannah Road. To reach this line, Confederate forces had to descend a sixty-foot bluff, cross the ravine, and climb the bank on the far side of the Tennessee River—all of this after thirteen hours of fighting. Although two brigades did reach the other side, they could not hold on and withdrew.

During the night, the Union received thousands in reinforcements. The Confederates had no additional men to give.

On the second day, the Union troops advanced and forced the Confederates back. By the afternoon, General Beauregard withdrew to Corinth. Despite the loss of one of its divisions and severe damages to the remaining four, the Battle of Shiloh was a decisive Union victory. Corinth and Memphis were within Union range.

FORT PILLOW STATE HISTORIC PARK

3122 Park Road, Henning, TN
PHONE: 731-738-5581
WEB: www.tn.gov/environment/
parks/FortPillow
HOURS: Open daily 8AM – sunset.
ADMISSION: Free.

In April 1864, Nathan Bedford Forrest's Confederate troops attacked Fort Pillow. Southern forces easily overran the fort, and the Union surrendered. Many Northerners were killed after the surrender. When the atrocities were investigated, the battle was declared a massacre by the Committee on the Conduct of the

Fort Pillow State Historic Park

War. A Visitor's Center at Fort Pillow State Historic Park includes a small museum and information on the site. Each April the site is host to an Anniversary Reenactment Weekend, other special events are scheduled throughout the year.

MUD ISLAND RIVER PARK AND MISSISSIPPI RIVER MUSEUM

Mud Island, Memphis, TN

Mud Island River Park and Mississippi River Museum

PHONE: 901-576-7241
WEB: www.mudisland.com
HOURS: Open daily
April 10 – October 31.
ADMISSION: A fee is charged; children and seniors are discounted.

The fifty-two-acre Mud Island River Park and Mississippi River Museum can only be reached by pedestrian walkbridge and monorail. The museum, located on an island in the Mississippi River, houses ship models and several Civil War exhibits, including one on the Battle of Memphis.

SHILOH NATIONAL MILITARY PARK

Shiloh, Tennessee and Corinth, Mississippi

PHONE: 731-689-5696 (Shiloh Battlefield), 662-287-9273 (Corinth Civil War Interpretive Center)

WEB: www.nps.gov/shil

HOURS: Open daily; closed Christmas Day.

ADMISSION: A fee is charged.

Stream of American History

Shiloh Battlefield and Corinth Battlefield comprise Shiloh National Military Park. Shiloh Battlefield is comprised of 4,200 acres with markers, monuments, and over 200 cannons to interpret the battle. The park experience includes battlefield tours, orientation films, and museum exhibits. Interpretive programs are offered daily in the summer, and living history events are hosted throughout the year. The park is also home to Shiloh National Cemetery and the Shiloh Indian Mounds National Historic Landmark.

The Corinth Battlefield includes the Corinth Civil War Interpretive Center, which features interactive exhibits and multimedia presentations. The center stands near the site of Battery Robinett, a Union fortification witness to bloody fighting during the October 1862 Battle of Corinth.

Silent Guns of Shiloh

THE BATTLE OF FORT DONELSON

February 12–16, 1862

The Confederacy's first major defeat, this battle was also the first victory for Union Brigadier General Ulysses S. Grant. Winning Fort Donelson gave the Union control of the Cumberland and Tennessee Rivers, main arteries into the Deep South.

Like the Mississippi River, control of the Cumberland River was needed by both armies to achieve their tactical goals. For the South, control of the river was imperative to maintaining control of Tennessee and Kentucky. For the North, the river provided access to Mississippi and Alabama. On February 2, 1862, Brigadier General Ulysses S. Grant left Cairo, Illinois, with 17,000 Federal soldiers and a flotilla of gunboats under the command of Flag Officer Andrew H. Foote. His objective was to win control of the Cumberland River.

Confederate Monument, Fort Donelson National Battlefield

Lower River Battery, Fort Donelson National Battlefield

In a joint land and water operation, Grant moved on Fort Henry, eleven miles north of Fort Donelson. After a two-hour battle, Grant took Fort Henry on February 11, 1862, sending Confederate forces fleeing to Fort Donelson.

On February 13, Grant encircled Fort Donelson. Probing Confederate lines indicated that a direct assault would be fatal; instead, Grant lay siege to the Fort while Foote attacked from the river. Foote's four ironclads, however, were no match for the Confederate water batteries. All four Union gun ships were badly damaged, and Foote was wounded. On February 15, as Grant contemplated his next move, Confederate General Gideon Johnson Pillow, aided by Brigadier General Nathan Bedford Forrest's cavalry, left the fort and attacked Grant's men with such force that the Confederates soon controlled the road leading to Nashville. In a tactical error, troops did not continue their attack or push on to Nashville. Grant acted quickly and soon regained all lost ground.

On February 16, Generals Floyd and Pillow fled the fort south by water, leaving Brigadier General Simon B. Buckner in command of the demoralized fort. When Buckner requested terms for surrender, Grant's now famous reply was "no terms except unconditional and immediate surrender can be accepted." Grant and Buckner were old friends from West Point and after the surrender, discussed the battle. With Fort Donelson in hand, the Federal army was poised for a move into the Deep South.

FORT DONELSON NATIONAL BATTLEFIELD ——

U.S. Highway 79, Dover, TN
PHONE: 931-232-5706, ext. 101
WEB: www.nps.gov/fodo
HOURS: Open daily 8AM – 4:30PM; closed Thanksgiving, Christmas, and New Year's.
ADMISSION: Free.

Fort Donelson National Battlefield covers 536 acres, about twenty percent of the core battlefield, the fort itself, and earthen rifle pits and river cannon batteries. The park also includes Fort Donelson National Cemetery, established in 1867; a Visitor Center; and the Dover Hotel, site of Buckner's headquarters and his surrender. Two rooms of the Dover Hotel have been restored and are open to the public. Walking tours of the battlefield are marked. Additionally, a seven-mile driving tour of the battle is available. Inside the Visitor Center is a museum of Civil War relics and an audiovisual presentation.

National Cemetery, Fort Donelson

NATHAN BEDFORD FORREST STATE PARK

1825 Pilot Knob Road, Eva, TN
PHONE: 731-584-6356
WEB: tennessee.gov/environment/
parks/NBForrest
HOURS: Open daily.
ADMISSION: Free.

The Nathan Bedford Forrest State Park commemorates Forrest's Johnsonville raid which destroyed supplies intended to aid General Sherman's March to the Sea.

Forrest enlisted in the C.S.A. a month before his fortieth birthday. He had only about six months of school but had risen from poverty to become a wealthy businessman and Memphis alderman. His raids against the Union were so effective that Sherman declared, "Forrest is the very devil, and I think he has some of our troops under cower. . . . [He] must be hunted down and killed if it costs 10,000 lives and bankrupts the Federal Treasury. There never will be peace in Tennessee until Forrest is dead."

Photo right: Nathan Bedford Forrest State Park

JOHNSONVILLE STATE HISTORIC AREA

90 Redoubt Lane, New Johnsonville, TN
PHONE: 931-535-2789
WEB: tennessee.gov/environment/parks/Johnsonville
HOURS: Open daily 8AM – sundown.
ADMISSION: Free.

This 600-acre Johnsonville State Historic Area rests on the Tennessee River and commemorates the November 4, 1864, Battle of Johnsonville. General Forrest attacked the Union navy and inflicted immense damage when he sank many Union boats. Twelve of these vessels still remain in the river, although one has been reclaimed. In addition, an original cannon, redoubts, and rifle pits remain as they were during the battle. Interpretive tours are available.

THE BATTLES OF FRANKLIN AND NASHVILLE

November 30, 1864, December 15–16, 1864

These decisive battles marked the end of the Confederate Army of Tennessee.

By September of 1864, General William T. Sherman had successfully taken Atlanta. The Confederate army under General John Bell Hood, however, still posed a threat to Sherman's extensive supply line.

After Union troops captured Nashville in December of 1862, the Confederates withdrew to outlying towns and

Carter House

Bullet holes in the Carter House

regrouped. They did not attempt to retake the city until 1864, when Hood chose to attack Nashville rather than pursue Sherman. Confederate cavalry, led by General Nathan Bedford Forrest, preceded the 40,000-strong Confederate army.

On November 29, 1864, 32,000 Confederate troops cut off 36,000 Union troops from Nashville by encircling them at Spring Hill. Union troops under Major General John M. Schofield slipped out of the net during the night and fled to Franklin. Hood threw his army against the defensive works at Franklin. At first the South appeared to have the upper hand, driving the Union troops from Franklin and capturing all their guns. A countercharge in the afternoon, however, drove the Confederates back. The fighting lasted until midnight, costing Hood almost one-sixth of his force and any hope of retaking Tennessee. Although Hood besieged Nashville until December 16, there was no chance of victory, and the Army of Tennessee retreated.

None of the battleground remains, but markers commemorate the Battles of Nashville and Franklin. Each year in November, a memorial march in Franklin leaves Winstead Hill for the Carter House at 4:00PM, the time the Army of Tennessee went into battle.

NASHVILLE NATIONAL CEMETERY

1420 Gallatin Road South, Madison, TN
PHONE: 615-860-0086
WEB: www.bonps.org/natlcem/natlcem.htm
HOURS: Open during daylight hours.
ADMISSION: Free.

Nashville National Cemetery was established in January 1867; 16,485 Union soldiers are interred here. *Nashville National Cemetery* Over 4,000 of those remain unknown. Veterans from other wars are also buried here, and each Memorial Day a service commemorates wartime casualties.

BELMONT MANSION

1900 Belmont Boulevard, Nashville, TN
PHONE: 615-460-5459
WEB: www.belmontmansion.com
HOURS: Open daily; closed major holidays.
ADMISSION: A fee is charged.

Built in 1850, the restored fifteen-room Belmont Mansion was the home of Adelicia Acklen. Acklen preserved the house and its contents through the Civil War, three marriages, and ten children. Union scouts used the 105-foot-tall, brick water tower, which still exists, as a lookout point and to relay signals. The mansion itself served as the headquarters for Union General Thomas J. Wood during the battle. Guided tours of the house, which is located on the campus of Belmont University, last approximately one hour.

Photo above: Mansion with tulips

Photo left: Night view

TRAVELLERS REST

636 Farrell Parkway, Nashville, TN
PHONE: 615-832-8197
WEB: www.travellersrestplantation.org
HOURS: Monday – Saturday 10AM – 4PM; Sunday 1PM – 4PM; closed major holidays.
ADMISSION: A fee is charged; senior, military, and AAA discounts are available.

Built by John Overton in 1799, Travellers Rest is one of the oldest surviving houses in Nashville, and was once the centerpiece of a 2,200 acre plantation. Confederate General John Bell Hood established his headquarters here just before the Battle of Nashville, and some of the bloodiest fighting took place within sight of the house.

BELLE MEADE PLANTATION

Belle Meade Plantation

5025 Harding Pike, Nashville, TN
PHONE: 615-356-0501
WEB: www.bellemeadeplantation.com
HOURS: Monday – Saturday 9AM – 5PM, Sunday 11AM – 5PM; closed major holidays.
ADMISSION: A fee is charged.

Belle Meade Plantation was once a thoroughbred horse farm, but during the Civil War the home served as headquarters for Confederate General Chalmers. Costumed interpreters recall the days before the war with the sweeping front lawn and colonnaded facade of Belle Meade as the backdrop. This historic site includes eight buildings and an antique carriage collection.

TENNESSEE STATE MUSEUM

505 Deaderick Street, Nashville, TN
PHONE: 615-741-2692 or 1-800-407-4324
WEB: www.tnmuseum.org
HOURS: Tuesday – Saturday 10AM – 5PM; Sunday 1PM – 5PM; closed major holidays.
ADMISSION: Free.

Confederate Cannon, Tennessee State Museum

Tennessee was a major Civil War battlefield, with hundreds of battles and skirmishes, including Shiloh, Chattanooga, and Nashville. The Tennessee State Museum has one of the largest and best Civil War collections in the nation of artifacts from this epic struggle, including flags, cannons, and uniforms. Many of these artifacts are on display in the permanent Civil War exhibits.

THE CARTER HOUSE

1140 Columbia Avenue, Franklin, TN
PHONE: 615-791-1861
WEB: www.battleoffranklintrust.org
HOURS: Open daily; closed major holidays.
ADMISSION: A fee is charged.

Built in 1830 by Fountain Branch Carter, The Carter House is nationally known for its role in the Civil War. The house was caught in the center of the Battle of Franklin and still bears the scars of the battle, with more than 1,000 bullet holes still visible. The Visitor's Center includes a new video presentation, military museum, and museum shop.

The Carter House hosts various annual events with reenactors as well as the annual Candlelight Tour in early December. Guided tours available. Joint tickets are offered with Carnton Plantation.

Interior, Carter House

CARNTON PLANTATION

1345 Carnton Lane, Franklin, TN
PHONE: 615-794-0903
WEB: www.battleoffranklintrust.org
HOURS: Open daily; closed major holidays.
ADMISSION: A fee is charged.

In 1826 after his term as mayor of Nashville, Randal McGavock built Carnton Plantation. On the evening of November 30, 1864, after the Battle of Franklin, the McGavocks opened the home as a field hospital for Confederate soldiers. In 1866 the McGavocks designated two acres adjacent to their family plot as a Confederate cemetery where 1,500 Southern soldiers are interred, making this the nation's largest private Confederate cemetery. Home of the *New York Times* bestseller *Widow of the South*, Carnton is open for guided tours. Joint tickets are offered with The Carter House.

Carnton Plantation

WINSTEAD HILL PARK

U.S. Highway 31, Franklin, TN
WEB: www.franklintn.gov
HOURS: Open daily.
ADMISSION: Free.

From the high point of Winstead Hill Park, Gen. John Bell Hood commanded his Confederate soldiers in the Battle of Franklin. A relief map and several large granite markers at this privately-owned park provide historical interpretation of the events prior to and during the battle. A Memorial Assembly and brief program with speakers and reenactors is conducted annually in November.

LOTZ HOUSE

1111 Columbia Avenue, Franklin, TN
PHONE: 615-790-7190
WEB: www.lotzhouse.com
HOURS: Open daily; closed major holidays.
ADMISSION: A fee is charged.

Lotz House, which has been on the National Historic Register since 1976, is located in the heart of downtown historic Franklin at "ground zero" of the Battle of Franklin. Guided tours of the Lotz House are available as are walking Battlefield tours led by renowned historian Thomas Cartwright.

DR. MCPHAIL'S OFFICE

209 East Main Street, Franklin, TN
PHONE: 615-591-8514
WEB: www.visitwilliamson.com
HOURS: Open daily; closed major holidays.
ADMISSION: Free.

Built in 1815, Dr. McPhail's Office served as General Schofield's Union headquarters during the battle of Franklin. It is now a Visitor's Information Center.

RIPPAVILLA PLANTATION

5700 Main Street, Spring Hill, TN
PHONE: 931-486-9037
WEB: www.rippavilla.org
HOURS: Open daily; closed major holidays; December – March: call for winter hours.
ADMISSION: A fee is charged.

Little has changed in the 12,000 square-foot Rippavilla Plantation and its 1,500 surrounding acres since it housed the Council of War for General John Hood. Here, with troops camped on the grounds, Hood gave his generals their orders and informed them of the plan for the Battle of Franklin. The 1852 plantation also serves as the regional Visitor's Center. It includes a historic house museum and a museum of the Civil War Armies of Tennessee.

THE BATTLE OF STONES RIVER (MURFREESBORO)

December 31, 1862–January 2, 1863

Stones River was a Southern defeat in both territory and manpower.

After the Federal victory at Perryville, Kentucky, General Braxton Bragg withdrew his troops to Murfreesboro, southeast of Nashville. In Nashville, the Union under Major General William S. Rosecrans fortified the city and prepared to attack Bragg. Confederate President Jefferson Davis ordered Bragg to hold Murfreesboro if possible. The city was on the Nashville & Chattanooga Rail Line and the Nashville Pike. Abandoning Murfreesboro could open up East Tennessee to the Union.

Bragg decided to hold his position northwest at Stones River. He disregarded the open terrain with no natural holds for his flanks, the thick patches of low trees that could hide the enemy and hamper any offensive movements, and the possibility of flooding in this low country. It was an area in which he could concentrate his force and protect the roads leading to his supply depot in Murfreesboro. At dawn on December 31, 1862, Bragg decided to attack Rosecrans's right flank in a clockwise wheeling movement. This advance caught the Union

Fortress Rosecrans, Stones River National Battlefield

Cannons, Stones River Battlefield

completely off guard, as they had planned to attack Bragg in his right flank and had concentrated forces accordingly. After falling back to the Nashville Pike, the Union did not retreat but regrouped in a sharp angle. The Confederates were unable to break this strong position.

After five days of rain, the Stones River was becoming exceedingly difficult to ford. Bragg's cold, wet, exhausted men were no match for the fresh reinforcements which joined Rosecrans; Bragg withdrew from Murfreesboro.

Both sides lost heavily, but the North gained solid control of Nashville and also won the confidence of the citizens of the state. Throughout the Union, news of the victory at Stones River lifted spirits after two tough Union defeats at Fredericksburg, Virginia, and Vicksburg, Mississippi.

Hazen Monument, Stones River National Battlefield

STONES RIVER NATIONAL BATTLEFIELD

3501 Old Nashville Highway, Murfreesboro, TN

PHONE: 615-893-9501

WEB: www.nps.gov/stri

HOURS: Open daily.

ADMISSION: Free.

Stones River National Battlefield tells the story of one of the most important battles of the war at places like the Slaughter Pen and Hell's Half Acre. It also includes remnants of Fortress Rosecrans, a supply depot built by the Union, and Stones River National Cemetery, the final resting place of more than 6,000 Union soldiers.

Visitors may tour the battlefield on their own using an audio tour for sale or rent in the park visitor center, or they may take a cell phone tour of the park. Daily ranger programs are offered from May through October. Living history programs are presented monthly.

Photo right: Stones River National Cemetery,
Stones River National Battlefield

Photo below: Living history demonstration,
Stones River National Battlefield

EVERGREEN CEMETERY

519 Greenland Drive, Murfreesboro, TN

PHONE: 615-893-5641
HOURS: Open daily.
ADMISSION: Free.

Evergreen Cemetery is home to the "circle of the unknown dead" where 2,000 unknown Confederate soldiers are buried. Also interred here is Confederate General Joseph B. Palmer.

Evergreen Cemetery

Evergreen Cemetery

OAKLANDS HISTORIC HOUSE MUSEUM

900 North Maney Avenue, Murfreesboro, TN

PHONE: 615-893-0022
WEB: www.oaklandsmuseum.org
HOURS: Open daily except Monday; closed major holidays.
ADMISSION: A fee is charged.

The grounds of Oaklands Historic House Museum once served as the campgrounds for both Confederate and Union forces. The home itself was used as the headquarters for Union Col. William Duffield and his regiment. Duffield surrendered Murfreesboro to Confederate Cavalryman Nathan Bedford Forrest at Oaklands. The antebellum mansion has been completely restored.

Photo right:
Oaklands Historic House Museum

THE BATTLE OF CHATTANOOGA

November 24–25, 1863

*Union victory at Chattanooga helped open the lower South
to Union forces.*

Chattanooga, situated on the south side of the Moccasin Bend
of the Tennessee River just north of the Tennessee-Georgia
border, was a river port to cities west of the Cumberland Plateau. It was also the site of railroad lines running to Virginia
and Mississippi. In short, it was a major strategic position for
both sides.

After its defeat at Chickamauga, Georgia, the Union
Army of the Cumberland withdrew to Chattanooga. Its position was tenuous, however, as a result of the disorganization
and disarray that followed Chickamauga. Union commander,
General William S. Rosecrans was demoralized and unsure of
himself, and he had lost the confidence of Union leaders. Rosecrans was replaced by General George Henry Thomas, who
was ordered to hold Chattanooga at all costs. The Confederates, led by General Braxton Bragg, began a siege of Chattanooga by occupying Lookout Mountain to the southwest and
Missionary Ridge to the south and east of the city. Bragg also
stationed 1,000 men on the river to guard the route into the
city. Although these two positions succeeded in overlooking

View of Moccasin Bend from Point Park, Lookout Mountain

Cannon atop Missionary Ridge

the railroads to the east and west and the river on the west, it proved ineffectual in controlling supplies to the city in total.

While the Union strengthened its position, Confederate forces weakened. Bragg was so stringently criticized by commanders under him, that Jefferson Davis himself visited him to offer support. The president encouraged Bragg; however, Davis also stripped the general of 15,000 men.

Major General Ulysses S. Grant took the offensive on November 23 by ordering Hooker to attack the line on Lookout Mountain where only a handful of Confederate soldiers were stationed; with that successful attack, the first part of the battle was over. On November 25, General William T. Sherman repeatedly assaulted Missionary Ridge, but the line held. Then, troops under General George Henry Thomas attacked the center of the Confederate line on the ridge. The Confederates panicked and fled; the siege was over.

Victory at Chattanooga set the stage for the Union to move on to Atlanta. It also interrupted the Confederate's east-west communication and supply lines. After his defeat at Chattanooga, Bragg resigned.

SIGNAL POINT

Atop Signal Mountain, Chattanooga, TN
WEB: www.nps.gov
HOURS: Open daily.
ADMISSION: Free.

Overlooking both Chattanooga and the Tennessee River, the strategic point of Signal Mountain was controlled by the Union army from September to November of 1863. Since rugged terrain to the west of the mountain prevented easy transport to Chattanooga, the Tennessee River was the Union supply line to the city. Although the mountain was important in the Union victory at Chattanooga, no fighting took place in the area. It was primarily used to watch Rebel troop movements and to convey messages to Union commanders in the field.

POINT PARK AND LOOKOUT MOUNTAIN

110 Point Park Road, Chattanooga, TN
PHONE: 423-821-7786
HOURS: Open daily; closed Christmas.
ADMISSION: A $3 per adult (16 years and older) fee is charged for entrance to Point Park. Museum and Cravens House are free.
* Note: See Georgia for additional information concerning the battles of Chickamauga and Chattanooga.

Point Park, located on top of Lookout Mountain, contains several artillery battery positions that mark a small segment of the Confederate siege lines that once encircled Chattanooga. In the park's center is the New York Peace Memorial. At the top of the monument, a Union soldier and a Confederate soldier shake hands under one flag, signifying peace and brotherly love. A Visitor Center, the Ochs Museum and Observatory, and the Cravens House, which was used as a headquarters by Confederate and Union officers, are also located on Lookout Mountain. Marked trails offer walking tours, but most are strenuous.

Cravens House, Lookout Mountain Battlefield

Each year special programs, such as guided tours of several battlefield areas and Civil War encampments, are presented at Chickamauga Battlefield and Lookout Mountain to commemorate the battles of Chickamauga and Chattanooga. These events take place near the

Point Park Entrance

anniversary of the battles (September for Chickamauga, and November for Lookout Mountain). Near Christmas, Cravens House is decorated in Victorian-era decorations, and candlelight tours are offered. On the Saturday nearest to July 4, Chickamauga Battlefield hosts an evening "Pops in the Park" concert presented by the Chattanooga Symphony Orchestra. During the summer, reenactment organizations present special demonstrations and Civil War encampments at Chickamauga Battlefield and Lookout Mountain. The Visitor's Center features exhibits on the Battle of Chickamauga, the Fuller Gun Collection, a Civil War timeline, and a multi-media program depicting the Battle of Chickamauga.

CHATTANOOGA NATIONAL CEMETERY

1200 Bailey Avenue, Chattanooga, TN
PHONE: 423-855-6590
WEB: www.cem.va.gov
HOURS: Open daily dawn to dusk.
ADMISSION: Free.

On November 26, 1863, the day after the battle on Missionary Ridge, work began on creating a final resting place for Union soldiers who died in northwest Georgia and southeastern Tennessee. Interred at the site are James Andrews and seven of his men. In April 1862, James Andrews and twenty Union raiders stole a locomotive, named the General, at Big Shanty (now Kennesaw), Georgia. In an episode that became known as "The Great Locomotive Chase," they were pursued throughout northwest Georgia and captured near Ringgold. Later, Andrews and seven of the raiders were hanged in Atlanta. The "Raiders" were the first soldiers to receive the Congressional Medals of Honor. Andrews was a civilian and therefore not eligible. A monument to Andrews' Raiders stands near the graves of James Andrews and seven of his men, all of which are marked with a small replica of the locomotive.

Raiders' Monument,
Chattanooga National Cemetery

THE BATTLES FOR CHATTANOOGA MUSEUM

1110 East Brow Road, Lookout Mountain, TN
PHONE: 423-821-2812
WEB: www.battlesforchattanooga.com
HOURS: Summer hours: 9AM – 6PM; Regular hours: 10AM – 5PM.
ADMISSION: A fee is charged; children under 12 are discounted.

The Battles for Chattanooga Museum is a small, privately-owned museum that features a large electric map and a light and sound show that explains the Battles of Chattanooga.

Photo left: The Battles for Chattanooga Museum, foreground, and Point Park Gate, background

ABRAHAM LINCOLN LIBRARY AND MUSEUM

6965 Cumberland Gap Parkway, Harrogate, TN
PHONE: 423-869-6235
WEB: www.lmunet.edu/museum
HOURS: Open daily; closed Thanksgiving, Christmas, and New Year's Day.
ADMISSION: A fee is charged.

Abraham Lincoln Museum

When Tennessee seceded from the Union, the Cumberland Gap area of Harrogate remained loyal. In appreciation of this loyalty, President Lincoln instructed General Oliver Otis Howard to do something for the people of the area. In 1897 Howard began Lincoln Memorial University. The museum, on the grounds of the university, contains a large collection of Union and Confederate uniforms, basic soldier's gear, and one of the largest collections of Lincoln memorabilia.

ANDREW JOHNSON NATIONAL HISTORIC SITE ———

College and Depot Streets, Greeneville, TN

PHONE: 423-638-3551

HOURS: Open daily; closed Thanksgiving, Christmas, and New Year's Day.

ADMISSION: Free.

The Andrew Johnson National Historic Site features Homestead, the home of President Johnson from 1851 until his death in 1875. After Lincoln's assassination, Johnson became president and presided over Reconstruction. Also included at the site are a Visitor's Center, Johnson's original Tailor Shop, an earlier home where the family lived prior to moving into the Homestead, and the Andrew Johnson National Cemetery where President Johnson is buried.

TEXAS

On February 1, 1861, the twenty-fifth anniversary of Texas's Declaration of Independence from Mexico, Texas seceded from the United States of America and became a member of the Confederate States of America. The legendary governor, Sam Houston, had fought against the secession and for his courage, was driven from office.

Texas brought to the Confederacy considerable assets, sending to the Southern cause over 50,000 troops. In addition, the state had four times as many cattle and horses as all other Southern states combined, which promised a steady supply of meat and mounts. Few battles were fought in the state, and very little damage was done by the war; Texas rejoined the Union in 1869.

SEE
NEW MEXICO
PAGE 126

SEE
OKLAHOMA
PAGE 146

SEE
ARKANSAS
PAGE 20

Amarillo

Wichita Falls

Lubbock

Fort Worth   Dallas   Longview

Abilene   Tyler

Odessa   Midland

San Angelo   Waco

TREÜE DER UNION MON.

TX ST. CEMETERY

Comfort   Austin

SABINE PASS

Port Arthur
Sabine Pass

San Antonio   Houston

Del Rio   Galveston

SEE
LOUISIANA
PAGE 74

Eagle Pass   Victoria

Corpus Christi

Laredo

PALMITO RANCH

FT. BROWN

McAllen

Brownsville

0   100 Miles
0   100 KM

THE BATTLE OF PALMITO RANCH

May 12–13, 1865

The last land-based engagement of the Civil War.

The Battle of Palmito Ranch took place near Brownsville, Texas, along the Rio Grande, more than a month after General Robert E. Lee's surrender to General Ulysses S. Grant at Appomattox Court House, Virginia. Lee's surrender of the Army of Virginia had brought the Civil War to its symbolic end but not its actual end. The Confederate army in Texas still continued the rebellion.

On May 11, 1865, Union Colonel Theodore H. Barrett, commander of forces at the island of Brazos Santiago, Texas, dispatched an expedition composed of 250 men of the Sixty-second U.S. Colored Infantry Regiment and fifty men of the Second Texas Cavalry Regiment under the command of Lieutenant Colonel David Branson to the mainland to attack reported Rebel outposts and camps. Branson led his men toward Palmito Ranch but encountered much skirmishing along the way. Branson sent word of his predicament to Barrett, who reinforced Branson at daybreak on May 13 with 200 men of the Thirty-fourth Indiana Volunteer Infantry.

Palmito Ranch Battlefield

Monument, Palmito Ranch Battlefield

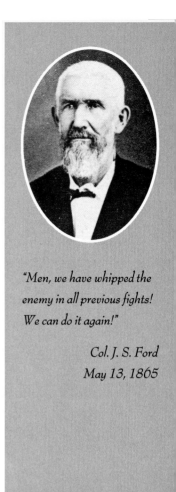

After the fighting stopped, Barrett led his force to a bluff at Tulosa on the river where the men could camp for the night. At 4:00PM, a large Confederate cavalry force, commanded by Colonel John S. "Rip" Ford, approached, and Union troops formed a battle line. The Rebels hammered the Union line with artillery. To preclude an enemy flanking movement, Barrett ordered a retreat. During the two-day battle, Ford's Confederate troops held off the Union and forced them to retreat to Boca Chica and ultimately to return to the island of Brazos Santiago.

The fighting at Palmito Ranch was the last land engagement of the Civil War. By holding off the Union army, the Confederacy's Trans-Mississippi Department was able to maintain control of the lower Rio Grande and Mississippi valleys a little longer.

Despite their victory, however, the Confederates were fighting a war that had already been lost. Fewer than two weeks later, the forces that fought to victory at Palmito Ranch were part of a Confederate surrender at New Orleans that put a final and complete end to the Civil War.

TEXAS STATE CEMETERY

909 Navasota Street, Austin, TX
PHONE: 512-463-0605
WEB: www.cemetery.state.tx.us
HOURS: Open daily;
office open weekdays.
ADMISSION: Free.

Texas State Cemetery was established in 1851; a Confederate
section was added in 1871. More
than 2,000 Confederate veterans
and their wives are buried in rows
of white marble tablets. In 1867
General Albert Sidney Johnston's

Fountain on Republic Hill and General Johnston's grave, Texas State Cemetery

body was moved to the Texas State Cemetery. Johnston led the Confederate charge at the Battle of
Shiloh and was fatally wounded there. The cemetery's Visitor's Center offers Internet access to biog-
raphies, photographs, and Confederate records of the buried.

TREÜE DER UNION (LOYAL TO THE UNION) MONUMENT

Just past the intersection of High Street and U.S. Highway 27, Comfort, TX
PHONE: 830-995-3131 (Chamber of Commerce)
HOURS: Open daily.
ADMISSION: Free.

In August 1862, a group of sixty-eight Union sympathizers, mostly comprised of German immi-
grants, left home to join Union troops in Louisiana, planning a route through Mexico. Their plans
were betrayed, and they were followed and attacked by Confederates. Nineteen Unionists died in
the battle, known as the *Nueces* Massacre, and Confederates killed ten more they had taken prisoner.
Seven additional men were hunted down and killed, more than two months later, at the Rio Grande.
Several of the Union sympathizers escaped to Mexico; some remained there for the rest of the war,
but three reached the Union forces in New Orleans. A limestone obelisk was erected in 1866 to
honor the slain. The names of the thirty-six fallen are inscribed on the monument.

PALMITO RANCH BATTLEFIELD

Texas Highway 4, Brownsville, TX
PHONE: 800-626-2639 (Convention and Visitor's Bureau)
HOURS: Open daily.
ADMISSION: Free.

Although much of the Palmito Ranch Battlefield is privately owned and is not open to public access,
historical markers along the Boca Chica Highway, or Highway 4, describe the battle and outline

much of the battlefield. A Visitor's Center is not available, but information can be obtained through the Texas Convention and Visitor's Bureau.

Palmito Ranch Battlefield

FORT BROWN

80 Fort Brown on the campus of University of Texas, Brownsville, TX
PHONE: 956-882-8200
HOURS: Buildings open during school hours; campus always open.
ADMISSION: Free.

Fort Brown was established in 1846 and utilized during the Mexican War. In 1861 Texas troops controlled the fort and used it to protect the Brownsville port which received cotton and war materiel. To extend a coastal blockade, Union forces took

Fort Brown

over the fort in November 1863, but eight months later a strong Confederate army retook the fort and controlled it until the end of the war. Today, the post headquarters, medical laboratory, guardhouse, hospital, and morgue still stand. The nearby Historic Brownsville Museum contains exhibits pertaining to Brownsville's Civil War past.

SABINE PASS BATTLEGROUND STATE HISTORIC SITE

Texas Highway 87, Sabine Pass, TX
PHONE: 512-463-6323
WEB: www.visitsabinepassbattleground.com
HOURS: Open daily.
ADMISSION: Free.

Sabine Pass was a major Confederate port for receiving supplies and material. Because of the Union blockade of gulf ports and those further east, the Confederates required that the Texas ports remain open. Fort Sabine and nearby Fort Griffin were constructed for this purpose. Twice, in September of 1862 and again in September of 1863, the Union attempted to gain control of the forts, with only brief success in 1862. Neither fort is still standing, but there is a monument to the Confederate Lieutenant Richard Dowling and his men who fought in the 1863 engagement. Walking trails are available. Each September the site hosts a tribute to Lieutenant Dowling.

VIRGINIA

Virginia did not join the parade of Southern secession until April of 1861, but it quickly became the most important state in the Confederacy. Virginia saw more battles than any other state—2,150 in all—and it was the birthplace of ninety-one Confederate generals, including Robert E. Lee and Stonewall Jackson. Richmond, Virginia, the Confederate capital, lay only 100 miles from Washington, D.C., and Virginia was of strategic importance to both sides for its farms, ironworks, and rail lines.

Most of the fighting in Virginia pitted two great Civil War generals and their armies—Robert E. Lee and his Army of Northern Virginia and Ulysses S. Grant and his Army of the Potomac—against one another in a contest that has become symbolic in American minds for the war as a whole. Rightly so, for when Lee surrendered to Grant at Appomattox Court House, although other armies in other states continued to fight, the Civil War was considered finally and officially over.

Virginia's rich Civil War heritage is unmatched by any other state, North or South. The Confederacy's most important state is now the nations' most important guardian of Civil War history.

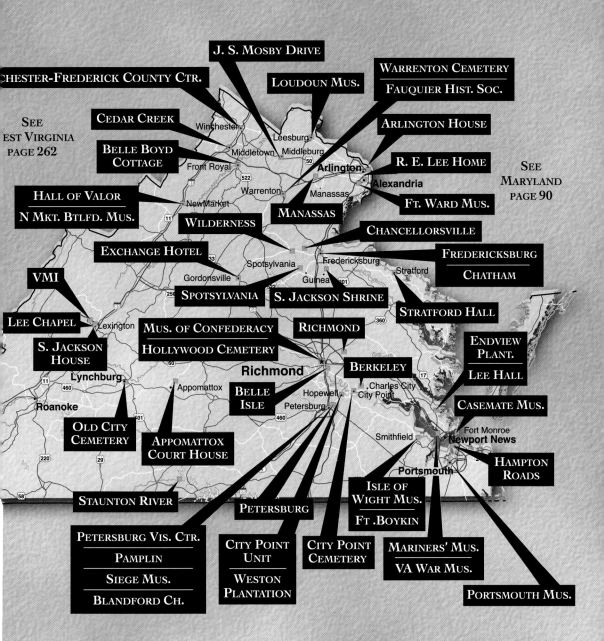

J. S. MOSBY DRIVE

WARRENTON CEMETERY

FAUQUIER HIST. SOC.

LOUDOUN MUS.

HESTER-FREDERICK COUNTY CTR.

CEDAR CREEK

ARLINGTON HOUSE

SEE
EST VIRGINIA
PAGE 262

Winchester

Leesburg

Middleburg

BELLE BOYD
COTTAGE

Middletown

R. E. LEE HOME

Front Royal

Arlington

SEE
MARYLAND
PAGE 90

522

Alexandria

HALL OF VALOR

Warrenton

Manassas

FT. WARD MUS.

NewMarket

N MKT. BTLFD. MUS.

11

MANASSAS

WILDERNESS

CHANCELLORSVILLE

EXCHANGE HOTEL

33

FREDERICKSBURG

Spotsylvania

Fredericksburg

Stratford

CHATHAM

VMI

Gordonsville

Guinea

201

SPOTSYLVANIA

S. JACKSON SHRINE

250

LEE CHAPEL

64

Lexington

STRATFORD HALL

360

S. JACKSON
HOUSE

MUS. OF CONFEDERACY

RICHMOND

ENDVIEW
PLANT.

HOLLYWOOD CEMETERY

BERKELEY

LEE HALL

60

Lynchburg

17

Appomattox

Charles City
City Point

CASEMATE MUS.

11

460

BELLE
ISLE

Hopewell

Roanoke

601

Petersburg

Fort Monroe
Newport News

OLD CITY
CEMETERY

460

Smithfield

220

29

APPOMATTOX
COURT HOUSE

HAMPTON
ROADS

Portsmouth

58

STAUNTON RIVER

85

ISLE OF
WIGHT MUS.

MARINERS' MUS.

PETERSBURG

PORTSMOUTH MUS.

FT .BOYKIN

VA WAR MUS.

PETERSBURG VIS. CTR.

CITY POINT
UNIT

CITY POINT
CEMETERY

PAMPLIN

SIEGE MUS.

WESTON
PLANTATION

BLANDFORD CH.

SEE NORTH CAROLINA PAGE 132

•Because of space constraints, all of
the sites listed on the following pages
are not shown on this map

0   100 Miles

0   100 KM

THE FIRST BATTLE OF MANASSAS (BULL RUN)

July 21, 1861

The Confederate victory at the first battle at Manassas made it clear that the war would be long and hard-fought.

The town of Manassas was an important railroad center between Washington and Richmond because it lay directly between the Confederate and Union capitals. It was obvious to many that conflict would occur between the two capitals, and civilians were eager to watch the fight. In the summer of 1861,

Stonewall Jackson Monument, Manassas National Battlefield Park

32,000 Confederate soldiers under General P. G. T. Beauregard set up defensive positions alongside a stream called Bull Run.

In mid-July Union Brigadier General Irvin McDowell led 39,000 men out of Washington toward Brigadier General P. G. T. Beauregard in a three-pronged attack. When McDowell's first probe into the Confederate flank at Manassas proved unsuccessful, he paused and spent the next two days devising a new plan of attack. He ordered General Patterson to keep General Joseph E. Johnston occupied in Winchester. Johnston, however, evacuated Winchester, leaving a cavalry screen to fool Patterson. Unaware of the deception, on July 21, McDowell directed a small group to feign an attack from the north while the main assault would come from the northwest. But the decoy attack was too weak. The Confederates realized the trick and left only a few men to fight against the Union. The remainder of the brigade left to meet McDowell.

The troop strength of the Northern army eventually drove Southern forces under General Barnard Bee back to Henry House Hill where a Confederate brigade under General Thomas Jackson waited to assist them. Bee rallied his troops with the words, "There stands Jackson, like a stone wall! Rally behind the Virginians!" The troops rallied and pushed the North into confusion. Thousands of Union troops began to move toward the rear where Northern civilians were watching the battle. A general melee ensued as both soldiers and civilians clogged the road in retreat. The first land battle of the war was over; victory belonged to the Confederacy.

Manassas proved to the citizens, however, that there would be no quick end to the war, and people began to plan accordingly. For example, a Manassas citizen named Wilmer McLean had his house damaged by the shots. After the battle, he moved to what he thought would be a safer location in Appomattox Court House, Virginia.

"The conduct of General Jackson also requires mention, as eminently that of an able, fearless soldier and sagacious commander— one fit to lead his efficient brigade. His prompt, timely arrival before the plateau of the Henry House . . . contributed much to the success of the day"

Brig. Gen. P. G. T.
Beauregard
August 26, 1861

THE SECOND BATTLE OF MANASSAS (BULL RUN)

August 28–30, 1862

The second battle of Manassas was also a victory for the Confederacy and opened the door for General Lee's invasion of the North.

A year after the First Battle of Manassas, the Northern armies had yet to win a major victory, and the South was hopeful that independence would soon be theirs. The Confederacy rested its hopes on General Robert E. Lee's Army of Northern Virginia. Lee, however, knew that if he were to succeed in northern Virginia, he had to defeat General John Pope's Union Army of Virginia before it joined the Army of the Potomac. These two forces would create a Federal fighting force twice the size of Lee's Confederate army. The fighting between Lee and Pope would climax in August 1862 at the Second Battle of Manassas.

On August 25, 1861, Jackson's foot cavalry flanked General Pope's right, cutting off his supply line from Washington. When Jackson's men fired from an unfinished railroad, Union troops from Wisconsin and Indiana (later called the Iron Brigade) quickly formed battle lines and marched to within 100 yards of the Confederates. Only darkness ended the fighting, which resulted in a thirty-three percent casualty rate.

Manassas Visitor Center, Manassas National Battlefield Park

Manassas National Battlefield Park

The next day, Pope continued the stalemate until Major General Kearny, the one-armed veteran of the Mexican War, drove against Jackson's left flank. Pope did not send reinforcements, and a Union retreat resulted. That evening, Generals Lee and Longstreet slipped in with reinforcements. On the third day, at what became known as the Deep Cut, Jackson slaughtered the Union army in thirty minutes of intense fighting. Pope fell back to fight until nightfall when he withdrew toward Washington where he was relieved of command and sent to the West to fight in the Indian wars.

Second Manassas was the climax of skirmishes between Generals Pope, Lee, and Jackson. In the end, General Pope and his men traced McDowell's steps back toward Washington.

This Union defeat was more devastating than the first; not only were the casualties higher but so were the stakes. After victory at Second Manassas, General Lee's confident Army of Northern Virginia was prepared to take the Civil War into Northern territory.

MANASSAS NATIONAL BATTLEFIELD PARK

6511 Sudley Road, Manassas, VA
PHONE: 703-361-1339
WEB: www.nps.gov/mana
HOURS: Open daily dawn to dusk; closed Thanksgiving and Christmas.
ADMISSION: A fee is charged.

Located twenty-six miles southwest of Washington, D.C., Manassas National Battlefield Park contains about 5,500 acres where the battles of the First and Second Manassas took place. The Henry Hill Visitors Center and Museum offers a battle map program as well as an audio-visual program that provides information on both battles. A twenty-five minute self-guided walking tour covers the major areas of the battles, and ranger-led tours are available during the summer months. A twelve-mile, twelve-stop driving tour includes the Groveton Confederate Cemetery where unknown Confederate soldiers are buried in mass graves. Only a few in the cemetery are identified. Period cannons on the grounds mark some of the original artillery positions. The historic Stone House is open weekends from 10AM to 4PM. During the battles, this house was turned into a field hospital.

Photo above: Old Stone House, Manassas National Battlefield Park

Photo below: Manassas National Battlefield Park

THE MANASSAS MUSEUM

9101 Prince William Street, Manassas, VA
PHONE: 703-368-1873
HOURS: Closed Mondays except
Monday Federal holidays.
ADMISSION: A fee is charged; children
are discounted.

The Manassas Museum

The Manassas Museum contains exhibits and photographs depicting the history of Manassas and features a large collection of Civil War artifacts and a video program: *A Place of Passages.*

The Manassas Museum system also includes the train depot, Liberia Plantation, an 1825 former Civil War military headquarters open for special tours and events, and Mayfield (Confederate) and Cannon Branch (Union) earthwork forts. Inside the depot, which also serves as a Visitor's Center, a small exhibit area illustrates the railroad's history and influence on Manassas and the two battles which occurred here. A walking/ driving Civil War Trails map is available at the museum.

Also of note in Manassas is the Manassas Industrial School/Jennie Dean Memorial, which was established in the 1890s by Jennie Dean, a former slave, for the purpose of providing African-Americans with a proper education.

CIVIL WAR MUSEUM AT THE EXCHANGE HOTEL

400 South Main Street, Gordonsville, VA
PHONE: 540-832-2944
WEB: www.hgiexchange.org
HOURS: See website for details.
ADMISSION: A fee is charged.

This former railroad hotel was converted into a Civil War hospital and served troops from the battles of Cedar Mountain, Chancellorsville, Trevilian Station, Mine Run, Brandy Station, Manassas, the Wilderness, and Fredericksburg. Although it was primarily a Confederate facility, it treated both sides. By the end of the war, over 70,000 men had passed through the Exchange Hotel/Hospital. Over 700 were buried on the grounds. After the war, the bodies of the Confederate dead were moved to a mass grave in Gordonsville's Maplewood Cemetery. Federal soldiers were reinterred in the national cemetery in Culpepper. Guided tours of the restored building are available. Annual Civil War Living History Encampments take place in June.

FORT WARD MUSEUM AND HISTORIC SITE

4301 West Braddock Road, Alexandria, VA
PHONE: 703-746-4848
HOURS: Fort open daily; closed major holidays.
Museum closed Mondays.
ADMISSION: Free.

Fort Ward is the best preserved of the system of forts and batteries built to protect Washington, D.C., during the Civil War. The Fort Ward Museum features an orientation video on the defense of Washington, a living history series and lecture series, bus tours, and changing exhibits. The museum focuses on the history of Fort Ward, Alexandria's role as a vital crossroads and supply center, and the lifestyles of soldiers and civilians during the war. The permanent collection includes: military equipment related to the infantry; artillery; edged and shoulder weapons; flags; musical instruments; medical equipment; uniforms and clothing accessories; cooking and mess equipment; artwork, primarily period prints of both Union and Confederate significance; documents; photographs; and artifacts excavated at Fort Ward. The museum also contains a comprehensive research library that is open to the public during regular museum hours; however, researchers should call ahead for reservations.

Northwest Bastion, Fort Ward Museum and Historic Site

Museum and Reconstructed Officer's Hut, Fort Ward Museum and Historic Site

BOYHOOD HOME OF ROBERT E. LEE

607 Oronoco Street, Alexandria, VA

Robert E. Lee lived in this home, which the Lee family rented, from the age of five to eighteen, when he entered the United States Military Academy at West Point. Sold in 2000, the home is now a private residence. A marker identifies the house.

THE LOUDOUN MUSEUM

16 Loudoun Street SW, Leesburg, VA
PHONE: 703-777-7427
WEB: www.loudounmuseum.org
HOURS: Friday and Saturday 10AM – 5PM; Sunday 1PM – 5PM.
ADMISSION: A fee is charged; seniors, students, and teachers are discounted; museum members, military and children under 4 are free

The Loudoun Museum is dedicated to the county's diverse history and contains rotating exhibits on the area's Civil War heritage. Artifacts from the Battle of Ball's Bluff are housed here as are exhibits that focus on the local citizens who were torn between the forces of North and South. The museum offers a twelve-minute movie and a self-guided Civil War Walking Tour of Leesburg.

BELLE BOYD COTTAGE

101 Chester Street, Front Royal, VA
PHONE: 540-636-1446
(Warren Heritage Society)
WEB: www.warrenheritagesociety.org
HOURS: Monday – Friday 10AM – 4PM.
ADMISSION: A fee is charged;
children 10 and under are free.

Belle Boyd, a Confederate spy, used friendships with Union soldiers and officers occupying Front Royal to gain information about troop movements. In one instance, Boyd eavesdropped on Union Generals Shields and Banks concerning

Belle Boyd Cottage

the upcoming Battle of Front Royal. The information she provided to General Stonewall Jackson helped win the battle for the Confederacy. The restored Belle Boyd Cottage is owned by the Warren Heritage Society. Exhibits at the Ivy Lodge Museum, located in front of the Belle Boyd Cottage, interpret the site and contain Civil War artifacts.

THE JOHN SINGLETON MOSBY HERITAGE AREA'S DRIVE THROUGH HISTORY

Virginia Highway 50, Middleburg, VA
PHONE: 540-687-6681 (Mosby Heritage Association)
WEB: www.mosbyheritagearea.org
HOURS: Tour route always open.
ADMISSION: Free; a fee is charged for Sky Meadows State Park (540-592-3556).

John Singleton Mosby, also called the Gray Ghost, is a legend in the Virginia counties of Fauquier and Loudoun. An unknown lawyer at the beginning of the war, Mosby identified the great advantage of guerrilla warfare in northern Virginia. He was first General J.E.B. Stuart's scout then was given his own command which eventually became the forty-third Battalion of Virginia Cavalry. Mosby led his rangers on raids throughout northern Virginia, wreaking havoc among Union lines, then disappearing without a trace. The area between Snickersville, Aldie, the Plains, and Markham became known as Mosby's Confederacy.

Route 50 has been named the John S. Mosby Highway, and is dotted with historical markers interpreting Civil War–era landmarks. The tour begins at the Mount Zion Church located at Route 860 and Highway 50. Built in 1851, the Mount Zion Old School Baptist Church served as a hospital, a prison, a barracks, and a soldiers' burial ground. The church was also a Civil War skirmish site in July 1864 between Mosby's Rangers and Union Cavalry. Other points of interest heading west on Route 50 from the church include the Historic Aldie Mill; the town of Middleburg; the Caleb Rector House; Goose Creek Stone Bridge; various homes of Mosby's Rangers; the town of Upperville; and other places instrumental in the life of Mosby. The driving tour ends at Paris, a pristine 19th century village.

Also of interest is Sky Meadows State Park just south of Paris on Route 17. This is the site of Abner Settle's home, Mount Bleak House, which is open to the public. The full tour can be downloaded for free on the Mosby Heritage Area website.

WARRENTON CEMETERY

Lee Street, Warrenton, VA
HOURS: Open daily.
ADMISSION: Free.

Although Warrenton saw no battle, it was surrounded by skirmishes and major engagements. Thousands of casualties were brought into Warrenton to be nursed or buried. This seven-acre cemetery includes Confederates from Alabama, Florida, Georgia, Louisiana, Mississippi, North Carolina, South Carolina, Tennessee, Texas, and Virginia. Approximately 200 Civil War dead, including Colonel John S. Mosby and many of his family, are interred here. Until recently, 600 Confederate soldiers were unidentified and buried in a common grave beneath a Confederate Memorial to the Unknowns. In 1995 a researcher at the National Archives in Washington, D.C., discovered the names of most of those soldiers, and a memorial wall inscribed with the 520 names now stands on the site.

FAUQUIER HISTORICAL SOCIETY AND OLD JAIL MUSEUM

10 Courthouse Square, Corner of Ashby and Waterloo Streets, Warrenton, VA
PHONE: 540-347-5525
E-MAIL: theoldjailmuseum@yahoo.com
WEB: www.fauquierhistory.com
HOURS: Tuesday – Sunday 10AM – 4PM; closed major holidays.
ADMISSION: Free.

This museum contains many Civil War artifacts, including memorabilia from Warrenton resident Confederate Colonel John Singleton Mosby's Rangers, as well as the bench from the front porch of Mosby's home in Warrenton. The museum also features a camp stool and bayonet which belonged to John Q. Marr, the first Confederate officer killed, and a collection of Black Horse Cavalry artifacts, including the frock coat of their commander, General William Henry Fitzhugh Lee. In celebration of the sesquicentennial, the museum will host a large display on the impact of the Civil War on Fauquier County.

Old Jail Museum

ARLINGTON HOUSE, THE ROBERT E. LEE MEMORIAL

On the grounds of Arlington Cemetery, Arlington, VA
PHONE: 703-235-1530
WEB: www.nps.gov/arho
HOURS: Open daily 9:30AM – 4:30PM; closed Christmas and New Year's Day.
ADMISSION: Free.

On a hill overlooking the grounds of Arlington Cemetery sits the family home of Confederate General Robert E. Lee. Lee lived here with his wife and their seven children before the outbreak of the Civil War. Upon his resignation from the United States Army, Lee moved his family deeper into Virginia. In the early years of the war, there was an attempt to preserve the house, but time and tension took their toll. Defenses were thrown up around the house, and many who viewed Lee as a traitor showered their feelings upon the house.

After the war, Lee's eldest son had the estate restored to the family, but already several thousand Union dead had been buried in the grounds surrounding the home. The U.S. government then purchased the property from the Lee family for $150,000, and fortifications around the property were absorbed into Fort Mayer. In 1925 Congress established the Robert E. Lee Memorial and began restoring the Greek Revival Mansion. The house contains pieces belonging to the Lee family, as well as period pieces. The home and grounds are open for self-guided tours.

THE BATTLE OF FREDERICKSBURG

December 11–13, 1862

The battle at Fredericksburg, Virginia, proved to be the greatest disaster of the war for the Union army.

Fredericksburg, located in northern Virginia between Washington and Richmond, was the site of four major engagements during the Civil War. Within a seventeen-mile radius of the city, more than 100,000 Americans became casualties.

In the autumn of 1862, General George B. McClellan was replaced by Major General Ambrose E. Burnside after McClellan failed to pursue the Confederate army after its defeat at Antietam, Maryland. McClellan was so slow that President Abraham Lincoln was prompted to write in 24, 1862, "I have just read your dispatch about sore tongued and fatigued horses. Will you pardon me for asking what the horses of your army have done since the battle of Antietam that fatigue anything?"

Burnside wanted to build upon the victory at Antietam by moving toward Richmond. He planned to use pontoon bridges to cross the Rappahannock River at Fredericksburg,

Sunken Road, Fredericksburg Battlefield

then move directly south to the Confederate capital of Richmond. He had to move quickly, however, to reach Fredericksburg before Longstreet and Jackson arrived to support General Robert E. Lee.

The Union army began moving on November 15, and the first division reached Stafford Heights overlooking Fredericksburg on November 17. Bridging equipment had not yet arrived, however, and the Federals were unable to cross the river. In fact, it took more than a week for the pontoons to come, and by that time Lee's army had taken possession of Fredericksburg. Although Burnside knew of Lee's movements, he believed that only part of Lee's army was in position. In truth, 78,000 were there. Burnside pushed ahead, and the disaster that followed ultimately earned him the nickname of "Butcher" Burnside.

On December 11 at 3:00AM, Union engineers began placing pontoon bridges in the Rappahannock. At daybreak, they were interrupted by minié balls from Confederate sharpshooters in town. After Union volunteers crossed the river and battled for control of the town, Lee allowed the bridges to be completed. On December 12, Union troops crossed the Rappahannock and plundered Fredericksburg.

On December 13, Burnside still believed he was facing only part of Lee's army and ordered attacks accordingly. One piece of land south of town exchanged sides between North and South throughout the day. Meanwhile, Burnside ordered an assault up Marye's Heights, just behind Fredericksburg, where Lee's men were entrenched in Sunken Road behind a stone wall at the base of the heights. Wave after wave of Union troops swarmed the hill, only to be mowed down by Confederate guns. By the end of the day, 8,000 Union troops, many from the Sixty-ninth New York "Irish Brigade," died attempting to reach the Heights. Men who were wounded froze to death that night in the torrential downpours. Burnside withdrew in defeat. Upon hearing of the loss of Fredericksburg, President Abraham Lincoln remarked, "If there is a worse place than Hell, I am in it."

"It is well that war is so terrible—we should grow too fond of it."

Gen. R. E. Lee
December 1862

FREDERICKSBURG BATTLEFIELD

1013 Lafayette Boulevard, Fredericksburg, VA
PHONE: 540-373-6122
WEB: www.nps.gov/frsp
HOURS: Open daily; closed
Christmas and New Year's Day.
ADMISSION: Free.

The Fredericksburg Visitor Center offers interpretive exhibits and films ($2 charge to view films) as well as exhibits and displays concerning the Battle of Fredericksburg. A self-guided driving tour includes the entire battlefield as well as Marye's Heights, a *Kirkland Monument, Fredericksburg Battlefield* national cemetery, Sunken Road, Chatham, and a monument to the Angel of Marye's Heights, nineteen-year-old Sergeant Richard Kirkland of the Second South Carolina Infantry. Kirkland was so moved by the cries of the wounded Union soldiers that he took as many canteens as he could carry and went among them, giving them some relief through water and compassion. Brochures and maps are available at the Visitor Center.

FREDERICKSBURG NATIONAL CEMETERY

1013 Lafayette Boulevard, Fredericksburg, VA
PHONE: 540-373-6122
WEB: www.nps.gov/frsp
HOURS: Open daily.
ADMISSION: Free.

Of the 15,429 Union soldiers here, only 2,643 are identified. The cemetery is not organized by state, unit, or campaign, but as the soldiers were brought in for burial. Various monuments do, however, commemorate units and campaigns. Most of the interred are privates; higher ranking *Fredericksburg National Cemetery* officers were often transported home by family members. This cemetery, part of the Fredericksburg and Spotsylvania National Military Park, sits behind the Fredericksburg Battlefield Visitor Center, and overlooks the Sunken Road.

The Southern dead are interred in the Fredericksburg Confederate Cemetery and the Spotsylvania Confederate Cemetery. Registers for the national cemetery and both Confederate cemeteries can be found in the Fredericksburg Battlefield Visitor Center.

CHATHAM

120 Chatham Lane, Fredericksburg, VA

PHONE: 540-371-0802

WEB: www.nps.gov/frsp/chatham.htm

HOURS: Open daily; closed Christmas and New Year's Day.

ADMISSION: Free.

Chatham was used as the headquarters of General Edwin V. Sumner during the Battle of Fredericksburg and now serves as headquarters of the Fredericksburg and Spotsylvania Battlefield Park. The elegant home of William Fitzhugh and Confederate Major J. Horace Lacy became the Union headquarters at various times for Generals McDowell, Burnside, Sumner, and Gibbon. In May of 1862, Lincoln visited the home.

After the battle of Fredericksburg, Chatham was converted into a hospital where Clara Barton tended to the wounded. Dr. Mary Walker and Walt Whitman also visited Chatham during the war. Graffiti scrawled by Union soldiers is still visible today. Five of its ten rooms are open to the public and contain exhibits and displays.

Photo right: Chatham

FREDERICKSBURG VISITOR CENTER

706 Caroline Street, Fredericksburg, VA

PHONE: 800-678-4748

WEB: www.visitfred.com

HOURS: Open daily 9AM – 5PM.

ADMISSION: Free.

The city is located on the banks of the Rappahannock River which served as a natural defensive barrier. Fredericksburg's position on the north-south rail corridor was strategic in keeping both armies supplied. On four separate occasions, the Union Army of the Potomac fought the Confederate Army of Northern Virginia in and around the city, leaving over 100,000 casualties and a scarred landscape in their wake. Information on historic walking tours and much more is available.

THE BATTLE OF CHANCELLORSVILLE

May 1–3, 1863

The Battle of Chancellorsville stands as the greatest Civil War victory for Confederate General Robert E. Lee.

After the crushing defeat at Fredericksburg, General Ambrose Burnside was relieved of his command and replaced by General Joseph "Fighting Joe" Hooker. In the spring of 1863, Hooker made plans to swing around and attack the rear of Lee's army at Fredericksburg. Lee discovered Hooker's plan, however, and fled to Chancellorsville, where he took up position protected by an area called the Wilderness. This terrain had dense and impenetrable underbrush, which provided excellent defense for the badly outnumbered Confederates. Hooker followed Lee and made for a high plateau marked by Zoan Church. Lee daringly split his small command in two and sent one group under General Jackson to meet Hooker. Jackson arrived at the ridge in time to drive Hooker back to Chancellorsville.

That night Lee and Jackson further divided their force,

Hazel Grove, Chancellorsville Battlefield

Ruins of Catharine Furnace, Chancellorsville Battlefield

and Jackson attacked Hooker's rear on the second day. Late that afternoon, Jackson's men roared out of the Wilderness, rolled over the Union army, and destroyed half of Hooker's line. On the third day, Confederate artillery aided the infantry surging across the fields around Chancellorsville and victory was secured.

Although Chancellorsville was a great victory for the Confederacy, elation soon mixed with mourning. On the evening of May 2, Jackson and his staff were reconnoitering the area. As they rode back to the Confederate lines, a North Carolina unit believed they were being attacked and fired on the Jackson group. Jackson was hit twice in the left arm and once in the right hand. His left arm was amputated that night.

Upon hearing that Jackson was wounded, Lee said, "He [Jackson] had lost his left arm, but I [Lee] have lost my right arm." Jackson died eight days later in Fredericksburg from pneumonia.

FREDERICKSBURG AREA MUSEUM AND CULTURAL CENTER

1001 Princess Anne Street, Fredericksburg, VA
PHONE: 540-371-3037
WEB: www.famcc.org
HOURS: Open daily; closed major holidays.
ADMISSION: A fee is charged; seniors, students, and AAA are discounted; children under 6 are free.

The Fredericksburg Area Museum houses seven permanent exhibitions and three changing galleries that interpret the history of the region. Exhibits focus on Virginia Indians; the settlement of the region during the Colonial Period; Fredericksburg during the Civil War, Revolutionary War, and WWI and WWII; African American history from slavery to Civil Rights; and perspectives on the community today. The museum is housed in the 1816 historic Town Hall/Market House and the 1927 Planters National Bank building. Visitors may also enjoy Fredericksburg's unique character in the adjoining historic Market Square, a public gathering space for centuries.

New exhibition gallery "Fredericksburg at War," Fredericksburg Area Museum and Cultural Center

CHANCELLORSVILLE BATTLEFIELD

9001 Plank Road, Fredericksburg, VA
PHONE: 540-786-2880
WEB: www.nps.gov/frsp/chanville.htm
HOURS: Open daily; closed Christmas and New Year's Day.
ADMISSION: Free.

There are 1,252 acres of Chancellorsville Battlefield remaining. The Visitor Center presents a twenty-two-minute movie, sea-

Photo right: Jackson Monument, Chancellorsville Battlefield

sonal walking tours, a bookstore, and numerous exhibits. A six-mile driving tour is marked with stops as a continuation of the Fredericksburg Battlefield. Stops include the ruins of the Chancellorsville Inn, Lee-Jackson Bivouac Site (the last time Lee would see Jackson), Catharine Furnace ruins, and the Visitor Center itself which marks the spot where Stonewall Jackson was hit by his own infantry. During the summer, a thirty-five minute guided walking tour is conducted to the site where Jackson was shot.

STONEWALL JACKSON SHRINE

12019 Stonewall Jackson Road, Woodford, VA
PHONE: 804-633-6076
WEB: www.nps.gov/frsp/js.htm
HOURS: Grounds open daily; closed Christmas and New Year's Day. Cottage open 9AM – 5PM Saturdays, Sundays, and Mondays only the end of October through the end of April; open daily May 1 through October 27.
ADMISSION: Free.

During the Battle of Chancellorsville, Stonewall Jackson was wounded by his own infantry in the darkness. Doctors at the field hospital amputated his left arm. Jackson was then taken about twenty-seven miles to a plantation in Guinea. There, an outbuilding that served as the plantation's office was converted into a small cottage for Jackson's recovery. Unfortunately, with his wife and young daughter by his side, Jackson died of pneumonia on May 10, 1863. The six-room cottage is furnished as it appeared at Jackson's death.

Stonewall Jackson Shrine

THE BATTLE OF THE WILDERNESS

May 5–6, 1864

The terrible battle fought in the thickest and roughest of terrain, the Wilderness has been called the "beginning of the end" for the Confederacy.

The Wilderness was a region ten miles west of Fredericksburg twelve miles wide and six miles deep, running along the south bank of the Rapidan River. It had been called the Wilderness since the first colonists to settle the area discovered that it could not be tamed. With Lieutenant General Ulysses S. Grant and his men advancing upon them in the spring of 1864, General Robert E. Lee saw the wild entanglement of the Wilderness as a possible ally. It was there that Lee would meet the Union advance.

Fighting began in the early afternoon of May 5 in the north and slowly spread southward as the Union forces came into line. By nightfall the Confederate line was solid in the north and ragged in the south. Lee, however, had only two-thirds of his army engaged. Reinforcements were due early the second day but were slow in arriving. When they did come, the Confederate counterattack brought the Union to a standstill.

140th New York Monument, Saunders Field, Wilderness Battlefield

Monument to Texans, Wilderness Battlefield

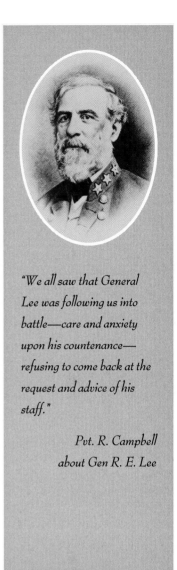

The Wilderness, which in the beginning was a friend to the Confederates, became a foe for North and South. The fighting was so fierce in the dry underbrush that fires broke out all over the battlefield, confusing the men on both sides. Fires were so strong that soldiers too wounded to move were burned to death. Both North and South suffered terrible losses and the battle itself was not a victory for either the Union or Confederacy, but Grant was the first Union general to press on south despite the number of casualties. The North, with far greater numbers, could endure the losses, unlike the South, whose every man was irreplaceable. The Civil War had become a battle of attrition; and the Wilderness sounded the death knell of the Confederacy.

WILDERNESS BATTLEFIELD

Virginia Highway 20 (Old Orange Turnpike), 16 miles west of Fredericksburg, VA
PHONE: 540-786-2880
(Chancellorsville Visitor Center)
HOURS: Open daily.
ADMISSION: Free.

The Chancellorsville Visitor Center provides brochures and maps for self-guided tours of Wilderness Battlefield, and there is an exhibit shelter with a historian on duty during summer months. Nearly 2,000 acres of the battlefield's dense woods remain. Confederate trenches along the Hill-Ewell Drive are still visible. During summer months, a forty-five-minute guided walking tour is available, depending on staffing. It leaves from the Wilderness Exhibit Shelter and covers the Gordon Flank Attack Trail. A driving tour visits Tapp Farm and Brock Road-Plank Road Junction.

Saunders Field, Wilderness Battlefield

SPOTSYLVANIA COURT HOUSE BATTLEFIELD

Virginia Highway 3 to County Highway 613 (Brock Road), Spotsylvania, VA
PHONE: 540-786-2880 (Chancellorsville Visitor Center)
HOURS: Open daily.
ADMISSION: Free.

The Battle of Spotsylvania followed directly after the Battle of the Wilderness and was a continuation of General Grant's Overland Campaign toward Richmond. While Grant headed

Ohio Monument at Bloody Angle, Spotsylvania Court House Battlefield

toward Spotsylvania, the Confederates marched toward Spotsylvania Court House. The two forces met on Spindle Farm, May 8, 1864. On May 12 at Mule Shoe Salient, intense small-arms fire and hand-to-hand combat in the pouring rain resulted in what is known as "Bloody Angle." With Confederate bodies filling the trenches, the sight was terrible and ghastly. Both sides were unsuccessful after thirteen days and 28,000 casualties.

Today, 1,448 acres of the battlefield remain. A self-guided driving tour includes stops at Bloody Angle and McCoull House. During the summer, a forty-five-minute guided walking tour leaves from the Bloody Angle stop. Although there is no Visitor Center at the battlefield, the Visitor Center at Chancellorsville provides maps for self-guided tours of Spotsylvania Court House Battlefield. It also has information on those buried at the Confederate Cemetery.

WINCHESTER-FREDERICK COUNTY CIVIL WAR ORIENTATION CENTER

Sponsored by the Shenandoah Valley Battlefields Foundation and
Located in the Winchester-Frederick County Visitors Center
1400 S. Pleasant Valley Road, Winchester, VA
PHONE: 1-877-871-1326; 540-542-1326
WEB: www.visitwinchesterva.com; www.shenandoahatwar.org
HOURS: Open daily 9AM – 5PM.
ADMISSION: Free.

Winchester-Frederick County was a strategic prize of importance during the Civil War. General Thomas "Stonewall" Jackson began his famous Valley Campaign in Winchester. At least six battles were fought here, and the town changed hands approximately 70 times; once, it changed hands 13 times in one day.

The new Winchester-Frederick County Civil War Orientation Center is the perfect place to begin exploration of Civil War sites in the Shenandoah Valley. A five-minute film orients visitors to the area. Brochures, maps, self-guided driving tours, and friendly travel counselors are on hand to help visitors plan their visits to Civil War sites. Ample parking, a gift shop with souvenirs, and restroom facilities are also available.

NEW MARKET BATTLEFIELD MILITARY MUSEUM

9500 Collins Drive, New Market, VA
PHONE: 540-740-8065
HOURS: Open daily March – November 1.
ADMISSION: A fee is charged; children are discounted; children under 6 are free

This military museum rests on the grounds of the Battle of New Market. The museum's collection of over 2,500 original artifacts is chronologically arranged in 130 displays and includes Stonewall Jackson's Bible. A self-guided walking tour of the battle site is included. An extensive book and gift shop is located in the museum.

LEE CHAPEL AND MUSEUM AT WASHINGTON AND LEE UNIVERSITY

Jefferson Street, Washington and Lee University, Lexington, VA
PHONE: 540-458-8768
WEB: chapelapps.wlu.edu
HOURS: Open daily; closed major holidays; see website or call for details.
ADMISSION: Free.

After the war, Gen. Robert E. Lee became president of Washington University; the name later changed to Washington and Lee, in his honor. Lee Chapel contains the Lee family crypt in which Lee, his wife, mother, father, and children are interred. Lee's horse, Traveller, is buried just outside the chapel. The museum contains exhibits on namesakes Generals and Lee and Washington.

Photo above: Lee Chapel, Washington and Lee University

*Photo left: Recumbent statue of Lee,
Lee Chapel, Washington and Lee University*

VIRGINIA MILITARY INSTITUTE MUSEUM

415 Letcher Avenue, Lexington, VA
PHONE: 540-464-7334
WEB: www.vmi.edu/museum
HOURS: Open daily 9AM – 5PM; closed December 23 – January 3.
ADMISSION: Free.

The VMI Museum is located on the institute's campus in Jackson Memorial Hall. Before earning his nickname "Stonewall," Thomas Jackson was a professor at VMI. The institute honors its famous alumnus at the VMI Museum. Among the museum's exhibits are the raincoat Jackson was wearing when he was shot; the hide of Jackson's horse, Little Sorrel; uniforms and weapons used by cadets in the Battle of New Market; and the Henry Stewart Antique Firearms Collection, including many Civil War–era pieces.

VMI's grounds are home to three notable monuments: Jackson Statue, Cadet Battery, and the New Market Statue. The Jackson Statue depicts General Jackson as he surveyed the field at Chancellorsville shortly before his death. Little Sorrel's bones are buried next to the statue. The guns preserved in the Cadet Battery monument were cast in 1848 and used by Jackson in cadet artillery training. The New Market Statue, also called "Vir-

VMI Museum

ginia Mourning Her Dead," is a memorial to the VMI cadets who fought at the 1864 Battle of New Market. This battle was the only incident when an entire school formed a single unit in battle. The statue honors the ten students who died in battle; six of the cadets are buried beneath the New Market Statue.

STONEWALL JACKSON HOUSE

8 East Washington Street, Lexington, VA

PHONE: 540-463-2552

WEB: www.stonewalljackson.org

HOURS: Open daily; closed major holidays. Call for winter operating hours.

ADMISSION: A fee is charged.

The Stonewall Jackson House was home to the Confederate General "Stonewall" Jackson and his wife Mary Anna just before the Civil War. The modest brick town house was the only home Jackson ever owned. Stonewall Jackson taught natural philosophy for ten years at VMI. The 1801 house and garden have been restored and include period furnishings and Jackson's personal belongings. Guided tours of the museum are available.

Photo left: Stonewall Jackson House

NEW MARKET BATTLEFIELD STATE HISTORICAL PARK/ HALL OF VALOR CIVIL WAR MUSEUM

8895 George R. Collins Parkway (State Route 305), New Market, VA

PHONE: 866-515-1864 (toll-free); 540-740-3101

WEB: www.vmi.edu/newmarket

HOURS: Open daily 9AM – 5PM; closed New Year's Day, Thanksgiving Day, Christmas Eve, and Christmas Day.

ADMISSION: Call for rates.

Located in Virginia's beautiful and historic Shenandoah Valley, the New Market Battlefield State Historical Park tells the story of one of the last major southern victories in the Civil War's "Breadbasket of the Confederacy." On May 15, 1864, Confederate forces under Maj. Gen. John C. Breckinridge defeated a larger Union army under the command of Maj. Gen. Franz Sigel on the Bushong family's farm near the town of New Market. Breckinridge's army included 257 Cadets from the Virginia Military Institute (VMI), facing their baptism of fire. Never before, nor since, has an entire college student body been called into pitched battle as were the VMI Cadets, ten of whom were killed or mortally wounded.

Established in 1967 and administered by VMI, the New Market Battlefield State Historical Park comprises nearly 300 acres of the core battleground, including the historic Bushong Farm and the Hall of Valor Civil War Museum. The Hall of Valor, one of the first Virginia museums accredited by the American Association of Museums, interprets the Battle of New Market and the saga of the entire Civil War in Virginia. Colorful dioramas, exhibits, and images describe the incredible acts of endurance and resilience demonstrated by soldiers of the North and South. The Hall of Valor also features an Emmy™ Award-winning film, *Field of Lost Shoes*, which depicts the battle in vivid detail. At the Bushong Farm, period room exhibits and markers describe the impact of war on the Shenandoah Valley's civilian population. Among annual Park programs are a Homeschool Day (March); the Battle of New Market Reenactment (May); Civil War Day Camps for children (July); and Spirits of New Market Lantern Tours (October). The Museum Store contains historical books, prints, ceramics, jewelry, toys, and souvenirs, including an extensive Civil War video collection.

Photo right:
Hall of Valor
Civil War
Museum

CEDAR CREEK BATTLEFIELD

8437 Valley Pike, Middletown, VA

PHONE: 540-869-2064

WEB: www.cedarcreekbattlefield.org

HOURS: Open daily April – October; open by appointment November – March; closed major holidays.

ADMISSION: Free; a fee is charged for special events and reenactments; children and active military are discounted.

On October 19, 1864, the Union dug in at Cedar Creek, not concerned about Confederate forces whom they had defeated at Kernstown and Fisher's Hill. General Sheridan, in fact, departed for a conference in Washington. Confederate General Early needed a quick victory to bolster his dwindling supplies and so tested the Union lines. Although this alerted acting Commander Wright of the Confederate intentions, the Union slowly gave ground until Sheridan's return inspired the Northern soldiers to regroup. In a counterattack, the Confederate line broke, and they fled south. Two future U.S. presidents, Rutherford B. Hayes and William McKinley, fought in the battle along with George Armstrong Custer. A museum, a Visitor's Center, a self-guided tour, and two battlefield monuments provide information on the battle. Each October, Cedar Creek Battlefield Foundation hosts a reenactment on the 308-acre site.

Cedar Creek Battlefield

"I again repeat that I am not responsible for this, and I say it with the earnestness of a general who feels in his heart the loss of every brave man who has been needlessly sacrificed today."

Maj. Gen. G. B. McClellan

NORTHERN COMMANDER:
Maj. Gen. G. B. McClellan

STRENGTH: 91,200

CASUALTIES: 16,000

SEVEN DAYS' BATTLES

June 25–July 1, 1862

Seven hard days of bloody battles saved the Confederate capital at Richmond from capture by the Union.

In May 1862, Federal forces were only seven miles from the Confederate White House in Richmond. Union commander, Major General George B. McClellan, was cautious and did not attack immediately. Instead, he waited for reinforcements. While McClellan waited, the recently appointed commander of the Confederate Army of Virginia, General Robert E. Lee, worked to fortify Richmond. Eventually, the Union initiated the Battle at Oak Grove on June 25.

This small battle commenced a week of fighting which would be known collectively as the Seven Days' Campaign. Particularly fierce fighting took place at Gaines' Mill. Here,

Watt House, Gaines' Mill site, Richmond National Battlefield Park

Union cannon overlooks battlefield from Malvern Hill,
Richmond National Battlefield Park

McClellan's troops under General Porter were entrenched along the Beaver Dam Creek with military bridges linking them to the main force. To attack, the Confederates charged across a cultivated field, down wooded slopes, and through Boatswain's Creek. Fighting that day was fierce, including hand-to-hand combat before the Confederates fell back for the evening. The second day saw what may have been the heaviest fighting of the war. Lee ordered an all-out assault, asking General Hood if he could break through Union lines. Hood succeeded with such force that a general Northern retreat ensued.

The seven days of fighting ceased at Malvern Hill on July 1. Confederate reconnaissance saw that the Malvern Hill plateau was suitable to mass its artillery against Union forces. This, combined with cannon on the left, would catch the Union in a deadly crossfire. Confederate artillery, however, could not get into position due to the wooded and swampy area and heavy Union fire. Lee began to look for another plan of attack but failed to notify his commanders of changes. Throughout the day, the Union prevented the Confederacy from serious assault. The next day, the Northern Army of the Potomac withdrew, relieving the Confederacy of any immediate threat to its capital, but at an extremely high price to the South. Lee lost one-fourth of his men, and the Confederate capital was again put out of the Union's reach. It would be three years before the Union got as close to Richmond.

RICHMOND NATIONAL BATTLEFIELD PARK ──────

Tredegar Iron Works, 470 Tredegar Street, Richmond, VA

PHONE: 804-771-2145

WEB: www.nps.gov/rich

HOURS: Open daily 9AM – 5PM; closed Thanksgiving, Christmas, and New Year's Day.

ADMISSION: Free; hourly parking charge.

Approximately 800 acres of Richmond National Battlefield Park are divided into ten units: Chickahominy Bluff; Beaver Dam Creek; Gaines' Mill (Watt House); Glendale (Frayser's Farm) where Union forces warded off Confederate forces; Malvern Hill; Drewry's Bluff; Cold Harbor; Garthright House; Fort Harrison; and Parker's Battery. A Visitor's Center sits on Chimborazo Hill, the site of a Confederate hospital, and offers orientation of the total park. An eighty-mile self-guided auto tour follows the Seven Days' Battles in chronological order. A narrated audio tour is available to purchase.

CHICKAHOMINY BLUFF

Chickahominy Bluff was a part of the outer Confederate line that formed Richmond's defense. Here, overlooking Mechanicsville and the Chickahominy River Valley, General Robert E. Lee watched the beginning of the Seven Days' Battles. The original earthworks are still intact.

BEAVER DAM CREEK

Ellerson's Mill, in the valley of Beaver Dam Creek, marks the point at which Lee's attack was stopped. The Confederates attacked the three-mile-long Union front here, but few Confederates crossed the stream due to heavy Union artillery and infantry fire.

COLD HARBOR

On May 31, 1864, Grant continued his incessant march toward Richmond, consistently driving around Lee's right to ensure that his army was resupplied from the tidal rivers; the next key was at the crossroads of Cold Harbor. The Southern cavalry reached Cold Harbor first, but General Phil Sheridan and the Union troops drove them out. Confederate General Anderson then advanced against Cold Harbor with two divisions. Sheridan, upon hearing this news, withdrew but returned under General Meade's order to hold the intersection at all costs, and Union forces retook it.

Although Cold Harbor was secured for the Union, Grant felt it necessary to attack again two days later, in an attempt to force Lee to retreat across the Chickahominy River. Nothing went well on June 3, to the extent that Grant "always regretted that the last assault at Cold Harbor was ever made." Lee was able to stave off the Union attacks and drive them into a stalemate. Although the Union advanced deeper into Virginia through another route that led to Petersburg, it was at a tremendous loss of life, half of which occurred that third day.

Cold Harbor is a unit of the Richmond National Battlefield Park. The national park currently manages 180 acres of the battlefield. There is a mile-long walking trail through trenches with explanatory stops to detail the fighting. A much longer hiking trail also explores the remote corners of the property. Cold Harbor National Cemetery is close by. Cold Harbor features a

Forest and Confederate Breastworks, Cold Harbor, Richmond National Battlefield Park

small visitor center that is open daily, except for Thanksgiving, Christmas, and New Year's Day, from 9AM to 5PM. It includes two electric map programs and a bookstore.

GARTHRIGHT HOUSE

The Garthright House was built in the early 1700s and served as a Union field hospital during the Battle of Cold Harbor. The house is restored but not open to the public; it can be viewed from the outside.

GAINES' MILL (WATT HOUSE)

Gaines' Mill was the site of extremely heavy fighting. During the summer of 1862, Lee ordered an all-out assault in an attempt to force the Union army back from Richmond. Hood found a gap in the Union line and penetrated with such force that a Union retreat ensued. The restored Watt House, built around 1820, was used as Union General Fitz John Porter's headquarters. A walking trail connects the home with the site where Texas and Georgia troops broke through the line and hastened Union withdrawal.

Photo right: Watt House at Gaines' Mill

DREWRY'S BLUFF

Northern troops referred to Drewry's Bluff as Fort Darling. The bluff was the guardian of the James River and prevented the capture of Richmond by water. Five Federal vessels attacked the bluff, including the iron-clad *Monitor*, but all were driven off. During the Civil War, this area served as the Confederate Naval Academy and Marine Corps Camp of Instruction. A self-guided trail gives details of the bluff's rich history.

Across the river from Fort Darling is Fort Brady, constructed by Union forces after the Battle of Fort Harrison. Fort Brady was built to anchor the Federal line from Fort Harrison. An overlook at the fort affords a panoramic view of the James River.

FORT HARRISON

Boatswain's Creek, Gaines' Mill, Richmond National Battlefield Park

After Cold Harbor, Grant, who had been deterred from capturing Richmond, crossed the James River and began a push against Petersburg. Union soldiers captured Fort Harrison on September 29. Union forces occupied and enlarged the fort, forcing a realignment of Richmond defenses. Several regiments of African-American Union troops were recognized on September 29, 1864, for gallantry, and fourteen soldiers received Congressional Medals of Honor.

A self-guided trail through Fort Harrison uses exhibits and plaques to provide details of the battle and the fort. In addition to Fort Harrison, the following sites—Battery Alexander, Forts Gilmer, Gregg, Johnson, and Hoke—contain remnants of Confederate defense works connected by miles of breastworks. Union soldiers are buried in Fort Harrison's national cemetery. A small visitor center is open May through August.

MALVERN HILL

On July 1, 1862, the last battle of the Seven Days' Battles took place at Malvern Hill. The Union army positioned itself between the steep slope of Malvern Hill and the swamp bottoms. The attacking Confederates were forced to advance across open ground. The Northern Army of the Potomac did not dig trenches but, instead, stood in parade-ground, line-of-battle formation across the gently sloping fields. Their artillery and infantry fire shattered the ranks of attacking Southerners. One Confederate officer later remarked, "It was not war—it was murder." A self-guided walking tour, about one-and-a-half miles long, winds through the battlefield.

GLENDALE (FRAYSER'S FARM)

On June 30, Union troops protected the crossroads at Glendale while McClellan's retreating army pushed south toward Malvern Hill. Throughout the afternoon, Confederates repeatedly assaulted Glendale but failed to take it. The Glendale National Cemetery features a summer-only visitor center with an electric map program and a general overview of both the Glendale and Malvern Hill battlefields.

PARKER'S BATTERY

Parker's Battery, a Confederate artillery work, was part of the defense of Richmond until the capital was abandoned in April 1865.

THE MUSEUM OF THE CONFEDERACY AND WHITE HOUSE

1201 East Clay Street, Richmond, VA
PHONE: 804-649-1861
WEB: www.moc.org
HOURS: Open daily.
ADMISSION: A fee is charged.

The Confederate White House was home to Jefferson Davis and his family while he was President of the Confederate States of America. The Museum's three levels of galleries feature items from the world's most comprehensive collection of artifacts related to the Confederacy, including "Stonewall" Jackson's forage cap, J.E.B. Stuart's LeMat pistol, and Robert E. Lee's field tent. The Museum's galleries are self-guided while the White House is viewed by guided tour only.

South Patio, The Museum and White House of the Confederacy

Center Parlor, The Museum and White House of the Confederacy

THE VIRGINIA HISTORICAL SOCIETY

428 North Boulevard, Richmond, VA
PHONE: 804-358-4901
WEB: www.vahistorical.org
HOURS: Tuesday – Saturday 10AM – 5PM; Sunday 1PM – 5PM; closed major holidays.
ADMISSION: A fee is charged; children and seniors are discounted. Members are free.

The Virginia Historical Society building houses the murals *The Four Seasons of the Confederacy* and the exhibition *The Story of Virginia, an American Experience*. The society's permanent collection contains many Civil War exhibits and features an impressive collection of Civil War artifacts, including General Lee's uniform and an extensive collection of Confederate-made weapons.

The Virginia Historical Society

HOLLYWOOD CEMETERY

412 South Cherry Street, Richmond, VA
PHONE: 804-648-8501
WEB: www.hollywoodcemetery.org
HOURS: Open daily, office open weekdays; closed major holidays.
ADMISSION: Free; a charge for brochure.

Hollywood Cemetery opened in the summer of 1849. Each day of the Civil War, bodies arrived from 10:00AM until noon for burial. Confederate soldiers were buried free of charge until the spring of 1862. As casualties mounted, however, the cemetery began charging one dollar to bury each soldier. Because of Northern blockades during the war, marble could not be obtained for headstones, and wooden markers were used. An estimated 14,000 Confederate soldiers are buried here in a Confederate soldiers' section marked by a pyramid dedicated to the women of the Confederacy who were prevented from being buried with their husbands and were interred elsewhere on the grounds. Other Confederates buried on the grounds include Generals George Pickett, J. E. B. Stuart, and Confederate President Jefferson Davis and his family. A bronze statue stands in memory of Davis, and a marble angel for Winnie, his daughter. Presidents James Monroe and John Tyler are also interred here.

VALENTINE RICHMOND HISTORY CENTER

VALENTINE RICHMOND HISTORY CENTER

1015 East Clay Street, Richmond, VA
PHONE: 804-649-0711
WEB: www.richmondhistorycenter.com
HOURS: Open daily.
ADMISSION: $7 – $10.

The Valentine Richmond History Center is dedicated to the life and history of the city of Richmond and includes artifacts from the Civil War era, as well as busts of many Confederate leaders. Public and group walking and bus tours of Hollywood Cemetery and other Civil War sites are available through pre-arrangement.

Valentine Richmond History Center

BELLE ISLE

An island in the James River, Richmond, VA
WEB: www.dcr.virginia.gov/state_parks/bel.shtml
HOURS: Open daily.
ADMISSION: Free.

Belle Isle is located in the James River and was the site of the Belle Isle prison camp for Union soldiers. A pedestrian bridge off Tredegar Street leads to what is now a city park.

*"I have only time to say
I have named you for the
command of the battery
under contract with Captain
Ericsson, now nearly ready
at New York. I believe you
are the right sort of officer to
put in command of her."*

Comm. J. Smith
to Lt. J. L. Worden
(Pictured above)

THE BATTLE OF HAMPTON ROADS

March 8–9, 1862

The first use of ironclad ships in battle.

At the beginning of the war, the South had naval personnel but no ships. The first logical step was to capture the Norfolk, Virginia, Naval Yard, a strategic port with all the resources to maintain a fleet. Following the attack on Fort Sumter in April, the Union chose not to risk valuable resources in protecting Norfolk. On April 20, 1861, Union troops set fire to the Norfolk Naval Yard. Northern forces left too early, however, and the Confederates hurried in, saved the dry dock, most of the important facilities, and the USS *Merrimac*. Although the ship had been burned to the water line, her hull and engines were only slightly damaged. She was hoisted up, repaired, and given the new name: CSS *Virginia*.

Now converted to the first armor-plated, cannon-mounted ship, the *Virginia* took its shakedown cruise to Hampton Roads, Virginia. There, the Union had instituted a blockade consisting of the sailing frigate *Congress*, the sailing sloop *Cumberland*, and the steam frigates *Minnesota* and *Roanoke*. The *Virginia* rammed the *Cumberland* below her waterline, sinking the Union sloop but tearing off the *Virginia's* ram. The *Virginia* turned to the *Congress*, which had run aground in shoal water, and brought all its firepower on the helpless ship. Within an hour, the *Congress* struck her colors, but when Confederate boarding parties approached, Union batteries fired upon them. Angered, Captain Franklin Buchanan ordered hot shot to be poured into the Union ship, setting it aflame. The *Virginia* then left the burning *Congress* and the other disabled ships for the next day.

When battle resumed the following morning, the *Virginia* encountered "the strangest looking craft we had ever seen before . . . an immense shingle floating in the water with a gigantic cheese box rising from its center; no sails, no wheels, no smokestack, no guns." This was the *Monitor*, the Union's answer to the Confederate ironclad. Its "cheesebox" was, in actuality, a revolving turret in which two cannons were mounted. The barely sea-

The Monitor *and the* Merrimac

worthy craft arrived at the entrance of the Chesapeake Bay on the evening of March 8. It took its position next to the disabled *Minnesota* and waited until morning.

On March 9, the *Virginia* began firing on the *Minnesota*, ignoring the shots from the *Monitor* for the first part of the morning. When the *Virginia* began exchanging shots with the *Monitor* they were from fifty to one hundred yards apart, sometimes close enough to scrape each other. Although the *Monitor* was more maneuverable, the *Virginia* could reload and fire faster. Neither vessel was seriously damaged after four hours of firing, at which time the *Virginia* broke off the combat and headed for Norfolk; the Battle of Hampton Roads was a draw. By its presence, the *Virginia* was able to prevent Union forces from using the James River for an offensive move into Richmond that spring.

Ironically, when Norfolk was abandoned in May 1862, the *Virginia* ran aground and was destroyed by her crew. The *Monitor* was lost in a storm off Cape Hatteras at the end of 1862 as she was being towed to waters off Charleston. The Battle of Hampton Roads ushered in a new type of naval warfare, one which the Union, with its resources, would dominate.

FORT BOYKIN HISTORIC PARK

7410 Fort Boykin Trail, Smithfield, VA
PHONE: 757-357-0115
HOURS: Open daily 8AM – dusk.
ADMISSION: Free.

Fort Boykin is located near the mouth of the James River and was initially constructed in 1623 to protect English settlers from the Spaniards. During the Revolutionary War, the colonists refortified the fort and used it again in 1812. At the start of the Civil War, the Confederates reinforced Fort Boykin to protect Richmond. In May 1862, Union gunboats sailed up the James River, fired upon Fort Boykin, and forced the Confederates to retreat. A walking trail includes remainders of Civil War gun salients and magazines. Confederate artifacts were excavated from a well and are on display at the Isle of Wight County Museum.

Fort Boykin Historic Park

HAMPTON ROADS NAVAL MUSEUM

1 Waterside Drive, Norfolk, VA
PHONE: 757-322-2987
WEB: www.hrnm.navy.mil
HOURS: Tuesday – Saturday 10AM – 5PM, Sunday 12PM – 5PM; closed Thanksgiving, Christmas Eve, and Christmas Day.
ADMISSION: Free.

This specialized naval history museum displays material on the battle of the ironclads at Hampton Roads, as well as other Civil War actions. An exhibit, which includes models of the *Monitor* and the *Merrimac*, help interpret the Battle of Hampton Roads. Material recovered from Civil War shipwrecks is also on display.

Naval exhibit, Hampton Roads Naval Museum

THE CASEMATE MUSEUM

Bernard Road, Fort Monroe, Hampton, VA
PHONE: 757-788-3391
HOURS: Open daily; closed Thanksgiving, Christmas, and New Year's Day.
ADMISSION: Free.

Fort Monroe was built between 1819 and 1834 to protect Hampton Roads, the entrance to Chesapeake Bay, and Washington, D.C. Ironically, when Robert E. Lee was in the Corps of Army Engineers, he helped complete the fort's construction. The fort was held by the Union throughout the war and served as the beginning point for the Union Peninsula Campaign. The fort cur-

The Casemate Museum

rently serves as the headquarters for the United States Army Training and Doctrine Command.

Located on the grounds of Fort Monroe and surrounded by a moat, The Casemate Museum's exhibits include the cell where Confederate President Jefferson Davis was incarcerated, weapons, uniforms, coastal artillery models, and drawings of Fort Monroe at the time of the Civil War. A self-guided walking tour of Fort Monroe is available.

THE MARINERS' MUSEUM

100 Museum Drive, Newport News, VA
PHONE: 757-596-2222
WEB: www.marinersmuseum.org
HOURS: Wednesday – Saturday 10AM – 5PM; Sunday 12PM – 5PM; closed Thanksgiving and Christmas.
ADMISSION: A fee is charged; students are discounted and children under 5 are free.

The Mariners' Museum protects the *Monitor* shipwreck sanctuary located off the coast of Cape Hatteras, North Carolina, and serves as the official repository for artifacts recovered from the Union's ironclad. Part of the museum is dedicated to the clash of the ironclads, and items on display include the *Monitor*'s anchor, lanterns, mustard jars, and, a more recent find, the propeller. One exhibit features a reconstruction of the *Monitor*'s turret and the "Geer Letters," a display of letters written by a crew member of the *Monitor* to his wife.

Crabtree Collection of Miniature Ships, The Mariners' Museum

VIRGINIA WAR MUSEUM

9285 Warwick Boulevard, Huntington Park, Newport News, VA
PHONE: 757-247-8523
WEB: www.warmuseum.org
HOURS: Open daily; closed Thanksgiving, Christmas, and New Year's Day.
ADMISSION: A fee is charged; children, seniors, and active duty military are discounted.

The Virginia War Museum contains artifacts from all of America's wars. Civil War exhibits include items from the Peninsula Campaign, including weapons, uniforms, personal items, artwork, and recruitment posters. The Civil War naval display features artifacts that include a naval uniform.

Virginia War Museum

LEE HALL MANSION

163 Yorktown Road, Newport News, VA
PHONE: 757-888-3371
HOURS: Open daily; closed major holidays.
ADMISSION: A fee is charged; children and seniors are discounted.

Lee Hall Mansion was built by Richard D. Lee (no relation to Robert E. Lee), who was a wealthy planter in the area. During the war, the mansion was used as a Confederate headquarters by Generals Magruder and Johnston. The original earthworks which surrounded the house are visible. The house features a Peninsula Campaign exhibit and rooms decorated with period furnishings.

Lee Hall Mansion

ENDVIEW PLANTATION

362 Yorktown Road, Newport News, VA
PHONE: 757-887-1862
WEB: www.endview.org
HOURS: April 1 – December 31:
Monday, Thursday, Friday 10AM – 4:30PM;
Saturday 10AM – 5PM; Sunday 12PM – 5PM.
January 1 – March 31: Thursday – Saturday
10AM – 4PM; Sunday 1PM – 5PM.
ADMISSION: Free.

Endview Plantation

Built in 1769, Endview Plantation functioned
as a Confederate hospital and headquarters for
Gens. McLaws and Toombs during the Peninsula Campaign of 1862. The plantation's former
owner, Dr. Humphrey Harwood Curtis, was instrumental in organizing the Warwick Beaure-
gards at the onset of war. The cannons roar again each spring as part of a Civil War reenactment.
Historical programs and children's summer camps are also offered.

BERKELEY PLANTATION

12602 Harrison Landing Road, Charles City, VA
PHONE: 1-888-466-6018
WEB: www.berkeleyplantation.com
HOURS: Open daily; closed Thanksgiving and Christmas Day.
ADMISSION: A fee is charged.

Berkeley Plantation was the
final stop of McClellan's Union
Peninsula Campaign and served
as the general's 1862 headquarters and as a base for 140,000
soldiers. President Lincoln visited Berkeley on two occasions
during McClellan's encampment. In 1862 Gen. Daniel
Butterfield composed "Taps,"
the now-familiar retreat played
at every military funeral. Civil
War artifacts are on display in
the main house.

Photo left: Berkeley Plantation

PORTSMOUTH NAVAL SHIPYARD MUSEUM

2 High Street, Portsmouth, VA
PHONE: 757-393-8591
WEB: www.portsnavalmuseums.com
HOURS: Open daily Memorial Day –
Labor Day; closed Monday September – May.
ADMISSION: A fee is charged
(please call for details).

Portsmouth Naval Shipyard Museum

The Portsmouth Naval Shipyard Museum chronicles the history of the City of Portsmouth and the Norfolk Naval Shipyard, from the colonial period through World War II. The museum's Civil War exhibit, *Resistance & Reunion*, discusses the role of the city and the shipyard (at the time known as Gosport Navy Yard) under both Confederate and Union occupation. The exhibit covers the destruction of the Navy Yard, construction of the CSS *Virginia*, the Battle of Hampton Roads, and life during occupation through the use of images, documents, relics, ship models, and weaponry.

STRATFORD HALL PLANTATION

483 Great House Road, Stratford, VA
PHONE: 804-493-8038
WEB: www.stratfordhall.org
HOURS: Open daily March – mid-December;
weekends January – March.
ADMISSION: A fee is charged.

General Robert E. Lee was born at Stratford Hall on January 19, 1807. Though he spent fewer than four years here, his later boyhood visits left an impression that carried throughout his life. He would write to his wife Mary on Christmas Day of 1861: "In the absence of a home I wish I could purchase Stratford. That is the only place I could go to, now accessible to us, that would inspire me with feelings of pleasure and local love."

A visitor center provides information concerning the plantation's history and the Lee

The bedchamber in the Great House where Robert E. Lee was born, Stratford Hall

Great House, circa 1738, Stratford Hall

family. Guided Great House tours are available. The 1,900-acre property on the Potomac River includes a gift shop, dining room open for lunch, as well as on-site lodging.

ISLE OF WIGHT MUSEUM

103 Main Street, Smithfield, VA
PHONE: 757-356-1223
WEB: www.co.isle-of-wight.va.us
HOURS: Open daily.
ADMISSION: Free.

Interpreting local history, the museum's exhibits include prehistoric fossils, Native American and Colonial artifacts, a country store, and artifacts from the two nearby Civil War–era forts: Fort Boykin and Fort Huger, two sites chosen in 1861 by Confederate engineer Colonel Andrew Talcott for defensive fortifications on the James River to protect Richmond.

Isle of Wight Museum

Isle of Wight Museum

THE BATTLE AND SIEGE OF PETERSBURG

June 15, 1864–April 1, 1865

The fall of Petersburg came only days before the surrender of the Confederate capital at Richmond and the end of the Civil War at Appomattox Court House.

Petersburg, located on the south bank of the Appomattox River, was a major Virginia shipping port. The Richmond and Petersburg Railroad funneled all major railroad lines into the city. Control of Petersburg was essential to a Union capture of Richmond.

Lieutenant General Ulysses S. Grant began his campaign to capture Petersburg in June 1864. General Robert E. Lee was aware of Grant's intentions and set up a horseshoe defense around Petersburg with its ends on the Appomattox River. When Grant attacked, his Eighteenth Corps captured a section of the Confederate line but did not press their success. The Confederates then built a new line, which could not be directly assaulted; thus Grant planned a siege of Petersburg.

Six major battles and numerous engagements, skirmishes, and assaults marked the siege. Throughout the summer and fall, Grant continued to hammer away at Lee, who had his 59,000 men spread over a thirty-five-mile line. Grant finally

Battle of Fort Stedman, Petersburg National Battlefield

The Dictator, Petersburg National Battlefield

gained control over the rails and forced Lee to supply his men by wagons. When winter set in, the men created log cities to protect themselves from the sleet and snow.

On March 25, 1865, Confederate forces stormed Fort Stedman on the north flank but were driven back with 5,000 casualties. On March 29, Grant ordered an all-out attack. After five days of fighting, Lee evacuated Petersburg on the evening of April 2, and by three o'clock on the morning of April 3, Grant occupied Petersburg.

Like Petersburg, Richmond was also evacuated and formally surrendered on April 3, 1865. The Confederate capital was in Union hands, and the Civil War was within days of its end.

The Crater, Petersburg National Battlefield

PETERSBURG NATIONAL BATTLEFIELD ————

5001 Siege Road, Petersburg, VA

PHONE: 804-732-3531

WEB: www.nps.gov/pete

HOURS: Open daily; closed Christmas and New Year's Day.

ADMISSION: A fee is charged.

Petersburg National Battlefield contains almost 2,700 acres of the original battle and siege area, including City Point, Five Forks, the battlefield itself, the siege line, and Poplar Grove National Cemetery. Information on a four-mile battlefield tour, a sixteen-mile siege-line tour, a driving

Five Forks Battlefield

tour, and short walking tours, which include wayside exhibits and audio stations, are available at the Visitor's Center. Points along the driving tour include Battery 8, captured by U.S. African-American troops and renamed Fort Friend; Battery 9, which U.S. African-American troops captured during the first day of fighting; Harrison Creek; Fort Stedman, the focus of Lee's attack on March 25, 1865; Fort Haskell, where Union artillery and infantry fire stopped the Confederate southward advance during the Battle of Fort Stedman; Taylor Farm; and The Crater, which marks the site where a Union mine exploded beneath a Confederate fort. During this episode, the Forty-eighth Pennsylvania Infantry, many of whom were coal miners before the war, dug a tunnel toward a Confederate fort. The explosion destroyed the artillery battery and left a crater about 170 feet long, sixty feet wide, and thirty feet deep. Union troops, instead of going around the crater, plunged directly into it and were unable to go any further. Confederate counterattacks retook the position, inflicting more than 4,000 Federal casualties. Ranger-guided tours of the Fort Stedman and Crater Battlefields are offered on a daily basis during the summers.

A roster of the soldiers interred at Poplar Grove is at the Visitor's Center. Of the 6,178 Union soldiers buried at Poplar Grove, only 2,139 are identified.

PETERSBURG VISITOR'S CENTER ————

19 Bollingbrook Street, Petersburg, VA

PHONE: 804-733-2400

HOURS: Open daily; closed Christmas.

ADMISSION: Free.

Petersburg's ten-month siege was the longest siege of any American city, and much of historic Petersburg is devoted to this period. The Visitor's Center offers information on walking tours of historic Petersburg along with maps that detail the Civil War Trail, an eighty-mile driving tour that follows the 1864–1865 overland campaign of Lee and Grant.

PAMPLIN HISTORICAL PARK AND THE NATIONAL MUSEUM OF THE CIVIL WAR SOLDIER

6125 Boydton Plank Road, Petersburg, VA
PHONE: 804-861-2408
WEB: www.pamplinpark.org
HOURS: Open daily year round.
ADMISSION: A fee is charged; children are discounted.

Pamplin Historical Park's three miles of walking trails feature reconstructed soldier huts, original picket posts, well-preserved earthworks, and artillery emplacements. A reconstructed military encampment reflects the variety of architectural styles used by the soldiers during the Civil War's final year. A renovated and refurbished 1812 plantation home, Tudor Hall, is also on the trail. A free audio guide is available. The museum's collection focuses on the life of an ordinary Civil War soldier, and exhibits range from a chaplain's sermon at a camp revival to a wounded and imprisoned soldier.

The National Museum of the Civil War Soldier, Pamplin Historical Park

SIEGE MUSEUM

15 West Bank Street, Petersburg, VA
PHONE: 804-733-2400
WEB: www.petersburg-va.org/tourism/siege.htm
HOURS: See website.
ADMISSION: A fee is charged.

Exhibits at the Siege Museum interpret the effects of the siege on the people of Petersburg. During the ten-month siege, supplies were scarce, and a chicken could sell for as much as fifty dollars. The museum's displays interpret life in Petersburg before, during, and immediately after the siege.

Photo right: Siege Museum

BLANDFORD CHURCH

319 South Crater Road, Petersburg, VA
PHONE: 804-733-2396
WEB: www.petersburg-va.org/tourism/blandford.htm
HOURS: See website.
ADMISSION: A fee is charged.

Blandford Church, circa 1735, was active until the early nineteenth century. During the Civil War, the building was used as a Confederate hospital after the Battle of the Crater. By the early 1900s, the Ladies Memorial Association of Petersburg restored Blandford Church as a Confederate Memorial Chapel and commissioned Louis Comfort Tiffany to design fifteen windows to commemorate the sacrifice of southern soldiers. The LMA was also responsible for approximately 30,000 Confederate burials in Blandford Cemetery.

Photo right: Blandford Church

CITY POINT UNIT

Far end of Cedar Lane and Pecan Avenue, Hopewell, VA
PHONE: 804-458-9504
WEB: www.nps.gov/pete
HOURS: Open daily; closed Christmas and New Year's Day.
ADMISSION: A fee is charged.

The City Point Unit is a part of the Petersburg National Battlefield and features Appomattox Manor. The home originally belonged to the Epps family, but during the war it served as General Grant's headquarters from June 1864 to April 1865. An orientation film and guided tours of Appomattox Manor are available.

Photo right: Appomattox Manor, City Point Unit

Weston Plantation

400 Weston Lane at the corner of 21st Avenue, Hopewell, VA
Phone: 804-458-4682
Web: www.historichopewell.org/weston-plantation
Hours: Open daily.
Admission: A fee is charged.

Weston Plantation

Built in 1789, Weston Plantation briefly served as Union Gen. Philip Sheridan's headquarters during the final siege of Petersburg. During the Civil War, thirteen-year-old Emma Wood lived there with her family. Later, at the age of seventy-five, Wood wrote her memoirs. The home features these experiences in period furnishings, and a guided tour is available.

City Point National Cemetery

10th Avenue and Davis Street, Hopewell, VA
Phone: 804-795-2031
Web: www.cem.va.gov
Hours: Open daily dawn to dusk.
Admission: Free.

More than 5,100 Civil War Union and Confederate soldiers are buried at the City Point National Cemetery. The interred Federal soldiers include more than 1,000 African-Americans.

Staunton River Battlefield State Park

1035 Fort Hill Trail, Randolph, VA
Phone: 434-454-4312
Web: www.stauntonriverbattlefield.org
Hours: Open daily.
Admission: Free.

One of the many minor engagements in the Siege of Petersburg, the Staunton River Battle occurred on June 25, 1864, when 492 old men and young boys from Southside, Virginia, joined fewer than 300 Confederate soldiers against 5,000 Union cavalry for control of the Staunton River railroad bridge. Although the Union wreaked havoc, they could not destroy the Staunton River Bridge. The bridge was burned during General Lee's retreat to Appomattox Court House but was rebuilt by the railroad within weeks of the end of the war. The current steel bridge was constructed in 1902 on the original stone piers. The park offers a walking tour of the battlefield, which includes remnants of earthworks, an earthen fort, and the rebuilt bridge. The Visitor's Center features exhibits and brochures on the history of the bridge and the battle.

THE SURRENDER AT APPOMATTOX COURT HOUSE

April 9, 1865

This was last Civil War battle in the east and the site of General Robert E. Lee's surrender.

After the battle of Sailor's Creek, General Robert E. Lee split his Army of Northern Virginia into two parts and headed to North Carolina to meet with General Johnston's army. The Union pursued and captured 8,000 Confederates, including most of Ewell's Corps and Anderson's Corps. Lee pushed on. Tired and low on rations, he and his men rested around Appomattox Court House, where they hoped to find the supplies Lee left at Farmville after the Battle of Sailor's Creek.

Lee soon found himself surrounded by Union forces in the west, south, and east. On April 7, General Ulysses S. Grant sent Lee a note suggesting surrender. Lee declined but asked about the terms. Grant replied on April 8 that the Confederates should give up their arms never to fight again and go home. Lee asked to meet and talk, but Grant said he would only meet if it were to discuss surrender. The last message of Grant's did not reach Lee until the morning of April 9. In the meantime,

Appomattox Courthouse, Appomattox Court House National Historic Park

Lee's Surrender to Grant, *Artist Unknown*

Lee met with his commanders to discuss options. Lee agreed to advance his cavalry to the front, attack, and possibly break through Union General Sheridan's line in the west. When the Confederates attacked, Sheridan pulled back, not out of weakness, but to allow Gibbon's infantry to join. Lee was forced to withdraw and called off the engagement.

Just after noon on April 9, Grant met Lee at the home of Wilmer McLean. (Ironically, McLean's former home was located on the battlefield at Manassas. After the battle, he moved to Appomattox Court House to get away from the war.) At the McLean house, Grant proposed the same terms as in his message and, at Lee's request, added that the Southerners could take their horses with them. Grant also authorized rations for Lee's men. The formal surrender ceremony was held April 12, 1865. Brigadier General Joshua Chamberlain, famous from Gettysburg, was given the honor of receiving Lee's surrender.

Only 22,000 Confederates were there to lay down their arms and furl their flags for the last time. Chamberlain formed his troops on either side of the road and saluted their enemies, who were once again their countrymen. Confederate General Gordon ordered his men to return the salute.

Although it would be another four months before all fighting ceased, Lee's surrender to Grant at Appomattox Court House symbolically ended the war.

APPOMATTOX COURT HOUSE NATIONAL HISTORIC PARK

Virginia Highway 24, Appomattox, VA

PHONE: 434-352-8987
WEB: www.nps.gov/apco
HOURS: Open daily; closed major holidays.
ADMISSION: A fee is charged.

Over twenty buildings in the Appomattox Court House Village have been restored to their 1865 appearance. This national historic site commemorates General Robert E. Lee's surrender to General Ulysses S. Grant. Ten historic buildings in the village are open to the public, including the McLean House, where Generals Lee

Parlor of McLean House, Appomattox Court House National Historic Park

and Grant met. Outside the village, the battlefield, Lee's headquarters, and Grant's headquarters are also open for touring. Orientation videos, maps, and self-guided walking tours of the village are

McLean House, Appomattox Court House National Historic Park

available at the Visitor's Center. During the summer, costumed interpreters conduct living history programs. A small Confederate cemetery is also located inside the park.

OLD CITY CEMETERY

401 Taylor Street, Lynchburg, VA
PHONE: 434-847-1465
WEB: www.gravegarden.org
HOURS: Open daily; office open daily 11AM – 3PM March – October; closed Sundays November – February.
ADMISSION: Free.

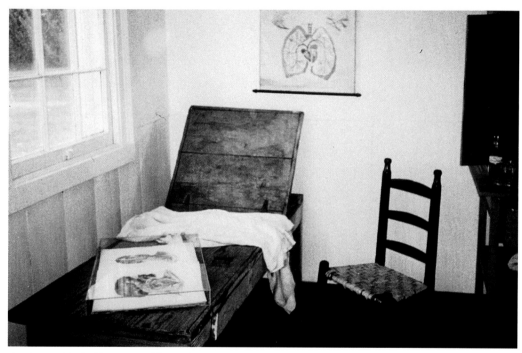

Pest House Medical Museum, Old City Cemetery

The Old City Cemetery contains the cemetery, the Pest House Medical Museum, a Potter's Field, and the site of the Quartermaster's Glanders Stables. A greenstone arch marks the entrance to the Civil War section where over 2,200 soldiers from fourteen states are interred and provides the setting for the 125-year tradition of the Memorial Day service. Eleven slaves who worked in the hospital are buried in the Confederate section. Two African-American soldiers, one Confederate, and the other Union, also rest in the cemetery. Originally, the cemetery contained the remains of 187 Yankee prisoners. Although their bodies were moved in 1866, their names still appear on a commemorative plaque.

The Pest House Medical Museum, next to the Confederate Section, relives the time of the smallpox epidemic and Dr. John Jay Terrell's successful efforts to stop the deadly disease. A self-guided tour is available with recorded narratives. Inside, tours are available by appointment.

WASHINGTON, D.C.

During the Civil War, the nation's capital was surrounded by a series of sixty-eight forts and ninety-three batteries with 837 guns to protect it from the foreign nation across the Potomac River. Although only one skirmish took place near Fort Stevens, Washington, D.C., was forever changed by the Civil War. Even the Washington Monument, the 555-foot obelisk that has come to symbolize our country, was affected by the war. Begun in 1848, construction was halted by the Civil War. When construction resumed, builders used marble from a different quarry, resulting in a noticeable color difference.

Directly west of the monument is the Lincoln Memorial. Lincoln's Gettysburg Address and Second Inaugural Speech are carved into the walls surrounding Lincoln's statue. The Emancipation Proclamation rests in the National Archives, only a few blocks away. Lincoln's presence is also felt nightly at Ford's Theatre, the site of his assassination.

Also situated on the Mall, the city's symbolic center, is the Smithsonian Institution's National Museum of American History. Items ranging from military relics to Civil War-era life are housed in the massive collection. Nearby, the National Portrait Gallery contains a number of Mathew Brady's Civil War photographs. Brady documented the battles and their terrible aftermath in photographs. Brady's work can also be seen at the Library of Congress.

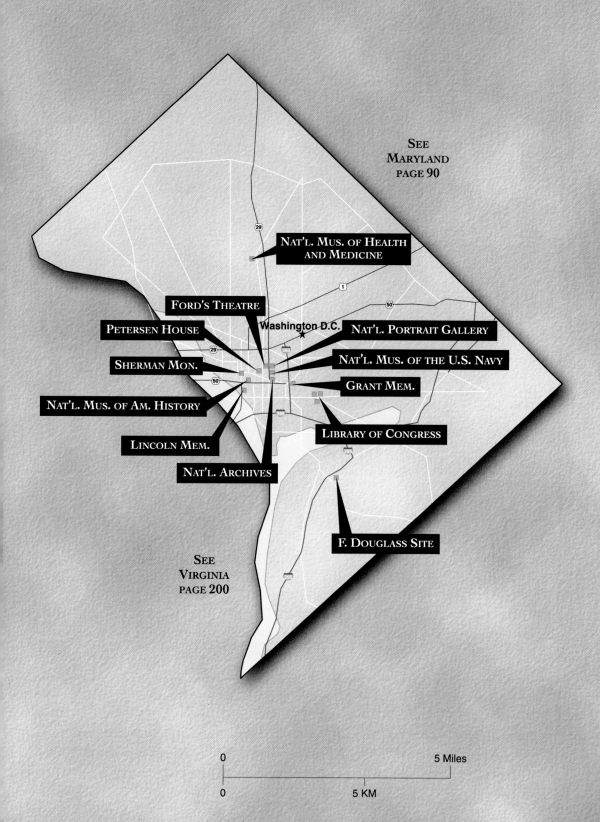

SEE
MARYLAND
PAGE 90

NAT'L. MUS. OF HEALTH
AND MEDICINE

FORD'S THEATRE

Washington D.C.

NAT'L. PORTRAIT GALLERY

PETERSEN HOUSE

NAT'L. MUS. OF THE U.S. NAVY

SHERMAN MON.

GRANT MEM.

NAT'L. MUS. OF AM. HISTORY

LINCOLN MEM.

LIBRARY OF CONGRESS

NAT'L. ARCHIVES

F. DOUGLASS SITE

SEE
VIRGINIA
PAGE 200

0   5 Miles

0   5 KM

NATIONAL MUSEUM OF HEALTH AND MEDICINE

6900 Georgia Avenue and Elder Street (at Walter Reed Army Medical Center, Building 54), Washington, DC
PHONE: 202-782-2200
WEB: www.nmhm.washingtondc.museum
HOURS: Open daily 10AM – 5:30PM; closed Christmas.
ADMISSION: Free.

The National Museum of Health and Medicine contains a great deal of information pertaining to Civil War medical practices. Among the exhibits are many Mathew Brady photographs and a model of the *Captain January*, the first hospital on water. This boat was used to transport the injured from one side of the Mississippi River to the other side. A popular exhibit, entitled *The Bullet That Killed Lincoln*, features the bullet fired at Ford's Theatre, casts of Lincoln's hands, and a description of the assassination. Another popular exhibit is a display of General Sickle's leg and the cannonball that blew the leg off. After its amputation, Sickle donated his leg to the U.S.; later he wanted the leg returned. He was told that it was now the property of the U.S. government. Until his death, Sickle made regular trips to visit his leg.

SHERMAN MONUMENT

Pennsylvania Avenue and 15th Street NE, Washington, DC
WEB: www.nps.gov/whho
HOURS: Open daily.
ADMISSION: Free.

Sherman Monument stands on the spot where, in 1865, General William T. Sherman reviewed his victorious army. The monument is located east of the White House and south of the Department of Treasury.

NATIONAL MUSEUM OF AMERICAN HISTORY

14th Street and Constitution Avenue NW, Washington, DC
PHONE: 202-633-1000
WEB: americanhistory.si.edu
HOURS: Open daily 10AM – 5:30PM; closed Christmas Day.
ADMISSION: Free.

The Smithsonian's National Museum of American History holds extensive collections that document the history of the men and women of the armed forces of the United States, including ordnance, firearms, and swords; uniforms and insignia; flags and banners; military and naval accoutrements; and more. *The Price of Freedom: Americans at War*, a permanent exhibition, surveys the history of America's military and explores ways in which wars have been defining episodes in American history. This exhibition includes an extensive section on the Civil War and includes such artifacts as the flag of the Eighty-fourth Regiment U.S. Colored Infantry, which fought in many campaigns of the Civil War in Louisiana and Texas; and the models of the ironclads *Monitor* and *Virginia*, better known as the *Merrimack*. Union Gen. Philip Sheridan's horse is also on display. Sheridan rode the horse, named Rienzi, to the town of Winchester in northwestern Virginia to turn a potential defeat for the Union forces into a victory. Rienzi was later renamed Winchester. One of the main attractions of the museum is the 1814, fifteen-star, fifteen-stripe flag that inspired Francis Scott Key to write *The Star-Spangled Banner*. For up-to-date information on displays and programs, please check the website prior to your visit.

LINCOLN MEMORIAL

23rd Street NE (west end of the Mall), Washington, DC
WEB: www.nps.gov/linc
HOURS: Open daily.
ADMISSION: Free.

The classical columns of the Lincoln Memorial anchor the eastern axis of the Mall. The white marble statue of Lincoln, designed and sculpted by Daniel Chester French, surveys the Reflecting Pool and, beyond it, the Washington Monument. On the walls, the words of Lincoln's Gettysburg Address and Lincoln's Second Inaugural Address serve as a constant reminder of the sixteenth president's place in national history. Ironically, the 1922 dedication ceremony, which was attended by Lincoln's son, Robert Todd, was segregated; African-Americans, including Booker T. Washington who gave a speech, watched from across the road. In 1963, Martin Luther King, Jr. chose the site to deliver his stirring "I Have a Dream" speech.

Lincoln Memorial

PETERSEN HOUSE

516 10th Street NW, Washington, DC
PHONE: 202-426-6830
HOURS: Open daily; closed Christmas.
ADMISSION: Free.

Across the street from Ford's Theatre National Historic Site is the house where Lincoln died. After the shooting, Lincoln was moved across the street to the Petersen boarding house. The bedroom where Lincoln died and the front parlor where Mrs. Lincoln sat through the night have been restored. Also on display is the back parlor in which Secretary of War Edwin Stanton interviewed witnesses to the assassination.

Photo left: Petersen House

FORD'S THEATRE NATIONAL HISTORIC SITE

511 10th Street NW, Washington, DC
PHONE: 202-347-4833
WEB: www.fords.org
HOURS: Open daily; Museum:
9AM – 4PM; Theatre: 9AM – 4:30PM;
closed Thanksgiving Day and
Christmas Day.
ADMISSION: Free; requires ticket
(can be reserved online).

On April 14, 1865, John Wilkes
Booth fatally shot President Abraham Lincoln at Ford's Theatre. The
interior is restored as closely as pos-

Exterior view of Ford's Theatre National Historic Site

sible to the building's original appearance. The president's box looks as it did on the night of the
assassination, although some of the pieces of furniture are reproductions.

Both Ford's Theatre and the Lincoln Museum underwent renovations completed in 2009.
The museum now allows for a richer visitor experience with topics covering Lincoln's presidency from his first arrival in Washington, Civil War milestones, and a look at life in the White

House. The museum also features video elements, audio
tours, and the National Park
Service collection of assassination artifacts, including the
murder weapon and other
memorabilia.

*Photo left: View from the stage
of the President's Box at Ford's
Theatre, following an 18-month
renovation*

NATIONAL PORTRAIT GALLERY

8th and F Streets NW, Washington, DC
PHONE: 202-633-1000
WEB: npg.si.edu
HOURS: Open daily 11:30AM – 7PM; closed December 25.
ADMISSION: Free.

The National Portrait Gallery, with the only complete collection of Presidential portraits outside of the White House, tells the stories of America through the individuals who have influenced American history and culture. The museum's collection of more than 20,000 paintings, drawings, photographs, sculptures, and new media features likenesses that are valued for both their subjects and the artists who created them. Part of the Smithsonian, this national museum contains portraits of many Civil War leaders, including Lincoln, Grant, and other generals. The museum also holds thousands of collodial wet-plate glass negatives by Mathew Brady.

NATIONAL MUSEUM OF THE U.S. NAVY

Washington Navy Yard, Building 76, Washington, DC
PHONE: 202-433-4882
WEB: www.history.navy.mil/branches/org8-1.htm
HOURS: Open daily; closed Thanksgiving, Christmas, and New Year's Day.
ADMISSION: Free.

The National Museum of the U.S. Navy features various items that illustrate the long and varied history of the U.S. Navy. Of particular interest is a Civil War 100-pound cannon taken from the CSS *Atlanta* which was captured by the U.S. monitor *Weehawken*.

NATIONAL ARCHIVES

Constitution Avenue NW (between 7th and 9th Streets), Washington, DC
PHONE: 202-357-5000
WEB: www.archives.gov/nae
HOURS: March 15 – Labor Day: 10AM – 7PM; Day after Labor Day – March 14: 10AM – 5:30PM; closed Thanksgiving Day and Christmas Day.
ADMISSION: Free.

The U.S. Constitution and Bill of Rights are on permanent display at the National Archives. The Emancipation Proclamation is housed here and is displayed in January to coincide with the Martin Luther King, Jr., holiday.

GRANT MEMORIAL

East end of the Mall, Washington, DC
WEB: www.nps.gov/gegr
HOURS: Open daily.
ADMISSION: Free.

At the time of the statue's dedication in 1922, the Grant Memorial was the largest cast sculpture in the United States. Today, it remains as the city's largest statue dedicated to a general. The 252-foot-long sculpture features a calm General Grant surveying seven charging horsemen and three horses hauling cannons through mud.

LIBRARY OF CONGRESS

1st Street SE, between Independence Avenue and East Capitol Streets, Washington, DC
PHONE: 202-707-8000
WEB: www.loc.gov
HOURS: Open daily, except Sunday, 8:30AM – 4:30PM;
closed Thanksgiving Day, Christmas Day, and New Year's Day.
ADMISSION: Free.

The Library of Congress is open to both visitors and researchers (those 16 years and older may obtain a research card). The Library's collections contain materials on the Civil War in many formats, including over 1,200 Civil War photographs, most of which were made under the supervision of Mathew B. Brady. These include scenes of military personnel, preparations for battle and the aftermath of battle, and portraits of Confederate and Union generals. Civil War–related collections also include

Main Reading Room, Library of Congress

maps, newspapers, manuscripts, genealogical assets, and books. Many materials have been digitized and are available via the Library's website. Guided tours are offered of the historic Thomas Jefferson Building which include the overlook to the Main Reading Room. Exhibitions highlighting the Library's Civil War collections are planned during the period of 2011–2015.

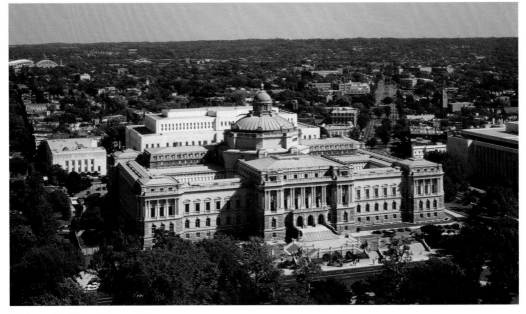

Jefferson Building, Library of Congress

FREDERICK DOUGLASS NATIONAL HISTORIC SITE

1411 W Street SE, Washington, DC
PHONE: 202-426-5961
WEB: www.nps.gov/frdo
HOURS: Open daily; closed major holidays.
ADMISSION: A fee is charged to view the house (reservations are recommended during the summer months); Visitor Center and grounds are free.

Born a slave, Frederick Douglass was one of the most ardent and eloquent speakers for abolition before and during the Civil War. Douglass purchased Cedar Hill, his final home, in 1877 and expanded the house from fourteen to twenty-one rooms. In addition, he purchased the adjoining land to expand its acreage. Seventy percent of the objects at Cedar Hill today belonged to Douglass, including portraits of his two sons who served in the 54th Massachusetts during the Civil War. Tours are available and begin with a film at the Visitor Center.

Photo above: Douglass's Study,
Frederick Douglass National Historic Site

Frederick Douglass National Historic Site

WEST VIRGINIA

At the beginning of the Civil War, both the South and the North began military operations to secure that region of Virginia which is now known as West Virginia. On May 14 , 1861, General George McClellan was assigned to command the Department of the Ohio which included the area of Western Virginia. McClellan's success in securing the area for the Union during the summer of 1861 led to his being named to command all of the Union armies.

During the remainder of the war, West Virginia saw fighting in its mountains and sent troops into battle under the banner of "The Army of West Virginia." The area was officially admitted as a state June 20, 1863, although the transfer of Berkley and Jefferson counties from Virginia to West Virginia was not recognized by Congress until March 10, 1866.

Today, West Virginia protects its rich Civil War heritage, through sites such as Harpers Ferry National Historical Park, where John Brown captured the city in 1859, and the Monongahela National Forest, which contains remnants of both Northern and Southern forts.

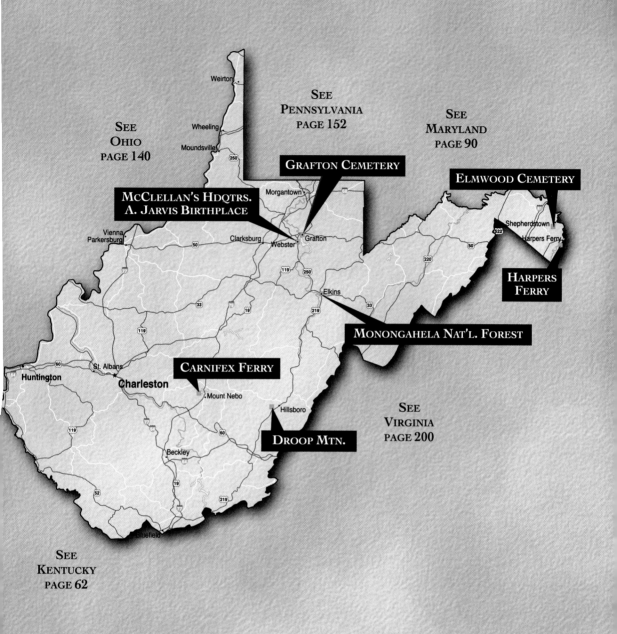

SEE
OHIO
PAGE 140

SEE
PENNSYLVANIA
PAGE 152

SEE
MARYLAND
PAGE 90

GRAFTON CEMETERY

ELMWOOD CEMETERY

McCLELLAN'S HDQTRS.
A. JARVIS BIRTHPLACE

HARPERS
FERRY

MONONGAHELA NAT'L. FOREST

CARNIFEX FERRY

SEE
VIRGINIA
PAGE 200

DROOP MTN.

SEE
KENTUCKY
PAGE 62

Weirton
Wheeling
Moundsville
Morgantown
Vienna
Parkersburg
Clarksburg
Webster
Grafton
Shepherdstown
Harpers Ferry
Elkins
St. Albans
Huntington
Charleston
Mount Nebo
Hillsboro
Beckley
Bluefield

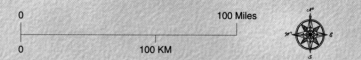

0   100 Miles
0   100 KM

BATTLE OF HARPERS FERRY

September 13–15, 1862

Harpers Ferry changed hands eight times during the war. Its railroad junction, its arsenal, its armory, and its location on the border between North and South made this small town strategically important to both sides.

Harpers Ferry is probably best known as the site of abolitionist John Brown's raid on a Federal arsenal in 1859. Brown saw himself as a prophet and messenger of God whose purpose was to free the slaves. In 1855, he followed his sons to Kansas with a large load of weapons to aid in keeping Kansas free but in the process helped the state earn the title of "Bloody Kansas." While there, Brown and four of his sons deliberately murdered five men on the banks of the Pottawatamie.

On October 16, 1859, Brown and twenty-one men came to Harpers Ferry, seized the armory and railway bridge, and took possession of the town. In addition, Brown had control of 100,000 weapons from the arsenal. When asked why and on what authority he acted, Brown replied, "To free the slaves, and by the authority of God Almighty."

Local militia blocked Brown's escape, and a company of marines, led by Colonel Robert E. Lee came to put down the uprising. Brown was captured and ten of his men were killed.

View of Harpers Ferry from Maryland Heights

Shenandoah Street in the Harpers Ferry National Historic Park

Brown was tried for treason; and on December 2, 1859, he was hanged at Charlestown. Among the soldiers observing the hanging was John Wilkes Booth. Northern sympathizers considered John Brown a martyr, and he became the hero of the song "John Brown's Body."

Three years later, in September of 1862, Lee, by then a Confederate general, returned to Harpers Ferry with his Army of Virginia, hoping to capture the arsenal himself on his way into Northern territory.

Lee divided his men into three columns, the first commanded by General Stonewall Jackson, the second by Brigadier General John G. Walker, and the third by Major General Lafeyette McLaws. These units advanced on the Union force led by Colonel Dixon S. Miles from three directions. In order to hold their lines, Union troops posted brigades on the high ground surrounding the city. After three days of siege, 12,000 Federal troops surrendered. An additional 1,400 Union cavalry had escaped under cover of darkness. Colonel Miles was killed by one of the last Confederate cannonballs to be fired as he prepared to offer surrender.

Lee then continued on to Antietam, Maryland. Only days after his defeat at Antietam, Lee abandoned Harpers Ferry to the Union and retreated into Virginia.

MONONGAHELA NATIONAL FOREST

200 Sycamore Street, Elkins, WV
PHONE: 304-636-1800
HOURS: Visitor's Center open weekdays; closed holidays.
ADMISSION: Free.

The 909,000-acre Monongahela National Forest contains Camp Allegheny and Cheat Summit Fort. The park's Visitor's Center provides free brochures detailing self-guided tours of the Civil War sites.

Cheat Summit Fort, Monongahela National Forest

CHEAT SUMMIT FORT

Cheat Summit Fort, also called Fort Milroy, was built by the order of Gen. George B. McClellan in July 1861. The fort, intended to stop a Confederate invasion, was believed to be impregnable by artillery or frontal assault from infantry or cavalry. Confederate Gen. Robert E. Lee attacked the fort on September 12, 1861, dividing his force to isolate and capture the fortification. Because of the density of the forest, neither side was aware of the strength of the other. The Southern troops of 1,500 believed they were outnumbered by the Northern troops, who, in actuality only consisted of 200 men. The Confederate forces retreated, leaving weapons and equipment. Although skirmishes continued for the next two days, Cheat Summit Fort was never captured. The main fortification of Cheat Summit Fort is well-preserved. Surface features, such as pit and parapet earthworks, cabin sites, and earthen mounds representing collapsed chimneys, are visible.

CAMP ALLEGHENY

Camp Allegheny, also known as Camp Baldwin or Camp Johnson, is a Civil War–era Confederate fortification located astride the Staunton-Parkersburg Turnpike in Pocahontas County, West Virginia. Camp Allegheny was built in the summer of 1861 by Confederate forces in an attempt to control the turnpike (which is now County Route 3). They hoped to bar Federal advances toward Staunton, Virginia, and the Shenandoah Valley. At an elevation of approximately 4,400 feet above sea level, the fortification is the highest in the eastern theater of the Civil War. The fort was constructed on the farm of John Yeager, and a large sugar maple grove supposedly was cut down for building cabins. Following the October 3, 1861, Battle of Greenbrier River at Camp Bartow (nine miles northwest), Confederate Gen. Henry R. Jackson moved his forces to this position. Here the Confederate army established winter quarters.

Camp Allegheny is extremely well-preserved and looks today much as it did in 1861. The area includes three rows of stone piles and surface depressions representing the remains of at least thirty-five cabins. The hillside above this point contains a shallow trench which indicates the location of General Milroy's attack during the December 13, 1861, battle.

CARNIFEX FERRY BATTLEFIELD STATE PARK

Carnifex Ferry Road, off West Virginia Highway 129,
5 miles west of U.S. Highway 19 near Mt. Nebo, WV
PHONE: 304-872-0825
WEB: www.carnifexferrybattlefieldstatepark.com
HOURS: Park open daily; museum open weekends
Memorial Day – Labor Day.
ADMISSION: Free.

Carnifex Ferry Battlefield State Park commemorates
the September 10, 1861, battle where Union troops
led by General Rosecrans forced the Confederates
to evacuate their entrenched position on the Henry
Patterson farm overlooking Carnifex Ferry. Confederate Gen. John B. Floyd retreated to Meadow Bluff
near Lewisburg. This Civil War battle represented
the failure of a Confederate drive to regain control of
the Kanawha Valley; and as a result, the movement
for West Virginia statehood proceeded without serious threat from the Confederates.

Carnifex Ferry Battlefield State Park

A small museum contains exhibits on the area's
history. Several self-guided hiking trails are avail-
able. Each year the park hosts a Civil War Weekend during the weekend after Labor Day. The
two-day program features reenactors portraying Civil War camp life complete with Confederate
and Union camps, morning reveille, skirmishes, infantry and artillery drills, and other living history demonstrations.

DROOP MOUNTAIN BATTLEFIELD STATE PARK

HC 64, Box 189, Hillsboro, WV
PHONE: 304-653-4254
WEB: www.droopmountainbattlefield.com
HOURS: Open daily.
ADMISSION: Free.

Droop Mountain Battlefield, West Virginia's
oldest state park, was dedicated on July 4,
1928, as a memorial to the men who took part
in what is generally considered to be the largest Civil War battle fought on West Virginia
soil. Located in Pocahontas County, five

Photo right: Droop Mountain Battlefield State Park

miles south of Hillsboro, the park offers scenic mountain vistas, hiking, and picnicking but is most noted for its historic significance as the site of a fierce struggle which took place between the North and the South on November 6, 1863. The battle resulted from the movements of the Union army of Gen. William Averell, whose intent was to clear Confederate troops in the southeastern section of West Virginia and then strike at the Virginia and Tennessee Railroad. He was successful in forcing the army of Gen. John Echols into Virginia but failed to reach the railroad.

A museum contains exhibits of firearms, cannon shells, canteens, and other Civil War artifacts. The park features Civil War trenches, a lookout tower, memorials, and walking trails that include Musket Ball Trail, Minié Ball Trail, and The Horse-Heaven Trail, where all the dead horses from the battle were tossed in the ravine. In October of even-numbered years, the park hosts a reenactment of the battle.

GRAFTON NATIONAL CEMETERY

431 Walnut Street, Grafton, WV
PHONE: 304-265-2044
WEB: www.cem.va.gov
HOURS: Open daily.
ADMISSION: Free.

Grafton National Cemetery

Grafton National Cemetery was established in 1867 for the purpose of having all the Civil War dead reburied in a location accessible from all parts of the state. More than 1,250 Union troops were exhumed and reburied here. Records in the cemetery office indicate the location from which all bodies were disinterred. The 613 unknowns buried here are marked only by number. The cemetery also has the distinction of having interred the first casualty of the Civil War, Private Thornsberry Bailey Brown; a special monument commemorates his grave.

GENERAL MCCLELLAN'S HEADQUARTERS/ ANNA JARVIS BIRTHPLACE

U.S. Route 119 S/250 S, Webster, WV
PHONE: 304-265-5549
HOURS: Open Tuesday – Sunday April 1 – October 31; November 1 – second week of January, hours vary, call ahead.
ADMISSION: A fee is charged; children under 12 are free.

Here in June 1861, soon after the Battle of Philippi, Gen. George B. McClellan established his headquarters and began to prepare for the Battle of Rich Mountain. The headquarters was the first field headquarters of the Civil War. This house was also the childhood home of Anna Jarvis, whose efforts to honor her mother resulted in the founding of Mother's Day.

ELMWOOD CEMETERY

West Virginia Highway 480, Shepherdstown, WV
PHONE: 304-876-6352
HOURS: Open daily, dawn until dusk.
ADMISSION: Free.

Elmwood Cemetery is the final resting place of 577 Confederate soldiers, most from the Battle of Antietam, Maryland. Brochures describing the Confederate officers' burial sites are available.

HARPERS FERRY NATIONAL HISTORICAL PARK

171 Shoreline Drive, Harpers Ferry, WV
PHONE: 304-535-6029
WEB: www.nps.gov/hafe
HOURS: Open daily; closed Thanksgiving Day, Christmas, and New Year's Day.
ADMISSION: A fee is charged.

The first target in Virginia after secession and Stonewall Jackson's capture of the largest number of Union troops in the war highlight the Civil War history of Harpers Ferry. Because of Harpers Ferry's strategic location on the Baltimore and Ohio Railroad at the northern end of the Shenandoah Valley, Union and Confederate troops moved through Harpers Ferry frequently. The town changed hands eight times between 1861 and 1865. Four years of warfare resulted in a garrison town under martial law, military hospitals, partisan warfare, and a base of operations for military campaigns. Fortifications, trench lines, and ruins remain on a landscape one soldier described as "carved out by nature for some great tragedy."

The expansive park features hiking trails and auto stops across battlefield terrain and 20 original buildings, each focusing on a different era of Harpers Ferry's history. John Brown and Civil War museums offer a variety of exhibits, artifacts, and films. Guided walking tours and self-guided tours are available seasonally.

Photo left: Harpers Ferry National Historical Park

INDEX

*(Page numbers in **bold** indicate maps.)*

PHOTO CREDITS